Soil ecology is an exciting new textbook for all those concerned with the environment. The author meets the increasing challenge faced by environmental scientists, ecologists, agriculturalists and biotechnologists for an integrated approach to soil ecology. Intellectually enticing and yet eminently readable, the book sets out both fundamental theory and principle to give the reader a thorough grounding in soil ecology.

The author emphasises the interrelations between plants, animals and microbes. The fundamental physical and chemical properties of the soil habitat are clearly set out, enabling the reader to explore and understand the processes of soil nutrient cycling, the ecology of extreme and polluted soil environments and the potential of soil biotechnology.

The book will appeal to advanced undergraduates and graduates in environmental science, plant science, ecology, microbiology and agriculture.

Soil ecology

Soil ecology

KEN KILLHAM
Department of Plant and Soil Science, University of Aberdeen

with electron micrographs by
RALPH FOSTER, CSIRO Division of Soils, South Australia

CAMBRIDGE
UNIVERSITY PRESS

Published by the Press Syndicate of the University of Cambridge
The Pitt Building, Trumpington Street, Cambridge CB2 1RP
40 West 20th Street, New York, NY 10011-4211, USA
10 Stamford Road, Oakleigh, Melbourne 3166, Australia

First published 1994
Reprinted 1995

Printed in Great Britain at the University Press, Cambridge

A catalogue record for this book is available from the British Library

Library of Congress cataloguing in publication data

Killham, Ken.
Soil ecology / Ken Killham ; with electron micrographs by Ralph
Foster.
    p. cm.
Includes bibliographical references and index.
ISBN 0–521–43517–X — ISBN 0–521–43521–8 (pbk)
1. Soil ecology.   2. Soil science.   3. Biogeochemical cycles.
I. Title.
QH541.5.S6K54   1994
574.5′26404—dc20   93-26150   CIP

ISBN 0 521 43517 X hardback
ISBN 0 251 43521 8 paperback

KW

To Pauline

Contents

Foreword

Most books in the field of soil science are discipline oriented and deal in considerable detail with the particular field favoured by the author. This book departs from this practice and under the title of *Soil ecology* deals with the whole range of soil science. To some this may appear unnecessary, but when we consider the complexity of the soil matrix and the environment in which soil organisms and plant roots exist, there is a need to explain the chemical, physical and mineralogical properties of soils in which organisms occur. Without this firm foundation provided by an understanding of these non-biological factors in soil, it is impossible to understand how different components of soil biota operate and interact. Within the field of soil biology and soil ecology, the tradition has been to specialise in particular components of the topic, for example soil microbiology, soil biochemistry, soil zoology etc. In this book, Dr Killham has covered all these aspects of soil biology and adopted an integrated approach to the subject. It is this approach that will make this book so valuable to scientists and students working in the fields of soil and plant science and in environmental research.

Progress in science is made up of a series of steps, and often a step up from the previous level of knowledge depends on the development of new techniques. In soil microbiology, for example, the development of selective agars enabling the isolation and study of individual groups of bacteria and fungi improved our understanding of the ecology of these organisms against the background of the total populations. Later within this subject we see the development of studies on the organic compounds released from healthy plant roots. These studies greatly improved our understanding of the energy supplies for microorganisms in the rhizosphere and depended upon the development of paper chromatography for amino acid and sugar analyses and the development of ^{14}C-labelling techniques developed in other areas of science. The application of electron microscopy to ultrathin sections of soil and rhizosphere was another technique which greatly advanced our understanding of the microecology of organisms in soil and their locations in relation to clay minerals, organic matter and particulate plant residues.

As the writing of this book has been underway, soil ecology is once again poised on the threshold of major advances due to the development of techniques of genetic manipulation of microorganisms and DNA fingerprinting. It will be possible to 'tailor make' microorganisms to perform different tasks in soil, e.g. biological control of root diseases, detoxification of toxic compounds, oxidation and removal of pesticide residues, hydrocarbons etc. and to track microorganisms in the environment. These techniques will be of little value unless more is known about the interactions between the components of the soil biota, e.g. interactions between bacteria and protozoa, bacteria and earthworms, bacteria and fungi. This book goes a long way towards addressing these questions of the interactions between the different components of the soil biota and the influence of soil physical and chemical properties on these interactions.

This book provides a comprehensive cover of the topic 'soil ecology' – it defines the soil environment; how this affects the survival of different components of the soil biota under stress; it deals with pollution, manipulation of microorganisms within the environment, the use of genetically modified organisms and the use of DNA technology. Knowledge of all these topics will be essential if we are to manage the soil biota to improve plant production and protect the environment.

Soil is one of the most heterogeneous environments that exists in nature and existing within this complex matrix are soil biota ranging from virus particles through to macrofauna. From this complex environment comes most of the food needed for the world population. This highlights the absolute importance of improving our understanding of this complex environment.

In this book, in which Dr Killham integrates the chemical, physical and biological properties of soil, readers will have a tool that will go a long way towards giving them the understanding of soil ecology relevant to research in production, agriculture and on environmental problems.

A. D. Rovira,
Chief Research Scientist,
CSIRO Division of Soils,
Glen Osmond, South Australia

Introduction

A great many books have been written on the soil ecology of microbes, of plants and, to a lesser extent, of animals. Integration of these themes, however, has largely remained unchallenged. This book has been written in an attempt to fulfil this challenge and to identify both the theory and applications of an integrated approach to soil ecology.

Never before has the need to understand the fundamental principles of soil ecology been so great. The urgency of feeding the world's growing population (partly through realising the potential benefits of modern biotechnology), of combatting soil pollution as well as responding to climate change has given soil ecological research vital importance.

Modern techniques, particularly involving molecular biology, are enabling study of soil ecology at a scale and with sensitivity never dreamed possible by the pioneers of the subject in the late eighteenth and early nineteenth centuries. This picture now emerging is one of immense heterogeneity with much of the soil's biological activity being restricted to niches or 'hot spots' such as the rhizosphere, fresh plant/animal residues, and the guts of decomposer organisms. The remaining bulk soil seems to be a zone of relative starvation or oligotrophy where activities and population densities are relatively low and may sometimes be maintained by novel growth strategies.

Since emerging from the primordial sea, a community has evolved to colonise the heterogeneous soil environment and penetrate all but the finest pores, adapted to life even under the most extreme conditions of water stress, temperature, acidity/alkalinity, aeration/redox and energy/nutrient supply.

Countless interactions of the components of the soil's biota have developed. Some of those involving plants and microbes, such as the mycorrhizal symbiosis, may have been necessary to create favourable nutrient/water relations to facilitate the transition from water to land. We are still discovering the complexity of soil biological interactions and this understanding will enable us to manipulate them for man's benefit.

The heterogeneity of soil in terms of soil particle and pore distribution causes a bewildering complexity of spatial compartmentalisation of soil organisms and the soil's other resources. Soil microbes in small pores and in sites of low pore connectivity, for example, may be well protected from protozoal attack but the advantages of this protection may be weighed up against the reduced substrate/nutrient supply associated with a pore microhabitat deep within a soil aggregate. Substrates, enzymes and organisms may also be attached to the surfaces of soil particles, restricting possible activity until some disturbance (through cultivation or soil animal activity, perhaps) disrupts the soil matrix.

The conditions which soil organisms experience must no longer be determined from bulk measurements – microbial adsorption to surfaces, colonisation of pores, and the development of thick mucilaginous sheaths of individual cells on biofilms, for example, provide protected microsites about which we know very little, but must characterise before we can usefully introduce microbial inocula (genetically engineered or otherwise) into the soil.

One of the weakest links in our understanding of soil ecology relates to the involvement of animals, relying too heavily on limited research carried out many decades ago. This role of soil animals in mixing soils, in aggregate formation/disruption and turnover, in primary and secondary decomposition, in microbial interactions in the gut, in microbial transport through soil, and in a whole host of other aspects of soil ecology, has been identified, but seldom reliably quantified under field conditions.

The challenge to the soil ecologists has never been greater, but neither has the opportunity!

Ken Killham
Aberdeen

1 *The soil environment*

INTRODUCTION

Soil consists of mineral material, the roots of plants, microbial and animal biomass, organic matter in various states of decay, as well as water and a gaseous atmosphere. The uneven distribution of these components provides a great variety of conditions at all levels of scale from field to soil micropore, and sets a challenge to all those who sample the soil to study its composition and function. A whole spectrum of interacting physical and chemical factors contributes to the varied nature of the soil habitat, and hence determines the composition and activity of the soil biota at a particular site and time. This chapter presents the most significant of these habitat-determining soil factors, particularly at the microsite level, and considers some of their more important interactions.

THE SOIL AS A SOURCE OF ENERGY AND NUTRIENTS TO THE BIOTA

Different components (plant roots, microbes and animals) of the soil biota have different dependencies on the soil environment for their energy and nutrient supply. Plants and photoautotrophic microbes obtain their energy from sunlight, and also, along with chemoautotrophic microbes (energy from oxidation of inorganic compounds) acquire their carbon directly from the atmosphere largely as carbon dioxide. In addition, a number of specialised microbes and plant root/microbial associations are able to directly fix free atmospheric nitrogen. Apart from these obvious exceptions, the remaining soil biota obtain their energy and nutrients directly from the soil resource either from minerals, from organic matter or from other components of the living soil biomass.

1

Soil minerals as a source of nutrients

The soil biota obtain a significant proportion of their nutritional requirement from the weathering of soil minerals, predominantly secondary minerals. These secondary minerals, such as secondary silicates and oxides of iron and manganese, tend to be present in the fine silt and clay fractions of the soil. Nutrients from weathered minerals enter the soil solution and then reach the sites of biological activity through a combination of mass flow and diffusion.

In some cases, members of the soil biota accelerate the rate of mineral weathering, usually through the production of organic acids, thus encouraging mineral solubilisation. An example of this is the lichen association between an alga and a fungus, where the lichen thallus will often colonise and weather bare rock surfaces and hence initiate soil development. Ectomycorrhizal fungi, often dominating the microflora of forest soils, also release acids (organic acids from fungal metabolism) that accelerate nutrient supply from weathering minerals. Biological acceleration of mineral weathering also occurs when chemoautotrophic bacteria are involved in inorganic acid production. The most striking example is where sulphur oxidation carried out by species of the genus *Thiobacillus* produces considerable amounts of sulphuric acid, which accelerates the weathering of a wider range of sulphur-bearing minerals.

The soil mineral fraction, as well as being an important source of soil nutrients, also serves as a nutrient sink. Negatively charged clay minerals in soil tend to attract nutrient cations (e.g. NH_4^+, Ca^{2+}, Mg^{2+}, K^+ etc.). The cations may become adsorbed (adsorption simply refers to the adhesion of a substance to a solid surface). Cations held in this way are readily released back into the soil solution by a process known as ion exchange. This involves exchange with other cations including hydrogen ions. Because clay minerals generally have many sites for these exchangeable cations, they are referred to as having a high cation exchange capacity. In addition to simple surface adsorption of cations, interlayer clays such as illites can fix ammonia, rendering it less biologically unavailable, because the ammonium ion can substitute for potassium in the expanded clay lattice. The fixed ammonium can, however, be used by plants because it is released when plants take up potassium, although it is virtually unavailable to microorganisms for processes such as nitrification. In weathered soils, hydrous oxides of iron and aluminium can fix, and render unavailable, considerable amounts of nutrient phosphate.

Clays also have a key controlling role in soil nutrient supply, as they form sites for adsorption (through a variety of mechanisms) of nutrient-mineralising enzymes as well as of substrates, products, and soil microbes themselves. Generally speaking, adsorption of enzymes on to clay particles decreases enzyme activity, but also has the effect of stabilising the bound enzyme against attack by proteases and other denaturing agents. Clays such as montmorillonites with large surface areas will provide the most effective sinks for enzyme adsorption. The presence and type of clays, therefore, will have a profound effect on nutrient flow in soils.

Soil organic matter as a source of nutrients

The organic-matter content of the soil, consisting of plant, animal and microbial residues in various stages of decay, represents the dominant source for microbial nutrition.

All soil heterotrophs, the group that generally makes up the largest part of the soil microbial and animal biomass, required pre-formed organic carbon for growth. Most of the soil's heterotrophs are saprophytes, utilising dead organic matter. The breakdown of cellulose, comprising the largest amount of most plant residues, is a good example of this saprophytic activity. Cellulose is a polymer or chain of glucose units. The first stage of breakdown involves splitting of the chain or depolymerisation into progressively shorter units. This depolymerisation is carried out outside the decomposer cell (i.e. extracellularly). The resulting glucose units are readily assimilated into the microbial cell (i.e. for intracellular utilisation) where they serve as a source of energy and provide carbon for cellular growth. The initial depolymerisation is carried out by a rather specialised group of cellulolytic microbes, which includes bacteria such as species of *Bacillus* and *Pseudomonas*, fungi such as *Aspergillus* and *Trichoderma*, and actinomycetes such as *Streptomyces* and *Nocardia*. The subsequent utilisation of glucose is carried out by a vast range of heterotrophic soil microbes.

The picture of cellulose decomposition is representative of the breakdown of most components of soil organic matter where a large molecule, often a polymer or chain of simple units (e.g. chitin, a polymer of amino sugars; proteins, chains of amino acids; nucleic acids, chains of nucleotides; hemi-celluloses, chains of sugars and uronic acids; lignin, a polymer of aromatics etc.) is first depolymerised by rather specialised microbial enzyme systems. This then releases simpler units that serve as a substrate for a much wider group of soil microbes. In addition to supplying carbon, the soil organic matter also releases organically bound nutrients, particularly nitrogen, phosphorus and sulphur, that had previously been incorporated into living tissue. This release of organically bound nutrients is known as mineralisation. Some examples of these important mineralisation reactions are given below.

(i) Nitrogen release from organic matter, e.g. deamination of amino acids.

$$
\begin{array}{ccc}
\text{COOH} & & \text{COOH} \\
| & & | \\
\text{H}_2\text{N-C-H} & & \text{C=O} \qquad \text{released ammonia} \\
| & \longrightarrow & | \\
\text{CH}_2 & & \text{CH}_2 \quad + \text{NH}_3 \uparrow \\
| & & | \\
\text{CH}_2 + \text{H}_2\text{O} & \quad\overset{\frown}{} & \text{CH}_2 \\
| & & | \\
\text{COOH} & \text{FAD} \quad \text{FADH}_2 & \text{COOH} \\
\text{Glutamic} & & \text{Ketoglutaric} \\
\text{acid} & & \text{acid}
\end{array}
$$

(ii) Phosphorus release from organic matter, e.g. phosphate cleavage from a phosphate monoester.

$$
\begin{array}{ccc}
\text{O} & \overset{\text{phosphatase}}{} & \text{O} \\
\| & & \| \\
\text{ROPOH} + \text{H}_2\text{O} & \longrightarrow & \text{ROH} + \text{HOPOH} \\
| & & | \\
\text{OH} & & \text{OH}
\end{array}
$$

(iii) Sulphur release from organic matter, e.g. sulphate cleavage from a sulphate monoester.

$$
\text{R.O.SO}_3{}^- + \text{H}_2\text{O} \xrightarrow{\text{sulphatase}} \text{ROH} + \text{H}^+ + \text{SO}_4{}^{2-}
$$

A diverse soil microbial population produces nutrient-mineralising enzymes such as deaminases, phosphatases and sulphatases, and these microbes are particularly abundant in the rhizosphere (the region of soil close to the plant root) where organically bound nitrogen, phosphorus, sulphur and other nutrients are continually released.

The importance of the biological release and cycling of nutrients from organic matter should not be understated. Ninety-five per cent or more of nitrogen and of sulphur is in an organic form in most surface soils. Although the proportion of phosphorus in organic forms is often smaller than for nitrogen and sulphur, release of phosphorus from organic forms still represents by far the dominant form of nutrient supply to the biota, most forms of inorganic phosphorus being highly insoluble.

A considerable source of carbon and nutrients in soil organic matter is in the form of plant root exudates. Rhizosphere microbes are, by definition, dependent on these rich exudates, which largely comprise varying amounts of soluble carbohydrates, organic acids and amino acids, but also contain significant concentrations of fatty acids, sterols, vitamins and enzymes (Curl & Truelove, 1986). Although the quantity and quality of root exudates depends on a host of environmental (e.g. temperature, pH, light, etc.) and plant related (e.g. plant type, stage of development, health, mycorrhizal infection) factors, root exudation generally represents about 5% of the carbon that plants photoassimilate (Lambers, 1987). In addition to exudation, roots slough off cell material that also yields a range of readily degradable organic substrates to the soil microbes.

In addition to soil microbes, the soil macrofauna are also of great ecological importance in terms of breaking down soil organic matter to access this considerable nutrient reservoir. Soil animals involved in the breakdown of dead soil organic matter are termed saprophagous, and include earthworms, termites, ants and millipedes. The soil macrofauna not only break down soil organic matter for themselves, but are also particularly important in comminuting organic matter for enhanced microbial attack and in microbial inoculation of the material that they process through their guts.

Different types of soil organic matter tend to have a different composition of soil animals as well as soil microbes. Acid, mor humus (raw, acid, fibrous and poor in nutrients) tends to be dominated by small mites, enchytraeid worms and springtails (Collembola) and these are associated with a thriving fungal community. In more neutral, mull humus (more decomposed, crumbly, and rich in nutrients), one finds a soil animal population rich in larger invertebrates such as earthworms, slugs and millipedes associated with a more bacterial, microbial community. In most soils of near neutral pH, the earthworm is the most important soil animal with respect to nutrient cycling. The earthworm tissue and cast are enriched in certain nutrients relative to the bulk soil and earthworm ingestion of organic material greatly accelerates the rate of nutrient cycling. Even in acid organic soils, a very considerable proportion of the soil consists of faecal pellets from soil animals. These compacted pellets of primary-processed organic matter show little of the character of the original plant debris, but also very little of humus. The pellets become a very rich substrate for a vast array of soil microbial activity which completes the process of humification (a more detailed discussion of the humification process is provided in Chapter 4).

Like the clay fraction of the soil, the organic fraction also serves as a sink as well as a source for soil nutrients. Cationic nutrients are adsorbed on to the exchange sites of soil particles where they are relatively available, although ammonium is sometimes fixed more stably by soil organic matter. The mechanisms of this fixation are uncertain. Organic matter, again as does clay, immobilises enzymes, organic substrates and microbes to modify the rate of biological reactions in a variety of ways. Humic acids, for example, generally inhibit biological decomposition reactions through mechanisms such as complexation of substrates, enabling selective blocking of enzyme catalysis.

The two previous sections have considered the soil mineral fraction and the soil organic matter fraction as a source and sink for nutrients. Separate consideration of the soil mineral and organic matter fractions as sources and sinks for nutrients is convenient for discussion, but does not present a truly accurate picture of the soil, implying that these fractions are always separate. Of course in reality, clay and organic matter are often tightly bound and intimately mixed in the soil, as is the case with clay–humate complexes.

More detailed consideration of soil organic matter as a source of energy and nutrients is found in Chapter 4.

Living biomass as a source of nutrients

There are a number of ways in which soil organisms 'directly' acquire nutrients from other soil organisms.

Ingestion (followed by enzymatic digestion) of organisms by predators in soil takes on a variety of forms. Phagotrophic soil protozoa such as *Sarcodina* may directly ingest many thousands of bacteria in a life cycle between cell division, whereas some soil fungi can entrap nematode worms with their hyphae and then, slowly, enzymatically digest their immobilised prey.

It is becoming increasingly clear that plant root systems can transfer nutrients by direct root fusion and, as has been more recently discovered, by mycorrhizal fungal links (Read, Francis & Finlay, 1985). This latter nutrient-supply mechanism, although as yet of unknown significance, may have a key role in nutrient acquisition by the root systems of certain natural plant communities.

Table 1. *Approximate dimensions* (μm) *of soil constituents and of water-filled pore and water films at varying water tensions*

Soil particles	stones	2000
	coarse sand	200–2000
	fine sand	50–200
	silt	2–50
	coarse clay	0.2–2
	fine clay	0.2
Plant material	root hairs[a]	7–15
	fine roots[a]	50–1000
	roots	1000
Microbes	viruses	0.05–0.2
	bacteria	0.5–1.0
	actinomycetes[a]	1.0–1.5
	fungi[a]	0.3–10
Some soil animals	protozoa	10–80
	nematodes[a]	500–2000
	mites	500–2000
	earthworms[a]	2–5000
Water-filled pores	−10 kPa	<30
	−100 kPa	<3
	−1000 kPa	0.3
Water films	−100 kPa	<0.003
	−1000 kPa	few molecules thick

[a] Cross-sectional diameters.

STRUCTURAL ASPECTS OF THE SOIL HABITAT

The relative dimensions of soil particles in Table 1 suggest that size exclusion of components of the soil biota may operate in some soils. Colonisation of a soil pore, for example, may be limited by the size of the neck of that pore so that only the smallest soil bacteria are located within the pore. There is no simple relationship, however, between the size distribution of soil particles and the size distribution of the corresponding soil biota. This is because the amount and nature of the pore space in soil is not only determined by the relative proportions of various-sized particles (i.e. soil texture), but also by the way these particles are aggregated (i.e. soil structure).

Figure 1 shows a soil aggregate, emphasising two important features of aggregation in relation to the distribution of the soil biota. The first is that aggregation controls the pore distribution (about half of the volume of well-aggregated soils consists of pore space) and hence the soil water distribution, critical to the growth and survival of the soil biota (it should be remembered from Table 1 that pore size, along with the activity of soil water, determines the degree to which the pores will be water filled). The second is that the aggregation may enable simple size exclusion of components of the soil biota. For example, soil microbes may be free from protozoal attack in a soil pore because the latter are physically excluded from the pore. Microbial populations in small (2–100 µm) pores may therefore often be protected in contrast to those in larger pores. It is partly as a result of physical protection of organic matter through microbial exclusion (the organic matter may also be chemically protected by processes such as clay–organic complexation) that the turnover of soil organic matter may be measured in hundreds and even thousands of years).

In terms of plant root growth, the structural aspects of the soil habitat are of critical importance. The rate at which a root system extends into the soil is considerably influenced by the degree to which it must exert pressure to enlarge soil pores which are smaller than root dimensions. This is because roots are unable to reduce their diameter to enter small pores. Soils facilitating plant root growth, therefore, tend to have an adequate range of continuous large pores that roots can enter easily. Pore space both within and between aggregates varies greatly, largely because of varying clay content, but it also varies with soil depth. From this simplified picture, it would appear that soils with a high clay content have too few large pores to enable optimal root growth. In addition, however, soils can develop a macrostructure, also mediating root system growth, caused by the development of larger cracks and fissures. These are mainly formed by the presence of swelling clays (smectites, which cause soil to crack on drying), the burrowing activity of soil animals such as earthworms, and from the decay of plant roots.

Compaction of soil reduces the soil pore volume, largely by reducing the size of the larger pores. This affects root growth directly as a result of increased mechanical impedance, and also indirectly affects root growth because of changes to the soil water regime, nutrient flow and to aeration.

Structural aspects of the soil are extremely important in governing the occurrence and activity of soil animals. This is because, in general, soil animals tend to prefer moist, but well-aerated soil. Loams, intermediate in

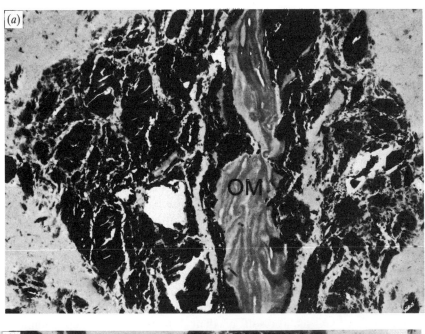

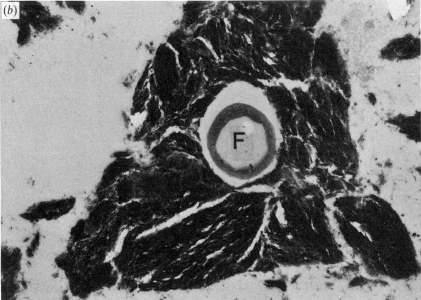

Figure 1. Transmission electron micrographs (TEMs) of aggregates held together by (*a*) amorphous organic matter (OM) (× 33 000) and (*b*) a fungal hypha (F) (× 7200).

texture between sand and clay, and with a well-aggregated structure will, therefore, tend to support the highest populations of earthworms and other soil animals.

Not only are structural aspects of the soil habitat important in influencing the nature and activity of the soil biota, but also the activity of the soil biota itself directly affects soil structure. There are two main mechanisms through which plant roots exert an influence on soil structure. Firstly, the plant encourages development of a good 'crumb' structure by development of an extensive root mat that enmeshes and separates soil particles. Grasses are known in particular to mediate this process. Secondly, the plant root exudes mucilaginous polysaccharides, which can have a strong binding effect on soil particles. Soil microbes, particularly the filamentous fungi, also have a direct enmeshing effect, which assists in the formation of stable aggregates, and the soil microbial biomass also produces polysaccharides that bind soil particles together. Plant and microbial production of polysaccharides may be a key mechanism in aggregating soil mineral particles and establishing physical protection of a fraction of the soil organic matter. The effects of soil animals on soil structure are considerable, particularly with respect to earthworms, which, as a result of their burrowing, open up channels (enabling increased infiltration of water and increased root penetration) and reduce the bulk density (the weight of oven-dry soil per unit volume) of the soil. This process is particularly important in tropical soils if a mulch of crop residue is left on the soil surface to encourage earthworm activity and minimise soil structural problems.

SOIL WATER

The degree to which the soil pore space is water filled is of fundamental importance in determining soil biological activity. Soil bacteria and protozoa tend to live in the soil water at all times. When the soil dries out, this water is restricted to thin films around the soil particles (Table 1). Soil fungi can, however, grow across the air-filled pore spaces. Large soil animals such as earthworms tend to occupy the larger pore spaces that are generally filled with air and only become water filled when the soil is saturated. In addition to providing these various niches and spatial compartmentalisation for different components of the soil biota, the nature of the pores holding the soil water also determines the availability of this water and soil aeration, as

Neck diameter of largest water-filled pore (μm)

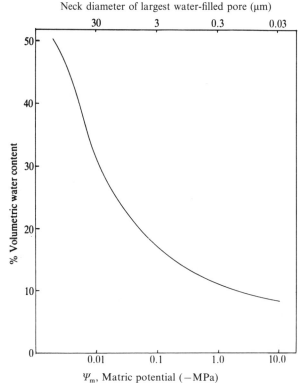

Figure 2. A soil moisture release curve, showing the relationship between volumetric water content, matric potential, and diameter of largest water-filled pore.

well as the supply of soluble nutrients, and regulates osmotic potential, as well as the pH and Eh of the soil solution.

In any study involving soil biological activity, it is not sufficient simply to report the moisture content of the soil in question. This has little or no meaning in terms of how much of the soil water is available to the soil biota. A sandy soil, for example, may have a low water content, but most of this will be available to plant roots. A clay loam, on the other hand, may have a higher water content, but a roughly similar amount of water available to the plant roots. This is because the clay loam has more small pores from which water is more difficult to extract. The tension or suction required to withdraw water from a soil at a certain moisture content is referred to as the matric potential of the soil and is measured in pascals. Graphs of matric potential against water content are termed moisture release curves (Figure 2)

Table 2. *The relation between soil pore neck size and pore-water
availability to plant roots*

Pore neck size (μm)	Water potential and availability to plants when pores are water filled
approx. 30 or greater	> -10 kPa. Free supply under gravity.
0.3–30	-1000 to -10 kPa. Can be withdrawn by absorbing roots.
<0.3	< -1000 kPa. Cannot be withdrawn by roots.

and should always be referred to by the soil ecologist to provide information
on available soil moisture.

From Table 2 it can be seen that there is a clear relationship between
matric potential and the neck diameter of the largest water-filled pore:

$$\Psi_m = 0.3/d$$

where Ψ_m = matric potential $(-$kPa$)$
d = neck diameter (mm) of largest water-filled pore.

Table 2 shows which pore sizes provide water to plants, freely under
gravity, and where plants can withdraw it. The pore size distribution is
critical in water supply to the roots of growing plants. Ideally, a soil should
have a reasonable number of large pores to facilitate root extension, but also
a large number of small pores (0.3–30 μm) to sustain water supply to roots
during periods of drought.

Water stress

During relatively dry periods, plant evapotranspiration of water exceeds
inputs from rainfall and the soil water potential declines. The resulting water
potential deficit in the plant may at first be recovered at night when plant
roots continue to absorb soil water. In time, however, despite this slight night
recovery of turgor, the major factor determining the growth of the plant will
be the suction the roots must exert to overcome whatever force (i.e. matric
tension) is holding water in the soil pores. When the tension exceeds
approximately 15 bar or 1.5 MPa, the roots of most plants can no longer
extract any water and the plant will die (even though the soil still contains

significant amounts of adsorbed water and water held in small capillary pores). This is referred to as the permanent wilting power. At lesser matric stresses, however, the plant root cannot extract sufficient water to maintain full turgor and the plant will wilt. The plant will recover fully, however, on rewatering. This is the reversible wilting point and the matric potential at which it occurs varies greatly from one plant to another. Considering matric tension alone is an oversimplification because, as the soil pores dry out, the remaining water will tend to become increasingly saline. Thus, there are two components of water potential stress imposed on the soil system, a matric and an osmotic potential (there is also a gravitational component to soil water potentials, but this becomes negligible under water stress), both of which must be overcome for plant uptake of water to occur.

$$\Psi_t = \Psi_m + \Psi_o$$

where Ψ_t = total soil water potential
Ψ_m = matric potential
Ψ_o = osmotic potential.

In fact, over the small matric potential range between field capacity (the water potential of a water-saturated soil after it has been allowed to drain under gravity) and permanent wilting point, the osmotic component of soil water potential is generally very small and need not be considered in most cases. Over this range, only saline soils and recently fertilised soils (particularly in the vicinity of the fertiliser granule) will have an appreciable osmotic component of water potential stress.

The rate at which soils dry to exert stress on plant water uptake varies greatly depending on a number of factors, but losses of 4 mm day^{-1} can take place under strong drying conditions.

To ensure plant survival under dry soil conditions, roots must extend at a sufficient rate to maintain contact with pore space in which water potential is adequate for plant growth. This capacity for root extension is a key feature in the high drought resistance of plants such as alfalfa. Other adaptations to drought tolerance are the development of deeper and highly branched root systems and the ability to rapidly regenerate roots once a period of water stress has passed.

Microbial water relations are quite different from that of the plant. Although not all soil microbes are tolerant to water/salt stress, some can grow under stresses more than an order of magnitude greater than most plants. Microbes are, in effect, permeable bags, without significant turgor,

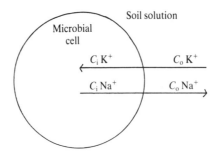

Free energy $\Delta G = \Delta G$ (Na transport) $+ \Delta G$ (K transport) $+ \Delta G$ (ATP hydrolysis)

where ΔG (K$^+$ transport) $= RT \log_e \frac{C_o K^+}{C_i K^+} + ZFV$

where C_i and C_o are concentrations inside and outside cell
Z is ion charge
V is potential difference across cell wall
T is temperature
R and F are constants

Figure 3. The energy costs to a microbial cell in a saline soil environment where cell integrity is maintained in part by selective transport of potassium (accumulation) and sodium (exclusion).

and with identical water potentials, both inside and outside the cell. Microbial cells counterbalance the water potential stress of their soil environment partly through selective transport of soil salts.

Figure 3 shows the energy budget of a cell selectively pumping out potentially toxic sodium and pumping in less toxic potassium – the energy for this work being supplied by ATP hydrolysis. Some microbial cells have an additional capability under water stress of synthesising organic cell solutes that are more compatible with their internal enzyme machinery than inorganic salts such as KCl. Actinomycetes, for example are particularly tolerant of water stress (Table 3) and this is partly because of the ability to synthesise intracellular proline (a highly soluble ring amino acid) as part of their osmoregulatory strategy. Clearly, synthesis of such an organic solute provides an ecophysiological advantage to a microbe in a soil environment subject to regular water stress. It is, however, energetically more expensive (but less disruptive to cell metabolism) than transport of simple inorganic salts and so the soil microbe must respond to water stress using the most energetically effective strategy. One must also bear in mind that the soil water potential can fluctuate dramatically and the microbe has to respond

Table 3. *Typical ranges of tolerance to water stress for soil microbes*

		Water potential (MPa)
increasing tolerance	Bacteria	0 to −10
	Yeasts	0 to −20
	Fungi	0 to −60
	Actinomycetes	0 to −70

correspondingly, either through the dumping (osmotic downshock) or the accumulation (osmotic upshock) of cell solutes. As a previously water-stressed soil is rewetted, the leakage and loss of expensively synthesised organic solutes represents an energy loss in an environment that by its very nature may be severely energy limited. Clearly, response to short-term fluctuations in water stress should ideally involve regulation of inorganic solutes only. Flushes of nutrients when soils are dried and rewetted may well partly result from the release of intracellular solutes.

Table 3 shows the approximate order (clearly, there are exceptions within these broad groups) of resistance to water stress amongst the major groups of soil microbes. Members of the actinomycetes appear to be amongst the best adapted of all and, after prolonged periods of extreme soil water stress, particularly in tropical and sub-tropical latitudes, actinomycetes often totally dominate the soil microflora.

The activity of some soil animals can be particularly adversely affected by the drying out of the soil pore space. Soil protozoa, for example, move through the soil water, grazing on a variety of soil microbes. The absence of a continuous film of water, thick enough to facilitate locomotion, severely restricts their activity. Further drying of the soil causes most protozoa to encyst, these protozoal cysts being incredibly resistant to prolonged water stress compared with the active (trophozoite) form.

Generally speaking, it seems then that the effects of matric and osmotic stress in the soil produce a total water stress against all soil organisms, to a greater or lesser degree. A good correlation is usually found between soil water content and soil biological activity. This relationship tends to hold to just above field capacity and then biological activity decreases as soils become waterlogged.

This section has provided the basic principles of how soil water stress affects the soil biota. A much more detailed account of the response of the soil biota to water stress can be found in Chapter 5.

Soil water and nutrient supply to the soil biota

Soil water not only directly affects the growth and activity of the soil biota but also mediates effects through the supply of nutrients to the organisms in question. This supply occurs through both mass flow and diffusion. The relative importance of the two processes depends on the amount of movement of the soil water. Where this movement is low, the dominant supply of nutrients is by diffusion. With increasing movement of soil water, however, mass flow becomes a greater and greater component of nutrient supply. This is particularly true for highly soluble nutrients such as nitrate.

Because of the demand for water by the plant root, there is generally a significant flow of nutrients towards the root. The considerable supply of root-exuded soluble carbon away from the root to the rhizosphere microbes can, therefore, only really be through diffusion. This diffusion of root-exuded soluble carbon supplies the rhizosphere microbial population with the bulk of their growth substrate.

Soil water being held at tensions of 50 mbar or 5 kPa (i.e. field capacity) or less will tend to drain from the soil under the influence of gravity. Nutrients, particularly those not attracted to soil particles by ion exchange, may well be lost from the soil as this drainage process occurs. Nitrate, in particular, being a highly mobile anion (i.e. being negatively charged, it is not attracted to negatively charged clay and organic matter particles) is readily leached in this way. The consequently high concentrations of nitrate in the groundwater of some areas receiving high inputs of nitrogenous fertilisers is an environmental problem of considerable current concern.

SOIL ATMOSPHERE

The degree to which the soil pore space is water filled has a profound influence on both the gaseous composition of the soil air and on the

Table 4. *Concentrations in air and soil air, diffusion coefficients, and water solubilities of the major gaseous components of the soil[a]*

	N_2	O_2	CO_2
Concentrations in air (%)	79	21	0.035
Typical soil air concentrations (%)	79	20–21	0.1–1.0
Diffusion coefficients in air ($cm^2 s^{-1}$)	2.1	2.1	1.6
Diffusion coefficients in water ($cm^2 s^{-1}$)	1.6×10^{-4}	1.8×10^{-4}	1.8×10^{-4}
Solubility in water	1.5	1.5	87.8

[a] Values given are for 20 °C.

composition of dissolved gases in the soil water itself:

$$\text{Soil water status} \rightarrow \text{Soil biological activity} \rightarrow \frac{\text{Soil } CO_2}{\text{Soil } O_2}$$

In well aerated soil, oxygen concentrations rarely will drop below 20% and CO_2 concentrations rarely will increase to above 1% (Russell, 1973).

Table 4 shows the typical ranges of concentration of the major gaseous constituents (N_2, O_2 and CO_2) of the soil. If a soil has a pronounced clay texture and/or is waterlogged, with a high level of biological activity, carbon dioxide concentrations as high as 10% may result.

A depth profile of carbon dioxide in the soil shows that concentrations generally increase with depth. Maximum biological activity, however, is usually close to the soil surface, as oxygen supply by diffusion is greatest. Maximum biological activity generally occurs at soil water potentials approximating to 40% of the soil's water-holding capacity, conditions usually found either soon after a rain event or just above the water table. At soil moisture levels greater than this, the rate of biological activity is generally limited by the rate of oxygen diffusion which is considerably slower in water than air (Table 4). Thus the shape and distribution of the soil pore space is of fundamental importance in determining the rate of oxygen and carbon dioxide diffusion to and from the zones of biological activity. If the biological respiratory demand exceeds the oxygen diffusion supply from the soil surface, then the oxygen concentration will approach zero (anoxic conditions). If biological activity is then to proceed, it can only do so anaerobically (i.e. in the absence of oxygen). A more detailed discussion of anaerobic biological activity is given in the following section on redox potential. Plant roots are unable to respire anaerobically and prolonged anaerobism will lead to the death of many plants. Some plants, however, provide pathways for oxygen diffusion into otherwise oxygen-starved depths of the soil. In this way, the plant creates an aerobic microenvironment around the root system. Plants with this adaptation are, not surprisingly, bog species and the rice plant, which is often cultivated in an artificially waterlogged paddy system.

Because only a few plants have developed a provision of their own root oxygen supply, in soils that are largely water filled (i.e. close to field capacity), it is oxygen supply to roots that tends to limit the growth of most plants. The largest soil pores ($> 30 \, \mu m$), which drain rapidly under gravity, become the main oxygen suppliers to roots, the water in smaller pores remaining full of stationary water through which oxygen diffuses at only a fraction (1/1000th) of the diffusion rate through air. It is this continuous replenishing of oxygen supply in drainage water that distinguishes a saturated but draining or flushed soil from a waterlogged soil where there is little or no movement of water. Replenishing of oxygen is both from diffusion of oxygen into soil water as well as from rainfall bringing dissolved oxygen into the soil.

The rate at which oxygen diffuses through the soil is an important determinant of soil biological activity and can be measured using a platinum electrode. The respiratory demand for oxygen from roots and microbes in soil can exceed $20 \, \text{g m}^{-2} \, \text{day}^{-1}$ and, if the replenishment of this oxygen ceased, oxygen in soil air could only maintain this respiratory demand for less than a day (Russell, 1973). Generally, of course, overall depletion of soil oxygen is less rapid and there is often great variability in relation to soil oxygen status, depending on the distribution of the pore space and on the distribution of available organic substrates that drive respiratory demand.

The overall oxygen status of a soil, although of value in interpreting crop growth, is not as useful as the status of individual aggregates in interpreting soil microbiological activity. Greenwood (1975) calculated the critical aggregate radius (i.e. assuming spherical aggregates) for the onset of anaerobic conditions at the centre of the aggregate for different respiratory oxygen demands at that centre. A derivative of Fick's law (the law governing rates of gaseous diffusion) was used in the calculation:

$$a^2 = 6CD/R$$

where a is the aggregate radius (cm)

$\quad\quad C$ is the difference in O_2 concentration between aggregate's surface and centre (ml O_2 ml^{-1})

D is the diffusion coefficient of O_2 through the water phase ($cm^2 s^{-1}$)
R is the respiration rate inside the aggregate ($ml \ O_2 \ cm^{-3}$).

For this calculation, one assumes that the switch from aerobic to anaerobic metabolism occurs at micromolar oxygen concentrations because of the very high affinity that cytochrome oxidase, the enzyme catalysing O_2 reduction in plants and animals, has for O_2. From the equation anaerobic conditions are predicted to occur in water-saturated aggregates of radius 1 cm or greater for typical levels of soil respiration. These conditions will be most likely found in clay soils in the spring when both moisture levels and biological activity are high. The fact that anaerobic processes do sometimes occur in most freely draining soils, however, suggests that anaerobic microsites often develop in soil and that Greenwood's theoretical calculations may overestimate the critical aggregate radius in which anaerobism occurs.

The soil atmosphere as a source of carbon and nutrients to the soil biota

Considerable research attention is currently being focused on the strategies that heterotrophic soil microbes adopt to grow in soil under conditions of low availability of carbon and other nutrients. Growth under these conditions is termed oligotrophy and is probably a common feature of microbial growth in soils where supply of available carbon and nutrients is often very low, particularly at the microsite level. An oligotrophic microorganism can be defined as 'one which predominates in a nutrient-poor environment, is isolated using a low nutrient medium and shows relatively high growth rates in culture at low concentratons of energy-yielding substrates' (Williams, 1985). As yet, it is not fully clear how soil microbes growing oligotrophically obtain their carbon supply, but it seems likely that, at these very low carbon concentrations in the soil solutions, the soil atmosphere may represent an additional carbon supply. It may be that soil microbial heterotrophs can fix atmospheric carbon dioxide, but this has yet to be substantiated. There have also been suggestions that oligotrophic soil microbes can scavenge hydrocarbons and other carbon volatiles from the atmosphere, although further research is required to identify how the soil atmosphere provides carbon for oligotrophic growth. It seems certain, however, that soil heterotrophs use strategies other than strict chemoheterotrophy to grow in environments of

low available carbon/nutrients, and that the role of the soil atmosphere as a supplier of this carbon and nutrients must be closely examined.

SOIL REDOX POTENTIAL

Non-photosynthetic biological activity in the soil (fungi, most bacteria, and soil animals) derives energy from the oxidation of reduced substrates, which may be either organic (for heterotrophic metabolism) or inorganic (chemo-autotrophic metabolism) in nature. Plants, of course, get this energy directly from sunlight. Electrons removed in these oxidations are passed down an electron transport chain inside the cell (Figure 4) which enables energy from the electrons to be harnessed as adenosine triphosphate (ATP). As stated in the previous section, unless the oxygen concentration in the soil water falls to micromolar concentrations, aerobes will then use oxygen to accept the 'spent' electrons, producing water. Oxygen is referred to as the terminal electron acceptor. When oxygen concentrations drop below this value, nitrate (NO_3^-) may replace it as the terminal electron acceptor (Figure 4), the nitrate reductase enzyme replacing cytochrome oxidase.

Once oxygen and nitrate have been used through respiratory demand, there follows a sequential reduction of possible electron acceptors. The

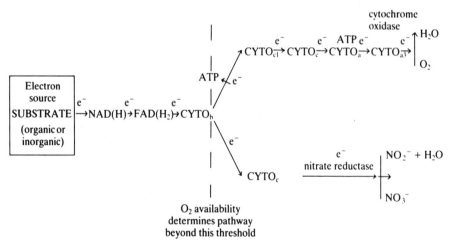

Figure 4. Electron transport mechanisms of denitrifying soil bacteria under aerated conditions (cytochrome oxidase) and under conditions of reduced oxygen tension (nitrate reductase). Cytochrome oxidase is always the preferred pathway when there is adequate oxygen.

Table 5. *Sequence of terminal electron acceptors used in the soil environment with associated redox potential scale at pH 7*

Terminal electron acceptor and ultimate reduced product	Environmental process	Redox potential at pH 7 (mV)	Soil biota involved
$O_2 + e^- \rightarrow H_2O$	Aerobic respiration	+820	Plant roots, aerobic, microbes, animals
$NO_3^- + e^- \rightarrow N_2$	Denitrification	+420	*Pseudomonas*,
$Mn^{4+} + e^- \rightarrow Mn^{3+}$	Manganese reduction	+410	*Bacillus* etc.
Organic matter $+ e^- \rightarrow$ organic acids	Fermentation	+400	*Clostridium* etc.
$Fe^{3+} + e^- \rightarrow Fe^{2+}$	Iron reduction	−180	*Pseudomonas*
$NO_3^- + e^- \rightarrow NH_4^+$	Dissimilatory nitrate reduction	−200	*Achromobacter*
$SO_4^{2-} + e^- \rightarrow H_2S$	Sulphate reduction	−220	*Desulfovibrio*
$CO_2 + e^- \rightarrow CH_4$	Methanogenesis	−240	*Methanobacterium*

acceptor in operation in soil at any time is determined by the soil redox potential, which, in simple terms, is a measure of the likelihood of a substance to gain (reduction) or lose (oxidation) electrons:

$$Eh = E_o + \frac{0.059}{n} \log \frac{[Ox]}{[Red]}$$

This is a simple Nernst-type equation

where Eh is the measured platinum electrode potential (mV)

E_o is the standard potential of the system (mV)

n is the number of electrons in the system

[Ox] is the electrons lost

[Red] is the electrons gained.

The sequence of reduction of terminal electron acceptors in the soil environment is shown in Table 5 with the approximate redox potential at which each reduction step occurs. Because Eh is a function of pH (Eh is measured relative to a standard potential from the hydrogen electron, assigned a value of 0 V at 1 mole, pH 0), there is a broad Eh range in which each reduction step may occur because of possible variation in soil pH. Nitrate, for example, may be used as a terminal electron acceptor (denitrification) at $+420$ mV at pH 7.0 or at -205 mV at pH 10.2.

It is a good general rule that the presence of electron acceptors of a higher oxidation state in soil will tend to inhibit respiration involving an electron acceptor of a lower oxidation state. For example, sulphate reduction will be inhibited by the presence of oxygen, nitrate, manganese (Mn^{4+}) and iron (Fe^{3+}).

The picture is further complicated by the fact that, as with soil aeration, there is enormous spatial variation in redox potential in the soil, particularly because of aggregate microsites of high biological activity. This means that, in reality, there is often more than one electron acceptor in operation at any one time in the soil. For example, under certain circumstances, NO_3^-, Mn^{4+} and Fe^{3+} may all be in operation as electron acceptors in soil simultaneously. Some soil microbes possess the enzyme machinery to use more than one terminal electron acceptor. Denitrifying soil microbes, for example, which are predominantly heterotrophic bacteria (species of *Pseudomonas*, *Bacillus* and *Alcaligenes* are common denitrifiers) are mostly able to use O_2, NO_3^- and Mn^{4+} as acceptors in that order of preference. Because of this ability to switch from aerobic to anaerobic metabolism, these bacteria are termed 'facultative anaerobes'. Bacteria that can only respire anaerobically are termed obligate anaerobes. Only when the soil environment provides for sustained anaerobic conditions do the obligately anaerobic bacteria prevail. Boggy sites often provide these conditions and are often characterised by sulphate reduction (1) and sometimes by methanogenesis (2).

$$CaSO_4 + 2CH_3CHOHCOONa \rightarrow$$

$$H_2S + CaCO_3 + 2CH_3COONa + H_2O \quad (1)$$

$$4H_2R + CO_2 \rightarrow 4R + CH_4 + 2H_2O \quad (2)$$

Sulphate reduction in soil is carried out mainly by the bacterial genera *Desulfotomaculum* and *Desulfovibrio*, and their electron donors include a range of carbohydrates, organic acids (particularly lactic acid) and alcohols. Methanogenesis may occur by a number of means, largely by the bacterial family Methanobacteriaceae, which includes the common genus *Methanobacterium*. In the case of reaction (2), carbon dioxide is the electron acceptor and some reduced organic species the donor. Microbial production of methane from reduction of carbon dioxide will only tend to occur when organic soils are waterlogged for a long period of time and other electron acceptors are exhausted.

Plants, soil animals, and almost all soil fungi, however, are only able to respire aerobically with oxygen as their terminal electron acceptor (obligate aerobes). Only plants specifically adapted to reducing conditions, through development of their own O_2 supply to the roots, can survive protracted anaerobic conditions in soils. This adaptation involves an increase in the cortical air space (aerenchyma) providing a channel for passage of air in plants such as rice and aquatic plants. The enhanced oxygen supply via the aerenchyma not only maintains the root system, but can also enable an aerobic rhizosphere microbial population to persist in an otherwise anaerobic soil. Generally, however, in anaerobic soils, root growth will be inhibited by the lack of oxygen supply. The plant suffers in a number of ways, including reduced water uptake (low oxygen reduces root permeability), restricted nutrient uptake, accumulation of toxic products of anaerobic metabolism, and various unfavourable hormonal responses. The pattern of carbon assimilation and distribution within the plant and rhizosphere is also fundamentally influenced by anaerobiosis. The book edited by Hook & Crawford (1978) provides an excellent review of the effects of anaerobism on plants.

Even in soils that are predominantly aerobic, products of anaerobiosis can diffuse to plant roots in aerobic sites and severely restrict their growth. Production of phytotoxins through the anaerobic breakdown of crop residues is a good example of this type of phenomenon. These phytotoxic products of anaerobic microbial decomposition reactions include acetic acid and other organic acids, a range of hydrocarbons and hydrogen sulphide. Soil anaerobiosis also adversely affects plant growth through the loss of nitrate, an important nutrient, by denitrification

$$NO_3 \rightarrow NO_2 \rightarrow NO \rightarrow N_2O \rightarrow N_2$$

Obligately aerobic bacteria and almost all soil fungi cannot survive prolonged anaerobic conditions in the soil. These organisms tend to decline in numbers when soils are subjected to flooding and subsequently anaerobic conditions. The greatest rates of decline are associated with soils of high organic matter content, presumably because of the formation of a range of fungitoxic products of organic matter decomposition under anaerobism. The products probably include ethylene and hydrogen sulphide. The decline of soil fungi as a result of even short periods of anaerobiosis may explain why mycorrhizal development is low in poorly draining soils.

Most soil animals are obligate aerobes and so, apart from non-active cysts, the numbers of active soil animals tend to be low in anaerobic soils. In fact, flooding arable soils to produce anaerobic conditions is a well practised means of controlling soil animal pests.

Where soil animals have adapted to anaerobic soil conditions (such as have some protozoa and nematodes) their strategies of metabolic adaptation in many ways closely resemble those of plants that grow in soils that are subject to anaerobiosis.

A more detailed discussion of the nature and effects of soil redox potential can be found in the review of Rowell (1981).

SOIL pH

A considerable area of the world's soils experiences a degree of either excess acidity or alkalinity that is sub-optimal for soil biological activity. Measurement and understanding of soil pH and its effects are, therefore, an integral part of studying soil ecology. The term pH is defined as the logarithm of the reciprocal of the hydrogen (H^+) activity

$$pH = \log(1/A_{H^+}) \quad \text{or} \quad -\log A_{H^+}$$

Soil pH, therefore, is a measure of the concentration of the hydrogen ions in soil water. Soil pH can also, then, be considered as a measure of the acidity of the soil solution, because acids are compounds that dissociate in water to produce hydrogen ions.

Under strongly acidic conditions, aluminium (if present) will also contribute to the pH measurement. Aluminium becomes increasingly soluble with greater acidity and is present in the soil solution as aluminium or aluminium hydroxy cations, which contribute to pH buffering because of their capacity for hydrolysis.

In soils that have a near neutral or alkaline pH, the exchange sites in the soil tend to become occupied by exchangeable base cations such as calcium (Ca^{2+}), magnesium (Mg^{2+}), sodium (Na^+) and potassium (K^+). When these cations replace hydrogen and aluminium ions on the exchange sites in the soil, the hydrogen ion concentration in the soil solution decreases with a concomitant rise in hydroxyl ions and, hence, in pH.

Soil biological growth, particularly of plant root systems, can cause short-term soil acidification because it tends to remove base cations such as calcium, sodium, potassium, and magnesium in exchange for hydrogen ions.

The nitrogen nutrition of the plant will have an important effect on pH relations, particularly of the rhizosphere soil. Plant root uptake of ammonium is balanced by the release of hydrogen ions into the soil. Plant root uptake of nitrate, however, is balanced by the release of bicarbonate and hydroxyl ions. The rhizosphere soil pH, therefore, is partly controlled by the source of mineral nitrogen to the plant, decreasing when ammonium is the dominant source of nitrogen, and increasing when nitrate predominates. Microbial decomposition of organic matter also tends to increase soil acidity through the production of organic acids. This tends to occur under wet, anaerobic conditions where fermentative microbes in the soil produce a range of organic acids including acetic, lactic, formic, butyric and propionic acid from plant residues. This type of situation develops in many moorland and forest soils, producing very acid litter. Soluble organic acids as well as larger fulvic acids are leached through the soil profile causing acidification and weathering, which leads to the formation of podzols with very low percentage base saturations (often less than 5%).

Generally, under anerobic soil conditions, the ultimate end product of the heterotrophic metabolism of microbes and animals in soil is carbon dioxide:

$$C_6H_{12}O_6 + 6O_2 \rightarrow 6CO_2 + 6H_2O + E$$

Carbon dioxide, produced eventually from the breakdown of almost every organic residue, will combine with water to form carbonic acid ($H_2O + CO_2 \rightarrow H_2CO_3$). This is a weak acid, which readily dissociates ($H_2CO_3 \rightleftharpoons H^+ + HCO_3^-$) yielding H^+ ions. The significance of carbon dioxide in soil pH relations is not always fully appreciated. The pH of a solution at equilibrium with carbon dioxide is represented by

$$pH = 6.04 - 0.65 \log P_{CO_2}$$

where P_{CO_2} is the partial pressure of carbon dioxide.

If soil biological activity produced a carbon dioxide level of 10% in the soil atmosphere, this will produce a dramatic pH shift in an unbuffered soil solution from pH 5.7 (at equilibrium with a background carbon dioxide level of 0.03%) to pH 4.4. Of course, this is an oversimplification for soil, however, because soil solutions are not unbuffered and biologically derived soil carbon dioxide levels only very seldom reach 10%. It nonetheless illustrates how important it is to trap CO_2 continuously in most sealed, soil incubation studies to prevent major shifts in soil pH.

Microbial oxidation of ammonium to nitrite (part of the process of nitrification) is another acidifying biological process:

$$2NH_4^+ + 3O_2 \xrightarrow{\text{Carried out by } \textit{Nitrosomonas}} 2NO_2^- + 4H^+ + 2H_2O + E$$

This process, however, is generally not strongly acidifying under natural conditions and it is only associated with a marked shift in soil pH after the input of an ammonium-based fertiliser or a manure, or in a weakly buffered sandy soil. Microbial oxidation of reduced sulphur in soil is potentially highly acidifying, but significant levels of reduced sulphur in soil are rare (after application of elemental S fertiliser or in the presence of sulphide-bearing ores).

A biological process that increases soil pH (i.e. causing alkalinity) is the hydrolysis of urea, catalysed by the enzyme urease.

$$CO(NH_2)_2 + H_2O \rightarrow H_2NCOONH_4 \rightarrow 2NH_3 + CO_2$$

Soil pH can rise by 2 or 3 units in the immediate vicinity of a urea fertiliser granule (Tisdale, Nelson & Beaton, 1985).

Soil pH most markedly affects plant growth through control of nutrient availability. High pH tends in particular to affect the plant adversely by reducing the availability (i.e. solubility) of manganese and iron to the root system. Phosphorus availability is also reduced because of formation of calcium phosphates. Marked soil acidification tends to affect the plant adversely through increased availability (often to the point of toxicity) of aluminium and also manganese. Sometimes other metals, because of their locally high concentrations, replace aluminium and manganese as the dominant phytotoxic components of low pH soil systems. Copper, for example, can become available at phytotoxic concentrations in mine spoil. Sometimes, plants growing in these situations exclude the copper by complexing the metal in fungal tissues that form a mycorrhizal association with the root system. Phosphorus availability is reduced at low pH, as well as at high pH, because of the formation of iron and aluminium phosphates. The main effects of soil pH on nutrient availability to root systems are summarised below.

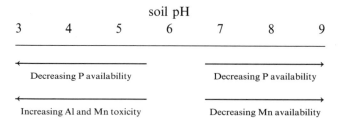

Soil pH has an important influence on the extent to which the plant root exudes carbon, carbon flow generally decreasing with increasing soil acidity.

Table 6. *Approximate pH tolerances of the major groups of soil microbes*

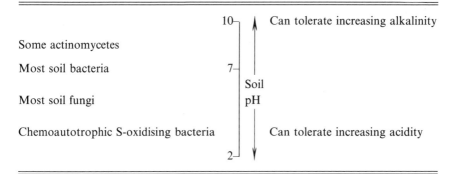

If less carbon is exuded by plants roots in acid soil, then less substrate will be supplied to the rhizosphere microbial population.

In the case of microbial activity, as with many other soil properties, it is the microsite variation in soil pH that is the most relevant determinant. Because of the swarm of cations within the double layer surrounding clay and organic colloids, the pH at the charged surface (out to 50–150 Å) can be a great deal more acid than the surrounding soil solution, although it remains unclear how much of this acidity will be experienced by a microbe attached to such a surface. A great deal of research is needed to understand the pH relations of microbes attached to soil particles, particularly as surface attachment can extend, rather than reduce, the lower pH limits of microbial processes. It may be that surface-attached microbes are protected by a thick, protective layer of polysaccharide through which protons can only diffuse slowly.

Table 6 shows the approximate pH range of the major groups of soil microbes. The most acid-tolerant S-oxidising bacteria (species of the genus *Thiobacillus*) can grow at pH 1, while the most alkali-tolerant streptomycetes can grow at pH 10. We are now discovering that, although different groups of soil microbes have well established pH optimum and ranges for growth, strains may somehow adapt to grow at pH values beyond the normal pH range of the species. Scientists, therefore, should not attach too great an ecological significance to published pH data for a particular organism. This is particularly true for chemo-autotrophic nitrification where it has long been considered (because of inappropriate *in vitro* evidence) that the process is negligible below pH 5, even though autotrophic nitrification occurs in soils considerably more acid than this.

Soil animals generally have fairly narrow pH requirements, although variation is considerable from one soil to another. Earthworms are generally highly sensitive to soil acidity and the range of pH tolerance of earthworms is such that species distribution is often highly indicative of soil pH (Swift, Heal & Anderson, 1979).

Earthworms have a mechanism of neutralising soil acidity, possessing calciferous glands on the sides of the pharynx. Other soil animals, including ants, are thought to operate this mechanism, although it is often the effect of calcium deficiency rather than the direct effect of pH that precludes many soil animals from acid soils.

In acid soils (below pH 5), such as coniferous forest and moorland soils, where acidity precludes the presence of earthworms, they are usually replaced by enchytraeid worms, which have considerable acid tolerance. The narrow pH range of many of the soil animals has an important bearing, of course, on the soil distribution of larger soil animals that feed on them. The absence of earthworms in acid soils, for example, contributes to ensuring the absence of large populations of moles, the earthworm being its primary prey.

SOIL TEMPERATURE

Temperature, a soil property of great biological significance, not only directly affects the rates of physiological reactions but also has many indirect effects on soil biological activity through temperature-induced changes to other aspects of the soil physicochemical environment such as diffusion rates, mineral weathering rates, redox potentials, water activity etc.

The ultimate source of heat energy for all soils is solar energy. About a third of the solar radiation incident on the soil plant system is reflected back to the atmosphere. The actual amount of energy that is not reflected (net radiation) depends on a variety of soil and vegetation properties (soil colour, slope, vegetation cover etc.). Some net radiation (about 5%) is used for photosynthesis while most (about 80%) is used to evaporate water. Only a small amount of incident light energy is available, therefore, to warm the soil. The degree to which the soil will warm per unit of energy is referred to as the specific heat capacity of the soil. Generally, however, it is the soil water content rather than the specific heat capacity that determines how much energy is needed to warm the soil – this is because of the specific heat capacity of water and also the heat of vaporisation of water (the energy involved in evaporating water).

Factors controlling the soil temperature regime, including diurnal and seasonal effects as well as factors such as vegetation status, moisture and soil depth, have been well reviewed (e.g. Russell, 1973).

As far as we know, there are no regions on earth (with the exception of sites of active volcanic activity) where terrestrial biological activity is absent because of temperature extremes. Sulphur-oxidising, thermophilic bacteria can grow at temperatures higher than 80 °C, on the other hand, psychrophilic 'snow-mould' fungi can decompose leaves buried under snow.

In most soils with a mesophilic microbial community, there is an approximate doubling of microbiological activity for each 10 °C rise in temperature between 0 °C and 30 °C/35 °C. Only a few degrees above the optimal temperature, there is a dramatic fall in activity as a result of thermal denaturation of proteins and membranes (thermophilic soil organisms possess great heat stability of these components).

Plant root systems are particularly sensitive to changes in soil temperature. A rise in soil temperature of as little as 1 °C can markedly stimulate both root and shoot growth and plant nutrient uptake. These mechanisms of growth effects due to changes in soil temperature are complex and include changes in water uptake, nutrient absorption, the budget of growth-related substances, and the temperature of the apical root meristem (Scott Russell, 1977). Soil temperature also influences the partitioning of photoassimilate within the soil/plant system, particularly with regard to root respiration, which markedly increases with soil temperature. To add further to these complications, temperature will not only affect the amount of carbon entering the soil from the plant root, but will also change the nature of this carbon supply. Because the rhizosphere microflora are dependent on this supply of carbon, soil temperature is, therefore, a fundamental control of the interaction between plant roots and the soil microbial biomass. The effect of changing soil temperature on this control, however, varies enormously with plant species, growth stage and other interacting soil parameters such as moisture status and pH.

There is considerable controversy concerning the significance of micro-biological activity at or near to freezing point in soil. Although we have long known of sub-freezing bioactivity in Arctic environments, far less information is available concerning more temperate latitudes. Soil researchers often assume that storing of soil samples under refrigeration at or around 4 °C will prevent biological activity. Such assumptions can give particularly misleading results in nitrogen-cycling studies where nitrification rarely proceeds significantly below 7 °C, but ammonification, because it is carried out by a much wider group of microbes, may be maintained at a slow rate down to freezing point. Certainly, ammonium accumulates in soils in autumn and spring and in stored soils. The mechanism of NH_4 accumulation in refrigerated soil samples and in soils in autumn/spring is shown below.

$$\text{Soil organic matter} \xrightarrow{\text{Mineralisation}} NH_4^+ \xrightarrow[\substack{\text{Low-temperature} \\ \text{block operates} \\ \text{here first}}]{\text{Nitrification}} NO_3^-$$

Freeze–thaw activity can selectively accelerate biological processes, particularly the microbial mediation of gaseous nitrogen loss via denitrification and NH_3-volatilisation. It may be that freeze–thaw action in soil accelerates these processes of N-loss through mechanisms such as carbon mobilisation (due to disruption of soil biomass and of hydrophobic organic matter residues) or by the reduction in oxygen supply to the soil (due to freeze–thaw alteration of pore structure).

Soil temperature is a factor of paramount importance in terms of the distribution and activity of the soil animals. Soil animals are generally very sensitive to overheating and will tend to migrate down the soil to avoid high temperatures. This is largely because of the excessive respiratory oxygen demand associated with these temperatures. There is also considerable literature evidence (e.g. Kühnelt, 1961) that the respiratory enzymes of soil animals are quite easily damaged by high soil temperatures. Generally, soil animals are less sensitive to extremes of low temperature. Some soil animals such as earthworms migrate down the profile, if possible, to avoid frost under wintry conditions. Many other soil animals, including springtails (Collembola) and mites (Acari), can often be frozen in the soil, but will renew activity with the onset of warmer soil conditions. It should be remembered that observed reductions in organic matter decomposition/turnover in soil with decreasing soil temperature are often as much, if not more, a consequence of reduced soil animal activity as microbial activity.

Finally, it must be emphasised that soil temperature may be interacting with other factors such as soil moisture to regulate biological activity. A rise in soil temperature, for example, can only have a marked stimulatory effect on soil biological activity if the moisture status of the soil is not limiting the activity. Similarly, the rewetting of a drought-affected soil will only markedly stimulate biological activity when temperatures permit. There is some uncertainty regarding the mathematical nature of this interaction between moisture and temperature, whether or not it is additive, involves a multiplication factor, or involves a 'threshold' principle where one of the factors may dominate in a particular situation.

SOIL LIGHT

Apart from affecting soil temperature as described in the previous section, light is also a primary determinant of soil biological activity. Generally speaking, light is a parameter only directly affecting the distribution and activity of organisms on or very near to the surface of the soil. The small amount of light penetration below the soil surface varies from one soil to another and is most markedly affected by the nature of the vegetation cover, topographic factors, and the nature of the pore space at the soil surface. This latter parameter is controlled by soil type, and also by the activity of burrowing soil animals and plant roots.

Light provides the energy source for the photoautotrophic component of the soil biota. About 5% of net solar radiation (total solar radiation at the earth's surface minus that reflected) is used for photosynthesis reactions in various components of the soil biota. These include the plants, the soil algae and the photoautotrophic soil bacteria. The photoautotrophs possess chlorophyll to enable them to convert sunlight to energy. The microbial photoautotrophs in soil only contribute very slightly to the total microbial biomass and are almost entirely restricted to the soil surface. Only occasionally do soil environmental conditions, particularly in temperate latitudes, enable soil surface blooms of algae to contribute significantly to the total soil microbial biomass. This is because of the soil algal requirement for adequate moisture, which limits growth in the summer months. Where light and moisture do permit blooms of algal growth on the soil surface, their production of polysaccharides is thought to often make an important contribution to aggregate stabilisation and, hence, establishment and maintenance of good soil structure.

Light may be an important agent in soil in triggering the activity of animals, particularly insects, living near the soil surface (Wallwork, 1970).

We should always bear in mind that it is light that ultimately provides the energy to drive the soil ecosystem. It is as a result of the death and decomposition of photoautotrophs (largely plants) and to a much lesser extent chemoautotrophs that inputs of chemical energy as fixed carbon are made to the soil enabling the whole soil heterotrophic community to proliferate (Figure 5).

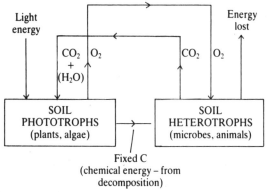

Figure 5. The interconversion of energy in the soil/plant system. It is the input of light energy that drives the whole system.

SOIL MICROSITES

The soil is far from homogeneous in relation to all the soil parameters discussed in this chapter – minerals, organic matter, living biomass, structure, water, atmosphere, redox, pH, temperature and light. Some of these properties vary over a few micrometres in the soil whereas others may not change over several kilometres. A small soil aggregate may have an anaerobic centre while the surface remains aerobic. Two distinctly different types of biological processes would, therefore, be occurring even though the sites might be less than a millimetre apart.

The soil biota consists of different sized organisms (see Chapter 2) and these inhabit the soil on vastly differing scales. The habitat for a bacterium may be a micropore of a soil aggregate, to the wall of which the bacterium is attached. On the other hand, an individual tree root system may occupy more than a thousand cubic metres of soil.

Soil must be considered at the microsite level to understand interactions between different components of the soil biota. This is particularly important in prey–predator relations where differences in size between prey and predator can facilitate predator exclusion in a range of soil microsites. It is also important in assessing substrate turnover and nutrient flow in soils, because pore location will not only determine access for microbial attack, but will also influence the moisture regime under which any activity occurs.

The microsite variation in distribution of the soil's living and non-living components are intimately related. The location and activity of an individual soil microbe may be caused by the occurrence of a tiny fragment of organic matter within the soil matrix, even though many more microbes may be located in the rhizosphere of a nearby root.

Understanding the microsite variation of the soil provides one of the greatest challenges to the soil ecologist, particularly because any study of the soil necessitates microsite perturbation. To date, we have only developed an integrated understanding of the role of microsites in soil ecology. The study of plant growth, for example, has enabled us to obtain an integrated measurement of the net products of microsite processes because the plant root system resolves the soil mosaic at a level necessary to optimise nutrient uptake (Anderson, 1987). To resolve and study individual microsites requires *in situ* techniques with great sensitivity. Modern molecular techniques involving the marking and *in situ* detection of components of the soil biota may, coupled with more traditional soil micromorphological methods, enable us to better characterise the soil at the microsite level.

CONCLUSIONS

The aim of this chapter has been to discuss the soil as a complex and varied habitat for biological activity. The physicochemical factors that most influence the soil biological habitat, and hence soil ecology, have been presented. Clearly, many of them are highly interactive and only a few of these interactions can be considered within the confines of this book. Furthermore, the interactions often occur at a microsite level. Only complicated computer modelling can ever attempt to formulate all of the possible interactions (at all levels in the soil), although field and laboratory investigations with increasingly powerful techniques will enable us to identify with greater certainty the dominant, selective factors and interactions governing the soil as a bio-habitat.

2 The soil biota

INTRODUCTION

The previous chapter considered the more important of the physical and chemical factors that contribute to make the soil a varied habitat (or range of microhabitats) and explained much of this heterogeneity in terms of distribution and function of the soil biota. This chapter briefly describes the chief components of the soil biota and demonstrates the incredible biodiversity of the soil community. Figure 6 illustrates some representatives of the main components of this community. The viruses, which are generally about 0.1 μm in length, are too small for realistic inclusion. Also for obvious reasons, the larger soil animals, such as moles and rabbits, cannot be considered.

The plant roots, microbes and animals that make up the soil biological community produce intracellular and extracellular enzymes that are responsible for much of the biogeochemical cycling in the soil. The ecological significance of soil enzymes is discussed in Chapter 4.

PLANT ROOTS

Since the classic work on plant root systems by Weaver (1926), a picture has gradually been emerging of plant root systems as an incredibly labile and varied component of the soil biomass. The volume of surface soil occupied by plant root systems obviously varies with the vegetation present and the soil environment for root exploitation but can be as much as 5% or more, although values of about 1% are probably more typical.

Root systems extend through the soil by division and elongation of cells at or near to the root tip. The root tip consists of a protective cap, which controls the geotrophic curvature of the root, surrounded by a film of mucilage, which is a largely polysaccharidic slime secreted by the outer cells

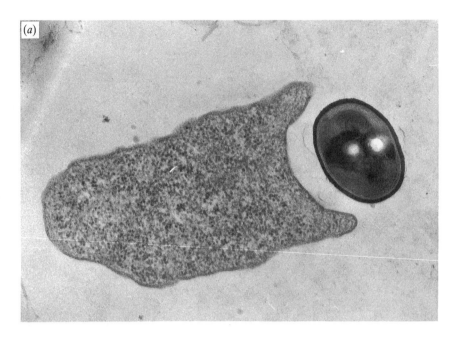

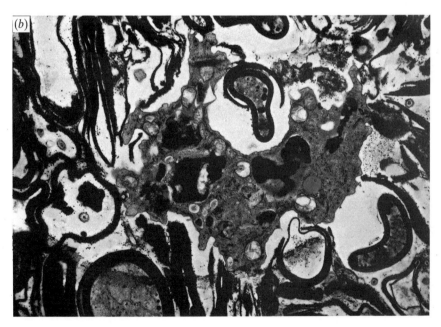

Figure 6. (*a*) and (*b*). *See caption on page* 37.

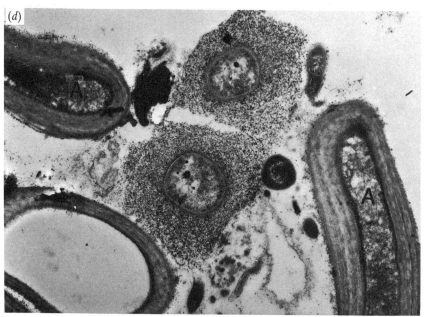

Figure 6. (*c*) and (*d*). *See caption on page* 37.

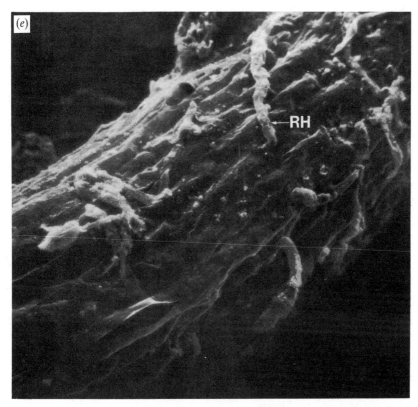

Figure 6. A collection of electron micrographs (EMs) showing some of the
different components of the soil biota. (*a*) and (*b*) Transmission electron
micrographs (TEMs) of (*a*) bacteria being ingested (× 30 000) and (*b*) having been
ingested (× 10 000) by amoebae in soil. (*c*) Scanning electron micrograph (SEM)
of a fungus in soil (× 5000). (*d*) TEM of arthropod parts (A) in soil (× 10 000). (*e*)
SEM of the root hair (RH) zone behind the zone of elongation of a plant root (× 570).

of the root cap. Behind the cap is the zone of the root (the meristematic
zone) in which cell division occurs. Behind the meristematic zone, the new
cells elongate and differentiate prior to maturation and the development of
root hairs. The extension of main root axes and of laterals through the soil
follows a similar story.

With very few exceptions, laterals are produced from main root axes
to enable a branched root system to develop in the soil. Although the rate
of extension of root members is largely a function of diameter (larger
meristematic areas facilitate greatest extension), there is considerable spatial

variation – intensive localised development of laterals, for example, can occur as a result of a favourable niche in the soil and can lead to interesting and unusual branching patterns in root systems.

Root systems vary enormously in their morphology, longevity, activity and composition as a result of both environmental and species differences, but their function is generally to supply the plant with water and mineral nutrients and to anchor it to the soil. A key feature of almost all plant root systems is an obligate requirement for aerobic conditions in the soil environment. Plant demand for soil oxygen is considerable – roots can often contribute 30% of total soil respiration. Usually, the supply of soil resources to the above-ground parts of a plant depends on the length of viable root available for absorption at that time in relation to plant demand, modified by root distribution with soil depth and by soil conditions.

Root systems are almost always associated with adjacent soil (rhizosphere) containing a denser distribution of microbes compared to soil without roots present. The term rhizosphere was introduced by Hiltner (1904) to rather narrowly define soil adjacent to legume roots in which bacterial growth is influenced by nitrogenous nodule exudates. The rhizosphere is now considered in a much wider sense to represent soil adjacent to any root where microbes are affected by the presence of the root. The extent of the rhizosphere will vary greatly but is generally considered to be the cylinder of soil that root hairs exploit and into which they release exudates.

The rhizosphere soil can be distinguished from the bulk soil on a physical, chemical and biological basis.

It is the movement of the growing root that contributes most to soil physical properties. The rates at which roots penetrate the soil vary with the plant and the environmental conditions, but rates of a few centimetres a day are not uncommon for root axes, with somewhat lower rates for laterals. As the root penetrates the soil fabric, it displaces its own volume and, in doing so, compresses the nearby soil. The clay minerals and soil particles may lie with their narrow dimension parallel to the root axis. There may be a zone of space around the root and, consequently, the pathway for water, nutrient, microbial, and even microfaunal movement may be more convoluted than in the bulk soil. Because of this, organic matter released by the root may accumulate close to the root. The water potential regime of the rhizosphere is very different from that of the bulk soil, generally being lower than the bulk soil; this causes a net mass flow of water towards the roots and can set up a nutrient gradient across the rhizosphere.

The chemical nature of the rhizosphere is quite different from the bulk soil, largely as a result of the release of carbon from the roots and the selective uptake of ions from the soil solution. The plant acts as a carbon pump, fixing carbon from the atmosphere as root exudates. Because microbial uptake provides a ready sink for this carbon, concentrations of available carbon around the root are not particularly high. Selective root uptake of ions from soil solution, however, causes some ions to be depleted in the rhizosphere while those that are not absorbed tend to accumulate. The rhizosphere also generally experiences greater rates of mineral weathering, and, depending on the ratio of cation:anion uptake by the roots, the rhizosphere pH may differ considerably from the bulk soil (see page 25).

The biological nature of the rhizosphere is discussed in Chapter 3 as an intense zone of interaction between plant roots and other components of the soil biota, particularly microbes.

The rhizosphere effect is not restricted to a proliferation of microbes. Root exudation of available carbon, through enabling microbial proliferation, can also cause the protozoal population density to increase in a classic predator/prey relationship, assuming soil water potentials are within the limits of protozoal activity.

As well as indirect associations between free-living rhizosphere and rhizoplane (root surface) microbes and the root, there are also more direct root/microbial associations where soil microbes become an integral part of the root itself. The symbiotic mycorrhizal and rhizobial/leguminous associations (Figure 7) fall into this latter category.

The interaction of plant roots with soil microbes, and animals, through the provision of photoassimilated carbon as root exudate, at first appears to be wasteful of the plant's resources. However, many of the microbes that receive this carbon provide direct benefit to the plant. Rhizobia, for example, supply fixed nitrogen to the plant root in return for photoassimilate. The mycobiont of the mycorrhizal association enhances the plant root's capacity for the uptake of phosphorus and many other soil nutrients. Free-living rhizosphere heterotrophs also provide a return to the plant for their carbon supply, such as through the provision of growth promoters, fixed nitrogen, mobilised soil nutrients and disease protection. Unfortunately the interaction of soil organisms with the plant root is not always beneficial to the plant. Many fungi causing soil-borne plant root diseases, for example, can grow saprophytically in the soil as a result of root carbon exudation, but may also attack as root pathogens. This is particularly true of fungi such as species of *Rhizoctonia* and *Pythium*, which are well known agents of plant root disease.

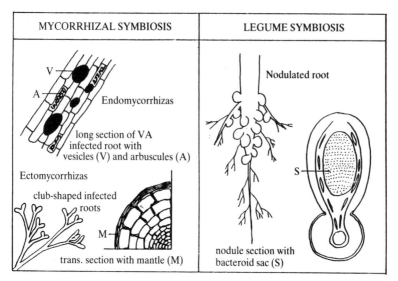

MYCORRHIZAL SYMBIOSIS	LEGUME SYMBIOSIS

Figure 7. Plant root/microbial interactions – the mycorrhizal and legume symbioses.

SOIL MICROBES – BACTERIA, ACTINOMYCETES, FUNGI AND ALGAE

Introduction

The microbial biomass in the soil is the driving force of most terrestrial ecosystems because it is this biomass that largely controls the rates of turnover and mineralisation of organic substrates. In recent years, a great deal of effort has gone into the measurement of the size of the microbial biomass and its associated nutrient pools. Sparling (1985) reviews many of the methods and approaches for this measurement.

This book will not dwell on measurement of the size of the microbial biomass. Far more relevant to the soil ecologist is the activity and potential activity of soil microbes as well as the interactions between soil microbes, between microbes and other components of the soil biota, and between microbes and the soil matrix.

Most of the soil represents a nutritionally poor or 'oligotrophic' environment. Microbes and their activity, therefore, are far from evenly distributed through the soil, being concentrated in certain niches or 'hot spots' such as the rhizosphere, guts of some soil animals, the vicinity of readily available organic and inorganic substrates, and the smaller, water-filled pores which exclude predators. Although less than 0.5% of the soil pore space is actually required for occupancy by microbes, there are few, if any, pores in the soil where microbes do not exist. The larger pores may be accessed by all microbes, while the smaller (pore neck diameters of the order of a few micrometres or so) micropores will tend to be accessed only by certain bacteria. Even smaller pores will be occupied by soil viruses.

True soil organisms (microbes and animals) are adapted to life in the soil. Gene mutations and genetic transfers of various kinds, in conjunction with natural selection processes, enable populations and communities of organisms to develop which are adapted in form and physiology to a particular soil habitat/niche.

Modern techniques of cell detection and enumeration such as specific DNA and RNA probes, immunological methods of detection, and fatty acid profile analyses are now available to the soil ecologist. The increasing use of these molecular-based techniques, with far greater sensitivity than traditional approaches, will greatly facilitate the study of soil microbial ecology.

Bacteria

The most common microbial cells in the soil are those of the single-celled prokaryotes. Despite their high concentrations in the soil, the bacterial biomass in soil is generally exceeded by the fungal biomass (Table 7).

Bacterial cells (Figure 8) lack a nuclear membrane, have a cell wall composed largely of mucopeptides, can be heterotrophic or autotrophic in their metabolism, and reproduce largely by binary fission (a form of asexual reproduction where a single division of the nuclear area, or chromosome, is followed by cytoplasmic division to form two daughter cells of equal size). A smaller number of bacteria reproduce by budding. Soil bacteria are generally of the order of 1–2 μm long and 0.5–1 μm in diameter, and the cell may be rod shaped (bacillus), spherical (coccus), or, more unusually, helical (spirillum) or S-shaped (vibrio). Bacterial cells in soil may be non-motile or motile. Motility is achieved by the use of flagella, which may be all around the cell (peritrichous flagella) or simply at one end of the cell (polar flagella).

Regardless of motility, most soil bacteria are adsorbed to soil particles by a variety of mechanisms, but often by simple ion exchange. Bacterial cells

Table 7. *Approximate range of biomass of each major component of the biota in a typical temperate grassland soil*

Component of soil biota	Biomass (t ha^{-1})
Plant roots	up to 90 but generally about 20
Bacteria	1–2
Actinomycetes	0–2
Fungi	2–5
Protozoa	0–0.5
Nematodes	0–0.2
Earthworms	0–2.5
Other soil animals	0–0.5
Viruses	negligible

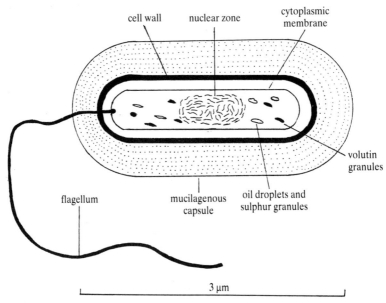

Figure 8. A diagrammatic representation of a soil bacterium.

and soil particles tend to have a net negative charge, and are held together via ionic bridges involving polyvalent cations.

Table 8 shows some of the major genera of the soil bacteria with their basic morphology and some of their other properties. Of the groups listed,

Table 8. *Some common soil bacteria and their main characteristics*

Genus	Gram stain	Cell shape	Motility	O_2 requirements
Bacillus	+	rod	+ (or −) peritrichous flagella	obligate aerobes and facultative anaerobes
Pseudomonas	−	rod	+ (or −) polar flagella	obligate aerobes and facultative anaerobes
Arthrobacter	variable	rod	−	obligate aerobes
Clostridium	+	rod	+ peritrichous flagella	obligate anaerobes
Nitrosomonas	−	rod	+ (or −) polar flagella	obligate aerobes
Micrococcus	+	sphere	−	obligate aerobes
Rhizobium	−	rod	+ (or −) peritrichous or polar flagella	obligate aerobes
Azotobacter	−	rod	+ (or −) peritrichous flagella	obligate aerobes

the *Arthrobacter* are generally the most prolific and, along with *Pseudomonas* and *Bacillus*, will usually dominate the bacterial population of most soils. Current understanding of which bacterial groups predominate in soils is based completely on the very limited traditional techniques of detection and enumeration (largely the plate count and related techniques) that have been available up until now.

The bacteria are divided into two main groups, the Gram-positive and the Gram-negative bacteria. The distinction is made by the Gram-staining procedure, which distinguishes between Gram-positive bacteria, which have a thicker cell wall (largely peptidoglycan, which consists of interlinked polypeptide and polysaccharide chains, with the rest made up of teichoic acid, a chain of sugar and glycerol units), and Gram-negative bacteria, which have a thinner cell wall, of almost pure peptidoglycan, surrounded by a thick, outer, lipoprotein-based membrane. The Gram-negative bacteria include the spirilla, most of the non-spore-forming rods with peritrichous flagella and all of the non-spore-forming rods with polar flagella. The Gram-positive bacteria include all the actinomycetes and most of the spore-forming rods.

The bacteria found in soil have numerous morphological and physiological adaptations that enable them to utilise more effectively the soil habitat. Often, one of the most striking morphological differences between a bacterium in the soil and the same species in a laboratory culture is the presence of a thick mucilaginous capsule around the soil bacterium. This capsule almost certainly has a number of roles, but it probably provides protection against a number of adverse aspects of the soil environment (e.g. desiccation, pH), and is involved in the attachment of the cell to soil particles.

Probably the most striking physiological adaptation to bacterial life (and other forms of microbial life) in soil is the ability to 'slow down' metabolic activity to enable growth under conditions of low supply of substrate carbon and nutrients. The most extreme example of this is oligotrophy (see pages 19 and 20) where the bacteria have developed numerous strategies to grow under carbon/nutrient starvation. Other soil bacteria have simply adapted to metabolise most efficiently at slow rates and obtain relatively high growth rates from the meagre resources generally available in the soil (the different growth strategies of soil microbes are discussed in more detail in Chapter 3, pages 80–6).

Differences in bacterial growth on rich laboratory media compared with the soil tell us a great deal about life in the soil. Some soil bacteria can have doubling times in the laboratory of under one hour. On the basis of these doubling rates, a bacterial colony would grow to exceed the mass of the earth itself in a matter of weeks! Clearly, because this has not happened in the soil (bacterial cells tends to divide only once or twice per year in soil), growth of bacteria (and other microbes) is strictly substrate limited for most of the time, with only brief flushes of intense activity. These flushes occur when substrate availability increases, perhaps through the addition of some plant or animal residue.

The composition of the bacterial population can often be used as an indicator of physicochemical conditions in the soil. The presence of actively growing bacteria such as *Clostridium*, for example, is indicative of anaerobic conditions, either in the bulk soil or just within microsites.

Bacterial cells tend to occur in small soil pores ($< 10\,\mu$m), probably because of protection from protozoal grazing and a favourable pore water regime. Most of these cells are found either individually or in microcolonies. It may also be that different bacterial communities exist in micropores within aggregates compared with those in larger pores and between aggregates. It has been suggested that intra-aggregate populations largely consist of Gram-negative bacteria and actinomycetes whereas the inter-aggregate populations include Gram-positive bacteria as well as other soil microbes (Hattori, 1973). This distribution of bacteria in relation to soil structure may reflect different survival strategies – the larger pores are more likely to dry out frequently so that spore-forming bacteria may be best equipped to survive, whereas the smaller pores containing the non-spore-forming bacteria will tend to remain water filled.

The bacteria have many varied functions in the soil. The decomposition of animal, plant and microbial residues is carried out by the heterotrophic bacteria. These bacteria tend to be the most numerous members of the soil microbial community and the degree of their substrate selectivity varies greatly from one bacterial species to another. Generally speaking, large organic polymers in the soil tend to be broken down by only a few specialised soil bacteria (or other microbes) whereas smaller organic molecules and sub-units of these polymers tend to provide a substrate for a much wider array of bacteria.

The chemoautotrophic bacteria in soil largely consist of the nitrifiers and, to a lesser extent, the sulphur oxidisers. Nitrification in soil is carried out largely by the chemoautotrophic bacteria *Nitrosomonas*, which oxidises ammonium to nitrite ($NH_4^+ \rightarrow NO_2^-$), and *Nitrobacter*, which oxidises nitrite to nitrate ($NO_2^- \rightarrow NO_3^-$). Sulphur oxidation in soil is largely performed by species of the genus *Thiobacillus*. More detailed discussion of the activity of the microbes involved in the cycling of nitrogen and sulphur in soil can be found in Chapter 4.

In addition to their role as decomposers, the heterotrophic bacterial community of the soil has a number of additional functions. Non-symbiotic nitrogen fixation is carried out by species of the genera *Azotobacter*, *Clostridium* and *Bacillus*, for example. *Azotobacter* is an obligately aerobic N_2-fixer, *Clostridium* is obligately anaerobic, and *Bacillus* facultatively anaerobic. The fixation is also carried out by cyanobacteria or blue-green algae although, because of their photosynthetic metabolism (photoautotrophism), the activity of these bacteria is largely restricted to the soil surface. The ability of the cyanobacteria to fix nitrogen and carbon dioxide directly from the atmosphere means that they have no dependence on preformed organic matter and can colonise bare rock surfaces and initiate soil formation. The cyanobacteria can also form part of the lichen association in conjunction with the fungi and these associations are also primary colonisers and initiators of soil formation. Symbiotic nitrogen fixation, largely in the nodules of leguminous plant roots, is the function of species of the genus *Rhizobium*, living in soil prior to infecting a legume as an aerobic saprophyte. The rhizobia infect and interact with around thirteen thousand different legume species. A number of other heterotrophic bacteria in soil are plant pathogens and, therefore, are the causal agents of many plant diseases. Plant pathogenic bacteria include species of *Agrobacterium* (causing, for example, gall diseases in many plants), *Pseudomonas* (largely sub-clinical plant pathogens) and *Erwinia* (a common cause of soft rots). These bacteria tend always to be associated with plant tissue, but are regularly reintroduced to soil in the residues of infected plants.

Actinomycetes

This group should strictly be included with the bacteria, as cell-diameter and composition of the cell wall of the actinomycetes defines them as Gram-positive bacteria. Actinomycete morphology (Figure 9), however, is mycelial and resembles the fungi in this respect, meriting their separate discussion. An actinomycete hypha is much smaller than a fungal hypha, typically being 10–15 μm long and 0.5–2 μm in diameter. As with fungi, growth of soil actinomycetes occurs from the hyphal apices with regular

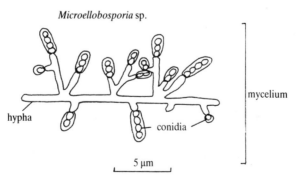

Figure 9. A soil actinomycete.

branching occurring behind the main apices of leading hyphae. The actinomycetes produce a reproductive spore, which is not as resistant to environmental adversity as the bacterial endospore. The spores of the actinomycetes are borne on aerial sporophores that are much more distinctive and characteristic than the hyphae of the substrate or vegetative mycelium. The dense production of a variety of sporophores by the soil actinomycetes can often be distinguished when the soil is examined microscopically.

Most soil actinomycetes are free-living saprophytes, able to decompose an enormous array of carbonaceous substrates. It is the degradation of some of the more recalcitrant polymers such as chitin, celluloses and hemicelluloses, particularly under conditions of high soil pH, however, for which the actinomycetes are regarded as being particularly specialised (in more neutral and low pH soils, the decomposition of these polymers is more commonly the domain of other bacteria and of numerous fungi). The soil actinomycetes are also important plant pathogens. *Streptomyces scabies*, for example, being the causal agent of potato scab in near-neutral and alkaline soils. Many soil actinomycetes exude antibiotics such as streptomycin as secondary metabolites (i.e. when active growth has ceased), both in culture for the enormous benefit of mankind, and in soil where the process may contribute to the competitive strategy of these microbes. Generally, the actinomycetes do not constitute the major part of the soil bacterial community. It is usually under soil conditions of either high pH, high water stress, or high temperature (many actinomycetes are thermophiles), that the actinomycetes really predominate.

A feature of the actinomycetes that is always of interest to those new to soil ecology is that some produce volatile terpene derivatives called geosmins, which contribute to the soil much of its earthy smell, particularly evident soon after rainfall.

Fungi

In terms of biomass (not numbers), it is the fungi that generally dominate the soil microbiota (Table 7). The fungi are eukaryotic and have a mycelial morphology comprising a mycelium or mass of tubes (hyphae) that enclose multi-nucleated cytoplasm (Fig. 10).

Fungal cell-wall composition is varied, but can consist of the polysaccharides chitin and cellulose, as well as significant amounts of proteins and glycoproteins. Typically, a fungal hypha is in the region of 2–10 µm in

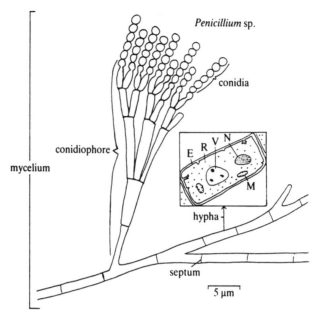

Figure 10. A septate soil fungus. Abbreviations: N, nucleus; V, vacuole with volutin granules; R, ribosome; E, endoplasmic reticulum; M, mitochondrion.

diameter, although some soil fungi have much broader hyphae, and so cell dimension is clearly much greater than for the soil bacteria and actinomycetes. Because of this, fungi are rarely found in soil micropores, being largely restricted to the interaggregate component of the soil matrix.

Fungi are heterotrophic in metabolism and are obligate aerobes. They are classified on the basis of both the form of the vegetative thallus and the reproductive structures (Figure 11).

The mastigomycotina and the zygomycotina are simple, aseptate (unicellular, i.e. hyphae without cross walls) fungi. The order Mastigomycotina reproduces asexually by motile zoospores and sexually to produce thick-walled oospores. Soil fungi belonging to the mastigomycotina include *Phytophthora* and *Pythium*. The Zygomycotina produce non-motile asexual spores in a specialised body or sporangium and reproduce sexually to form distinctive, thick-walled zygospores. Soil fungi belonging to this order include *Mucor* and *Rhizopus*. The order also includes endomycorrhizal-forming fungi such as *Glomus, Gigaspora* and *Acaulospora*, which are of paramount importance to the nutrition of most terrestrial, herbaceous plants.

The Mastigomycotina and Zygomycotina tend to mainly exist in spore

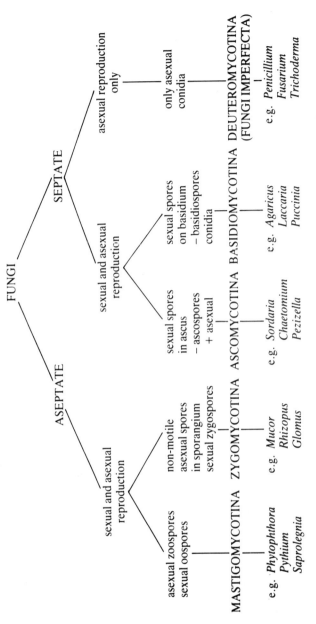

Figure 11. A simple classification of the soil fungi.

form until there is a readily available substrate, or in the case of the endomycorrhizal-forming fungi, when they are in the vicinity of plant roots.

The Ascomycotina, comprising both septate (with hyphal cross walls) fungi and unicellular yeasts, produce sexual ascospores that are held by a sac or 'ascus' that is contained by bodies that can take on a variety of closed (cleistothecia) and open (apothecia) forms. This fungal order includes the genus *Sordaria* found in the dung of herbivores at the soil surface, and soil/compost-inhabiting *Chaetomium*. Many of the Ascomycotina are plant pathogens, such as *Erysiphe graminis*, which causes powdery mildew, and again, tends only to exist in spore form in the soil.

The Basidiomycotina, also septate fungi, produce a sexual spore (basidiospore) on a specialised structure or 'basidium'. These basidia are usually borne on large fruiting bodies, which are such a characteristic feature of the surface of many forest soils and in meadows in the spring and autumn. Many of the Basidiomycotina form ectomycorrhizal associations with tree roots and are critical to the nutrition and growth of the tree. Examples of ectomycorrhizal Basidiomycotina are species of the genera *Pisolithus*, *Rhizopogon* and *Laccaria*, although possibly the best known example of all is *Amanita muscaria* or 'fly agaric', which has a distinctive red and white spotted appearance and is renowned as a poisonous fungus. The decomposition of the most recalcitrant of polymers, lignin (by 'white rot' fungi, which include almost all members of the Basidiomycotina except the Hemibasidiomycotina), and the breakdown of cellulose (by the 'brown rot' fungi such as *Poria*) are key activities of the Basidiomycotina, particularly in forest soils although some of these rotting activities also occur in the wood while it is still attached to the tree. A number of plant diseases are caused through attack by Basidiomycotina such as *Puccinia* (causal agent of cereal rust disease). Smut diseases are also caused by the Basidiomycotina.

The Deuteromycotina, or imperfect fungi, are so named because no sexual stage has been found for these fungi. If or when a sexual stage is identified these fungi, which comprise more than half of the species of the entire soil fungi community, are reclassified usually as Ascomycotina but sometimes as Basidiomycotina. This final order, generally including the majority of fungi viewed in soil by direct microscopy, includes *Penicillium*, from which Fleming first isolated penicillin and from which the drug is still commercially produced. This genus is frequently isolated from soil on to agar plates, largely because of its prolific production of asexual spores or 'conidia'. The Deuteromycotina also include causal agents of important soil-borne plant diseases. These fungi include species of *Rhizotonia* (*Rh. solani*, in particular, causes a variety of root rots), *Verticillium* and *Fusarium* (species of these fungi cause wilt disease in several plants).

Laboratory batch culture suggests that soil fungi grow as copiotrophs. This is when there is an adequate supply of nutrients and a carbon substrate. There is also increasing evidence to suggest that some soil fungi can be grown as oligotrophs (i.e. when there is a very low availability of nutrients and carbon substrates). Some of the possible mechanisms used by oligotrophic soil microbes are discussed in Chapter 1, pages 19 and 20. Regardless of how soil fungi scavenge carbon and other nutrients under oligotrophic conditions, the concept of oligotrophy has far-reaching implications to our understanding of soil ecology. The view that soil fungal activity can only be triggered by available nutrient and substrate supply from soil solution should be questioned in view of our increasing awareness of fungal oligotrophy where it appears some forms of carbon from the soil atmosphere may be scavenged.

Although fungi have a vast range of functions in soil, including their roles as plant symbionts, plant and animal pathogens, as oligotrophs, and even carnivores, by far the most important ecological role of fungi in soil is the decomposition of organic matter from the simplest sugars and amino acids to the most resistant polymers such as lignin and complex soil humic acids. Because of the generally greater fungal tolerance to acidity compared with bacterial heterotrophs, the decomposition of organic matter in more acid soils is predominantly a fungal process. Indeed, it is likely that in systems such as acid forest soils, which markedly favour the fungi to outcompete the bacteria, even processes such as nitrification and sulphur oxidation, generally considered to be the domain of the chemoautotroph, may also be of fungal origin. Even in non-acid soils, however, the fungal biomass typically exceeds the bacterial biomass (Table 7), and so the role of fungi in soil nutrient cycling, particularly in acidic systems, may therefore be considerable.

The role of soil fungi in forming symbiotic, mycorrhizal associations with most plant roots is of tremendous importance in terms of regulating nutrient uptake, disease resistance, water relations, and ultimately the growth of the plant partner in the association (Chapter 3, pages 66–71). In some cases, the adoption of a symbiotic strategy by a fungus has been associated with the loss of competitive saprotrophic ability, such as through the loss of cellulolytic and lignolytic enzymes, and with a stimulation of growth in the rhizosphere.

The production of spores by soil fungi, although primarily a reproductive strategy, does also provide a means of survival, to some extent, against adverse soil conditions. Many soil fungi also produce another type of reproductive structure consisting of a tight aggregation of fungal hyphae, often with a protective outer layer of very thick walled hyphae, which may be darkly pigmented with melanin. These structures are called sclerotia and, like the spores, provide a fungal structure more resistant to environmental stress than the normal hyphae.

Other fungal structures that are of considerable ecological significance in the soil are rhizomorphs and mycelial cords. These are filamentous aggregations of fungal hyphae. The main difference between them is that rhizomorphs extend by a single, autonomous apex whereas cords develop through the concerted growth of individual hyphae that form a firm mycelial framework (Cooke & Rayner, 1984). Rhizomorphs and cords are key structures for the channelling of nutrient resources by fungi as well as for mycelial extension. These features, as with sclerotia, are also associated with resistance to periods of environmental adversity in the soil. In certain of the ectomycorrhizal-forming Basidiomycotina, rhizomorphs may be a feature of the water relations of the tree host.

Algae

The soil algal population, being photoautotrophic in metabolism (algae evolve oxygen during photosynthesis) is largely restricted in its distribution/ activity to parts of the soil that are penetrated by sunlight. Thus, the soil surface and large cracks in the soil are the major zones of algal activity.

There are four groups of soil algae: greens (chlorophyta) such as *Chlorella* and *Chlamydomonas*, blue-greens (cyanophyta or cyanobacteria) such as *Nostoc* and *Anabaena*, diatoms (bacillariophyta), such as *Pinnularia* and *Navicula*, and yellow-greens (xanthophyta) such as *Heterothrix* and *Heterococcus*.

Strictly, the blue-greens are classified as bacteria, rather than algae, but, because of their many algal characteristics, are discussed in this section.

Algae in the soil may be either unicellular or filamentous (Figure 12). The algal cell contains the photosynthetic pigment chlorophyll and this may be either restricted to distinctive, localised patches or chromatophores (as is the case with the green algae), or may be more evenly distributed throughout the cell (as is the case with the blue-green algae where, along with the chlorophyll, the blue pigment phycocyanin is also present). The cell wall of soil algae is generally similar to that of the higher plants with cellulose representing the major constituent. Diatoms, however, are covered by a siliceous outer layer.

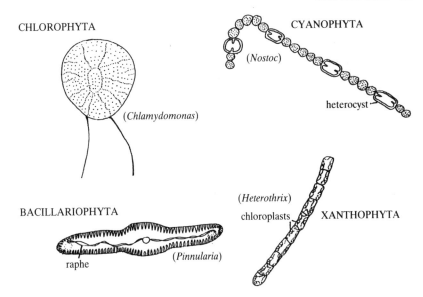

CHLOROPHYTA

(*Chlamydomonas*)

CYANOPHYTA

(*Nostoc*)

heterocyst

BACILLARIOPHYTA

(*Pinnularia*)

raphe

(*Heterothrix*)

chloroplasts

XANTHOPHYTA

Figure 12. Representatives of the soil algae.

In general, in temperate soils, the relative abundance and importance of the major algal groups is in the order: greens > diatoms > blue-greens > yellow-greens. In tropical soils, however, it is the blue-greens that are of greatest numerical and ecological importance.

Because the algae are photoautotrophs, they have no dependence on pre-formed organic matter in the soil and, therefore, have a key ecological role as primary colonisers on bare surfaces (such as volcanic and desert soils, and rock faces) that are exposed to the sunlight. This role is further reinforced by the production of carbonic acid as a result of the algal metabolism. The release of carbonic acid by the algal cell can accelerate the weathering of minerals and hence, along with the input of organic matter as dead algal cells, make a substantial contribution to soil formation, particularly in its primary stages. This role of the algae as primary colonisers and primary agents of soil formation is not restricted to free-living algae. Algal symbionts in the lichen thallus similarly contribute to these soil processes, although fungal metabolites, including a range of organic acids, also contribute to the mineral weathering activity of the lichens.

Algae also produce large amounts of extracellular polysaccharides, which can act as soil aggregating agents and this may be of considerable importance on bare soils and soils with relatively open vegetation where there is adequate sunlight and moisture. This soil-aggregating role of the algae may become a valuable process in developing and maintaining structural stability in badly degraded soils.

A further ecological role of the soil algae results from the ability of some algae to carry out non-symbiotic and symbiotic nitrogen fixation using the enzyme nitrogenase. These algae, therefore, are not only independent of preformed organic carbon, but also of fixed nitrogen. Non-symbiotic N_2-fixation by blue-green algae is not only of ecological importance in natural ecosystems but may also be of considerable agronomic significance as a major source of nitrogen to the rice plants under paddy cultivation. The site of nitrogenase activity in some of these blue-greens, the heterocyst, is a specialised, enlarged algal cell and is illustrated in Figure 12. Symbiotic nitrogen fixation is carried out by algae in the lichen thallus. Although rarely a true soil process, N_2-fixation by lichens can sometimes represent a significant input of nitrogen to soils.

PROTOZOA (MICROFAUNA)

The soil contains a rich variety of protozoa, small animals (microfauna, i.e. less than 100 μm in dimension) that predate the microbial population. In a gram of temperate, arable soil, it is not uncommon to find thirty or forty thousand protozoa. The protozoa are largely restricted to the top 15–20 cm of the soil profile, largely as a result of their dependence on a high density of microbial prey.

In terms of microhabitat distribution in soils, protozoa will tend to be located in pores, sizes partly determined by the dimensions of the protozoa themselves. The smallest flagellates, for example, may well be able to access pores with neck diameters of 10 μm or less. Larger ciliates such as *Colpoda*, however, may well only access pores with neck diameters of more than 30 μm or so.

As with microbes, protozoa have also adapted to a specialised life in the soil environment. Compared with their purely aquatic counterparts, soil protozoa tend to be much smaller (presumably to enable them to pass through the necks of soil pores to access their microbial prey), to lack external projections and be somewhat flattened (again to facilitate movement in soil) and to attach readily to substrates for efficient feeding.

There are three classes of protozoa in the soil. These are firstly and

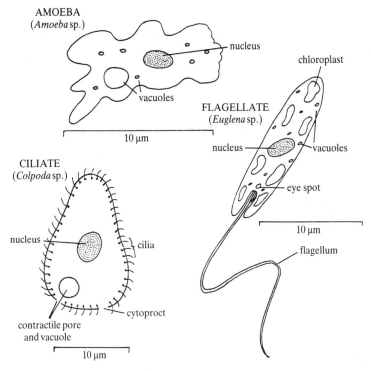

Figure 13. Representatives of the soil protozoa.

generally most importantly, the flagellates, then the amoebae, and thirdly the ciliates (Figure 13).

Soil flagellates, such as *Euglena*, possess between one and four whip-like flagella attached to one end of the organism. Movement of the flagella enable these animals to swim through the soil solution toward their microbial prey. The soil flagellates include the photosynthetically pigmented algal flagellates (including *Euglena*), their non-pigmented relatives, and the zooflagellates.

Soil ciliates, such as *Vorticella*, are also free-swimming protozoa. Movement is achieved, however, through the use of bands of small hairs or cilia of which there may sometimes be thousands on one organism. The cilia can also serve as a means of brushing food towards the cytosome (mouth) of the ciliate. The largest soil ciliates approach 0.1 mm in length. The ciliates can easily be distinguished from other soil protozoa by the presence of their cilia, and by their unique nuclear dimorphism.

The soil amoebae (sometimes termed rhizopods), including *Amoeba*, *Naegleria* and *Euglypha*, are of two types. One type, the naked amoebae, (e.g. *Naegleria* and *Amoeba*) simply consists of a mass of protoplasm enclosed by a flexible wall. The second type, the testate amoebae (e.g. *Euglypha*), have a rigid chitinous or siliceous shell with an opening from which project five strands of protoplasm or pseudopodia. The amoebae move through the soil solution by use of the pseudopodia which, in the case of the flexible amoebae such as *Naegleria*, may project from any point of the body. This means that they continually change shape as they move through the soil in search of their prey.

Although there are occasional examples of photoautotrophy among the protozoa, almost all are dominantly heterotrophic, requiring preformed organic matter as a food source, largely by preying and feeding on microbial cells (phagotrophic nutrition). Because of this dependence on microbes as a food source, protozoal activity is largely determined by the availability of suitable microbes as well as adequate soil moisture to facilitate locomotion.

Although the prey of the soil protozoa is dominantly of bacterial origin, some fungi are also grazed. Some amoebae, for example, graze only the asexual spores (conidia) of the fungus *Cochliobolus*. In some cases, therefore, protozoal grazing is highly selective, but more often there appears to be little species selection of prey, except on the basis of size and in terms of physical access (i.e. microbes, particularly bacteria, may be inaccessible to grazing because they inhabit pores with neck diameters that exclude the protozoa or where pore connectivity is limited). Protozoal access to microbial prey may be restricted, not only by pore size exclusion, but also by the formation of biofilms on soil particles. Only exposed cells on the surface of the biofilm will be available to the protozoa. Recognition of prey may be restricted if the cells are simply adsorbed to particles, rather than free in the soil solution.

Protozoa exist in two forms in the soil. When there are adequate numbers of microbial prey and when soil conditions, particularly those relating to soil moisture, are suitable, protozoa are active in the trophozoite stage. However, when conditions become unfavourable for the trophozoite stage, the protozoan may enter the cyst stage. The protozoan cyst, unlike the spores of the fungi, is primarily a structure to enable survival rather than reproduction. The rate and nature of encystment and excystment varies greatly from one species of protozoa to another, although it seems likely, on the basis of the water potential regimes of most soils, that soil protozoa may encyst for considerable periods or certainly that their activity must be severely restricted in soils except during or soon after rainfall or soil irrigation.

A great deal is still to be learned of the ecological significance of protozoa in the soil. Their food source is not restricted entirely to microbial prey. Protozoa are also involved in primary decomposition of soil organic matter. Protozoa take in and process fine organic particles, as well as occurring in the guts of a number of soil animals, such as termites, where they play a critical role in the decomposition of cellulosic debris (Swift, Heal & Anderson, 1979). A greater understanding of the ecological significance of the soil protozoa will only result from studies where protozoal activity is closely related to soil water potential and the pore space characteristics of the soil environment.

SLIME MOULDS

The slime moulds or myxomycota have close affinities with the protozoa, although because of their production of a walled spore, are sometimes classified with the fungi. The two main types of slime mould are the acrasiomycetes, or cellular slime moulds, and the myxomycetes, or true slime moulds. The cellular slime moulds are amoeboid organisms that prey on bacteria and small fragments of soil organic matter. They are common in soil and leaf litter, particularly when conditions are very wet. The true slime moulds consist of a plasmodium or naked, multinucleate mass of protoplasm. The feeding habit is similar to the cellular slime moulds, that is they engulf their prey or food particles by deformation. True slime moulds are most commonly isolated from moist, rotting wood and leaf litter on the surface of forest soils. The ecological significance of the slime moulds in soil is uncertain and they remain one of the most mysterious of all components of the soil biota.

LARGER SOIL FAUNA (MESO- AND MACROFAUNA)

Introduction

It is remarkable how varied a faunal community exists in the soil. Individual members of the community may spend all or only part of their life cycle in the soil. For example, members of the mesofauna (greater than 100 µm but less than 1–2 mm in dimension) with egg, juvenile and adult stages may spend one, two or all three of the stages in the soil environment.

Animal biomass differs enormously from one soil to another, but may often exceed 0.5 t ha^{-1}. Generally, the most important of these are the oligochaetes (the earthworms and enchytraeid worms), nematodes, arthropods (such as centipedes, millipedes, springtails and mites), molluscs (including slugs and snails), as well as large burrowing mammals (such as rabbits).

In general, the abundance and diversity of soil animals is greatest in soils of little or no disturbance, such as those of permanent grassland and natural woodland, where they play a vital role in nutrient cycling. In agricultural soils, the role of soil animals has recently been encouraged by the increasing use of minimum tillage, the reduction (in some cases) in pesticide applications, and the returning of crop residues to the soil. In addition to enhancing nutrient cycling, this should also enable farmers to benefit from the major contribution that soil animals, particularly earthworms, can make to good soil structure.

Although some soil animals are carnivorous, the most widespread eco-systematic activity of the soil meso- and macrofauna is the 'processing' and 'mixing' of organic detritus in the soil. Processing includes simple comminution of organic debris into smaller fragments, varying degrees of decomposition within the gut of the soil animal (both by the enzymes of the animal itself and its gut microflora), and the priming of decomposition through the covering of debris with a decomposer microbial inoculum. Clearly, there is a tremendous degree of synergism between the soil animals and microbes in terms of organic matter decomposition. Mixing of organic material through the profile by soil animals occurs through vertical and horizontal burrowing, particularly by the earthworms.

Oligochaetes – earthworms and enchytraeid worms

The contribution of the oligochaetes to soil fertility can be considerable. Where earthworms flourish, they represent the bulk of the soil animal biomass. They are intimately involved in the decomposition of soil organic matter, soil aeration, increased soil penetrability, and in the aggregation of soil particles. Earthworms may even influence nutrient movement in soils when their channels enable greater infiltration of rain water into the soil. One of the earthworms found in the UK, *Lumbricus terrestris*, can reach soil biomass levels of up to 2.5 t ha^{-1} (Table 7), representing up to 80% of total soil animal biomass. This population can pull leaf and other litter through the soil into burrows for rapid decomposition at a tremendous rate – well-developed earthworm populations can bury the annual litterfall of a mature woodland in a matter of months. The degree of selectivity, in terms of the type of plant litter processed by earthworms, is very variable. In some cases, such as *Lumbricus terrestris* and *Allolobophora longa*, there appears to be considerable discrimination between different types of litter material.

It is through the mixing and comminution of plant debris, rather than decomposition, that earthworms most contribute to ecosystem productivity. In most temperate ecosystems, as a proportion of energy flow through the decomposer system, earthworms rarely account for more than 5% (Lee, 1985). This contrasts with a corresponding figure of 90% or more for the microbial biomass.

In acid, moorland and forest soils, enchytraeids tend to replace the earthworm population in temperate latitudes, often with enormous population densities. More than one hundred thousand enchytraeid or 'pot' worms can be found in 1 m^2 of coniferous forest soil. This biomass, however, will be unlikely to amount to more than 0.1 t ha^{-1}, a fraction of the corresponding earthworm biomass likely to be found in the soil beneath a deciduous woodland.

The enchytraeids are the smallest of the oligochaetes ranging from the smallest species which measure less than 1 mm to the largest which can attain several centimetres. Although they can be isolated from most acid, organic soils, population density is strongly controlled by soil water potential, enchytraeids not being resistant to soil water stress.

Nematodes

Because of their role as important parasitic agents in arable agriculture, the nematodes have received considerable research attention. These non-segmented worms, typically 1 mm or so in length and less than 50 μm in diameter, are often present at very high population densities in soil (millions per square metre) and can attain biomass levels of 0.2 t ha^{-1} in some soils (Table 7). The nematodes are obligately aerobic and feed off the protoplasm of plants and algae, affecting primary production, and of heterotrophic microorganisms, affecting decomposition processes in the soil. These microbial- and plant-feeding nematodes commonly make up the majority of the nematode population in soil, with the plant feeders generally dominating in soils beneath established vegetation and with the microbial feeders prolific in decomposing organic matter. A number of nematodes are involved in parasitism of other members of the soil microfauna, particularly protozoa, but also other nematodes. These activities will regulate secondary decomposition in the soil and also the levels of plant-parasitic nematodes. Because of their size and their need for mobility, nematodes are active in water films in quite large (> 50 μm) soil pores and are generally most abundant in moist, coarse-textured soils. Although these soil conditions support active nematodes, nematodes that encyst can survive prolonged desiccation and other environmental adversities. Potato root eelworm disease is caused by the soil nematode *Heterodera*, a good example of a cyst-forming nematode. Although endoparasitic on the potato roots, the tough cysts of this nematode can persist in the soil for long periods, often reactivated by the exudates of a new potato crop.

Arthropods

Soil arthropods include saprophagous animals, which utilise dead plant material, as well as carnivorous animals. Millipedes are saprophagous soil arthropods, whereas centipedes are carnivorous. The mites include both carnivorous and saprophagous species. As is the case with other saprophagous soil animals, it is unclear to what extent soil arthropods carry out decomposition as a result of their own enzymes or through enzymes of their gut microflora.

Generally, the arthropods comprise a minor part of the soil animal biomass. There are exceptions to this, however, such as the acid humus of moorland and forest soil, which may be particularly rich in springtails and mites. The springtails of a forest soil have a significant effect on the nutrient dynamics of the forest ecosystem, largely as a result of their grazing of fungal saprophytes (Verhoeff & De Geoda, 1985).

Molluscs

Although there are many species of terrestrial molluscs, their diversity is only a fraction of their aquatic counterparts. Despite this, soil molluscs (or gastropods), although only a small component of the soil animal biomass, can be of considerable agronomic and ecological significance under damp soil conditions where they can often be responsible for intense herbivorous activity. Snails, in particular, with their high activity of the enzyme cellulase (catalysing the depolymerisation of cellulose) can cause considerable defoliation and damage of plants. Slugs are thought mainly to scavenge old plant material and debris, although under particularly favourable conditions, slug population densities in excess of a million per hectare can cause considerable, direct damage to living plants.

SOIL VIRUSES

These are the smallest life forms in soil and can only be observed with the aid of electron microscopy as it is unusual for a soil virus to exceed 0.3 μm in total length. Because of their size, viruses are able to enter soil pores that exclude all other components of the soil biota. Despite this, the soil itself is not the natural habitat for viruses and they can do no more than survive. The viruses are obligate parasites, only able to multiply within a host cell. The type of compatible host cell is used to classify the viruses. Bacteriophages and actinophages, for example, parasitise the cells of eubacteria and actinomycetes, respectively. Some viruses are active against particular plants and can sometimes be the cause of considerable economic loss to the farmer. Viruses cannot remain viable and infective in the soil for long periods of time, although they can be transferred from one host cell to another via virus-carriers such as fungi and mobile soil animals and can be protected from adverse soil conditions through adsorption to humic and clay colloids. An example of a soil virus of economic significance is the bacteriophage specific to *Rhizobium* spp., of critical importance to the legume association. It appears that the most effective control, to date, of this soil virus and of many others deleterious to farming, is through crop rotation to avoid the build-up of soil stocks of the virus.

Modern molecular biological techniques are fast revolutionising our study, identification, and even manipulation of soil viruses. Much of the latter will be stimulated by the exploration of viruses as possible agents of pest-control in agricultural and forest systems.

3 Ecological interactions between the soil biota

INTRODUCTION

A vast range of interactions (at the organism and population level) occur amongst the different components of the soil biota. Many of these interactions are short-lived and sporadic whereas others are more stable.

Table 9 (see page 63) describes the many types of biotic interaction that can occur in the soil, ranging from mutualism, where both partners benefit, to neutralism, in which no obvious benefit is accrued by either partner of the association. The term symbiosis applies to 'any association between two living organisms or populations, which, in the absence of environmental change, is stable'. Frequently, however, the term is used to describe associations that are of benefit to both participants although, strictly, the term for this is mutualism or mutualistic symbiosis.

PLANT/MICROBIAL INTERACTIONS

The legume/*Rhizobium* association

Introduction

Probably the best documented example of a plant/microbial interaction in the soil is the symbiotic association between the root of a leguminous plant and the soil bacterium *Rhizobium*. The association is of considerable ecological significance. It is a function of the association to fix atmospheric nitrogen and thereby supply a major input into the nitrogen cycle of many ecosystems. Other organisms and associations of organisms involved in N_2-fixation are discussed in Chapter 4, page 110. The benefits of this input have long been known and have been harnessed by agricultural civilisations

Table 9. *Different types of biological interaction that can occur in the soil*

Interaction	Definition
Symbiosis	An association between two organisms or populations, which, in the absence of environmental change, is stable.
(1) Mutualism	Both partners benefit.
(2) Protocooperation	Both partners benefit, but without the cooperation being necessary for their existence.
(3) Neutralism	Neither partner benefits.
(4) Commensalism	One partner benefits while the other is unaffected.
(5) Antagonism	One or both partners suffer.
(a) Competition	Two species limited by joint dependence on one nutrient.
(b) Ammensalism	One species inhibited by toxin from another.
(c) Predation	Ingestion of one organism by another.
(d) Parasitism	Organism obtaining nutrients from living tissue of another.
(6) Synergism	Association where combined activity exceeds sum of individual activities.

as ancient as the Egyptian and Chinese. At the global level, biological N_2-fixation, of which legume N_2-fixation is the major component, accounts for an input to terrestrial ecosystems of some 140×10^6 t of nitrogen. This is more than the combined input from artificial fertilisers (about 40×10^6 t) and from dry and wet atmospheric deposition (also about 40×10^6 t).

Formation of the nodule association

Rhizobia occur in the soil as free-living, probably motile (it is not known for certain whether rhizobia are motile in soil, even though there is motility in liquid culture) heterotrophic bacteria. However, the rhizobia only tend to grow well in rhizosphere soil where they are stimulated by the flow of carbon from the plant root. This stimulation is not restricted to legume roots and occurs under a broad range of soil/plant conditions, although effective nodulation only occurs for roots of leguminous plants. The association between the legume root and the rhizobia is initiated by the legume, which sends out a chemical signal to attract the then free-living, motile rhizobia. The rhizobia are attracted and bound to the surface of root hairs by a specialised glycoprotein molecule, lectin, produced by the plant. Rhizobia that are compatible with the legume root exude acidic polysaccharide, which facilitates selective adsorption to the plant lectin. The presence of the rhizobia causes the root hair to curl prior to invasion. This invasion is facilitated by invagination of the wall of the root hair into a tube or infection thread, and is rapid (only taking approximately two days from initial infection to colonisation of the base of the root hair). Having entered the host's root cytoplasm, both the bacterial cells and the surrounding host cells multiply to enable development of the nodule. Inside the nodule, the rhizobial cells cease their motile habit and take on a non-motile 'bacteroid' habit. The enzyme complex possessed by the nodule-forming rhizobia that enables them to fix atmospheric nitrogen is nitrogenase, a protein rich in iron and molybdenum.

The effect of soil conditions on rhizobia and on the nodulation process

Although effective legume nodules will form in a wide variety of soils, certain conditions will particularly favour the process. Nodulation is encouraged by neutral/slightly alkaline soil pH, the rhizobia generally being sensitive to high concentrations of available soil aluminium. Rhizobia are also sensitive to soil water stress and, probably being motile in soil, require an adequate water film to facilitate movement. The minimum thickness of this film for free movement is about 5 μm. The rhizobia are also affected by a variety of physicochemical factors associated with soil type. In addition, the state of the legume itself, of course, also largely controlled by soil conditions, will influence the nodulation process.

Energy and oxygen relations of the association

Fixation of nitrogen is an energy-requiring reaction and this is supplied by the host plant. Photoassimilated carbon is used, via the Krebs cycle (or, as it is often referred to, the tricarboxylic acid or TCA cycle) of the rhizobia, to generate energy in the form of ATP. The rhizobia are, therefore, a carbon drain on their host (Figure 14), although the plant is obtaining fixed nitrogen in return (Table 10). In young pea (*Pisum sativum*) plants, for example, one third of the net photoassimilate (i.e. total carbon photoassimilation minus shoot respired photoassimilate) can be diverted, via the phloem, to the root nodule (Pate, 1977). In fact, this supply of energy, in the form of photosynthate,

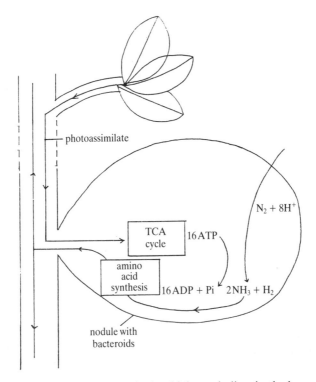

photoassimilate

N₂ + 8H⁺

TCA cycle

16 ATP

amino acid synthesis

16 ADP + Pi

2 NH₃ + H₂

nodule with bacteroids

Figure 14. The coupling of plant and microbial metabolism in the legume root nodule.

should be a primary regulator of nitrogen fixation. In a legume that is fertilised with mineral nitrogen, much of the carbon drain to the nodule should be available for photosynthetic activity and hence dry matter production. A cost of nitrogen fixation of 6.5 g C per g N can be estimated and this translates to a theoretical loss of 15–20 kg plant dry matter for every kg N fixed. This loss is rarely observed in the field, however, because, in reality, plants are rarely close to upper levels of productivity where the extra energy cost of fixation would become a significant burden.

Of the carbon diverted to root nodule, approximately 15% is stored in the nodule, nearly 40% is respired into the soil atmosphere by the nodule, and the remainder is re-translocated via the xylem to the above-ground parts of the legume plant (Pate, 1977). The flow of photoassimilated carbon to the nodule represents nearly as great a flow as that to the entire remainder of the legume root system.

Table 10. *Some of the main advantages to the plant and microbial partners in the legume/*Rhizobium *and mycorrhizal[a] associations*

Advantages to the plant	Advantages to the microbe
Legume	*Rhizobium*
(i) Fixed nitrogen from the atmosphere	(i) A habitat free of competition
	(ii) A steady supply of photosynthate carbon
Plant	*Mycorrhizal fungus*
(i) Increased nutrient uptake	(i) A habitat free of competition – sometimes the *only* habitat for growth
(ii) Access to organic forms of certain nutrients, e.g. N	(ii) A steady supply of photosynthate carbon (the exceptions to this are the orchid and monotropoid mycorrhizas where carbon flow is away from the fungus to the host)
(iii) Increased rootlet size and longevity	
(iv) Protection from pathogens	
(v) Improved water relations	

[a] For more detailed consideration of host benefits from the mycorrhizal association, see Chapter 7, page 199.

We know that the nitrogenase enzyme stress is highly sensitive to oxygen inactivation, and so a key feature of the legume symbiosis is the regulation of oxygen diffusion in the nodule (O_2 levels of less than $0.1\,\mu M$ are maintained) by means of a membranous sac comprising the pigment leghaemoglobin. Leghaemoglobin, which gives the nodule a pink coloration when crushed, tightly controls the oxygen supply to the nodule.

In recent years, there has been increasing use, largely in tropical soils, of rhizobial inocula to enhance nitrogen fixation in legumes and hence increase crop productivity. The use of these inocula, genetically engineered and otherwise, is discussed in Chapter 7, pages 182–6 and 204–5.

The mycorrhizal association – a plant root/fungus interaction

Introduction

A second plant/microbial interaction in the soil, also of great ecological significance, is that of the mycorrhiza. Mycorrhizas are formed by association between a plant root and a fungus and by far the majority of vascular plants are involved in these associations. There are a number of different forms of mycorrhizal association (Figures 7, 15 and 16), but in many cases the fungus involved (the mycobiont) enhances plant uptake of nutrients (major, minor and trace elements) from the soil, it increases rootlet size and longevity, it protects the root system from many pathogens, and it can also absorb and translocate water to the plant host (Table 10). The mechanism of enhanced nutrient uptake by mycorrhizal plants is mainly the increased soil volume exploited by the extra-matrical mycelium of the mycorrhizal fungus. Nutrients can therefore be transported from beyond the narrow nutrient depletion zone that surrounds the non-mycorrhizal roots. In addition to the mycorrhizal fungus exploiting the greater soil volume, the fungal mycelium can often absorb nutrients at lower solution concentrations than can the uninfected plant root. Thus, the kinetics of uptake differ between mycorrhizal and non-mycorrhizal plants.

The mycorrhizal association can also enable the plant host to access nutrients (particularly nitrogen) in an organic form that would otherwise be

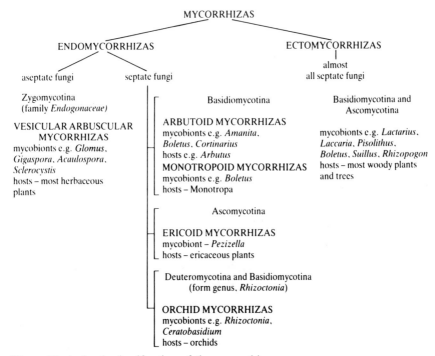

Figure 15. A simple classification of the mycorrhizas.

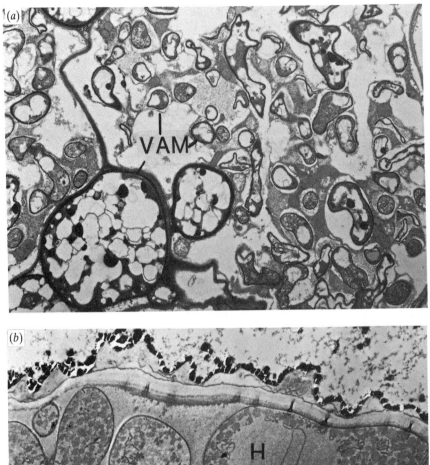

Figure 16. Transmission electron micrograph of the ecto- and endomycorrhizal association. (*a*) Demonstrates how the hyphae of Vesicular Arbuscular

unavailable (Stribley & Read, 1980). In addition, there is now clear evidence that some mycorrhizal plants can be connected via hyphal strands and this link provides a means of nutrient transfer from plant to plant (Read, Francis & Finlay, 1985).

The classification of the mycorrhizas in Figure 15 is very much a simplified picture. Both arbutoid and monotropoid mycorrhizas have many features that are often associated with ectomycorrhizas, such as a Hartig net and a fungal mantle or sheath (see Figure 7). On the basis of carbon translocation, the monotropoid and orchid mycorrhizas would appear to form a distinct mycorrhizal group as the mycobionts transfer carbon into their hosts, whereas the mycobionts of other mycorrhizas transfer carbon out of the host. The classification of mycorrhizas in Figure 15 is somewhat superficial, therefore, but it nevertheless enables some helpful distinctions to be made.

The effect of soil conditions on the development of mycorrhizas

Mycorrhizal development is strongly influenced by the available concentrations of soil nutrients. This is particularly true for the Vesicular Arbuscular (VA) Mycorrhizas (often simply abbreviated to VAMs) where the development of the association between the host and mycobiont is often strongly suppressed by high levels of available phosphorus and nitrogen. Soil pH is also a strong control of mycorrhizal development, altering the bioavailability of both nutrients and toxins, and for many VAMs, development is severely restricted in more acid soils. Soil water plays a key role in mycorrhizal development. For both endo- and ectomycorrhizas, both excessively low and high moisture regimes are generally inhibitory to development. Excessively high soil moisture is inhibitory when it leads to anaerobiosis, as all mycorrhizal-forming fungi, and indeed all soil fungi, are obligate aerobes. At low soil moisture status, reduced mycorrhizal development may be a direct result of water stress on both microbial and plant partners, or an indirect effect caused by changes in nutrient availability. Of course, the direct and indirect effects of water stress are very difficult, if not impossible, to factor out (see Chapter 5).

(*continued*) Mycorrhizal (VAM) fungi penetrate the host cortical cells and colonise the intracellular spaces ($\times 10\,000$). (*b*) Demonstrates how the hyphae (H) of the ectomycorrhizas penetrate and fill the intercellular spaces of the outer cortex (C) to form the Hartig net ($\times 14\,000$).

Formation of the mycorrhizal association

The association is initiated either by a fungal spore germinating on an appropriate root surface or rhizoplane, or by the meeting in the soil of a fungal mycelium and an appropriate root system. The rhizoplane is a particularly favourable environment for the germination process, providing much greater spore germination rates for mycorrhizal fungi than the bulk soil. As the fungal mycelium extends from these spore propagules, root invasion occurs, although the type of invasion will depend on the type of the mycorrhizal association. The fungi (largely Basidiomycotina) forming the ectotrophic mycorrhizas do not penetrate the root cells but simply form a sheath around the root with only intercellular penetration of root cortical cells. The fungi (largely Zygomycotina and Ascomycotina) forming the endotrophic mycorrhizas actually penetrate the root cortical cells and have a much more intimate association with the root.

Energy relations of the mycorrhizal association

As is the case for the legume, the microbial partner in the mycorrhizal association requires photoassimilated carbon from its plant host (the only exception to this is the orchid mycorrhiza where the developing orchid host receives a carbohydrate supply via the mycobiont) in return for the services previously mentioned (Table 10). This requirement can be considerable – about 4% of net photoassimilate in young, mycorrhizal faba bean (*Vicia faba*) plants was diverted into mycorrhizal fungal hyphae (Paul & Kucey, 1981). Of this diverted carbon, 25% is incorporated into the hyphae and 75% respired into the soil atmosphere. Where necessary, the plant host may increase its rate of photosynthesis (e.g. through increased leaf area) to prevent the diversion of assimilate from causing a reduction in overall growth. A major diversion of photoassimilate to the microbial partner is not restricted to the endomycorrhizas – the ectomycorrhizal fungal component of a forest stand accounting for 15% of primary productivity (Vogt *et al.*, 1982). This means that mycorrhizal roots are significant sinks for photoassimilate, perhaps diverting fifteen times more of this carbon than adjacent non-mycorrhizal roots.

Although rhizobia require a flow of photoassimilate from their host, they can also live in the soil environment as free-living heterotrophs and are, therefore, not dependent on their hosts for the sole means of vegetative growth. Some of the fungi that form mycorrhizal associations, however, cannot decompose soil organic matter and are, therefore, dependent on the plant host for maintenance of vegetative growth. Under these circumstances, existence in the soil in the absence of a suitable host is sometimes simply a survival exercise for the fungus, usually achieved through the formation of a resistant spore structure. This is particularly true for VAM-forming fungi such as *Glomus* and *Acaulospora.*

The rhizosphere – a zone of interaction between the plant root and the soil biota

The concept of the rhizosphere, as the zone of soil adjacent to a plant root where microbes are affected in some way by the presence of the root, was introduced in Chapter 2. A corresponding zone of influence termed the 'spermosphere', can be found adjacent to plant seeds in the soil. It is the rhizosphere, however, that is of most ecological significance in soil. Strictly, the rhizosphere does not just extend outward from the rhizoplane as illustrated in Figure 17. As well as this ectorhizosphere, it also must include the interior of the roots, or endorhizosphere, because both these regions provide a niche for an adapted microbial community. In addition to microbial changes due to the presence of the root, the root is also fundamentally affected by the presence of the rhizosphere microbes. Plant nutrient uptake through roots, for example, is influenced in a number of ways. Microbially mediated changes in root morphology/physiology, in nutrient phase equilibria (through pH and redox changes), in soil chemistry (through changes in mineralisation and weathering), in competition for nutrients (especially through rhizoplane blocking) and the formation of symbiotic associations (e.g. mycorrhizas, root nodules) between microbes and roots all contribute to this effect on nutrient uptake by plant roots (Nye & Tinker, 1977).

The presence of free-living microbes on or near the root considerably increases loss of carbon from those roots. The increased carbon loss is thought to be caused by the microbial production of compounds that increase the permeability of the plant root cells. These compounds probably include hormones as they are produced by many root-associated microbes and can increase plant cell permeability. Root efflux of carbon due to microorganisms can be increased by up to 100% compared with sterile roots (Barber & Martin, 1976). There is, however, a slight reduction in carbon loss (as a proportion of the carbon budget of the plant), if the roots have

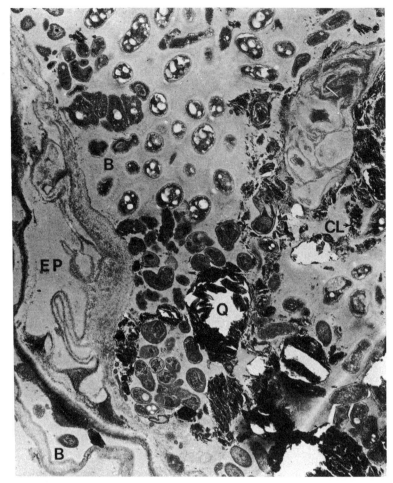

Figure 17. Transmission electron micrograph of the rhizosphere of clover, demonstrating epidermal cells of the root (EP), high concentrations of bacteria (B), as well as soil particles of quartz (Q) and clay (CL) ($\times 10\,000$).

symbiotic associations with microbes such as in the legume and mycorrhizal symbioses, although this may be largely offset by the greater carbon fixation rate of the plant hosts.

The 'rhizodeposition' of carbon causes the microbial population density in the soil to be massively enhanced in the rhizosphere, the best evidence for this coming from direct observation using electron microscopy. Not surprisingly, population densities of viruses also tend to be greater closer to the root, rhizosphere microorganisms often acting as vectors for viral diseases of plants.

Population densities in the rhizosphere are generally highest on the rhizoplane (root surface) itself, with a fairly steep population gradient (over a few millimeters) away from the root. Typically 4–10% of the rhizoplane is covered by soil microbes (Rovira *et al.*, 1974), although this figure is much higher if the roots are involved in direct symbiotic associations such as mycorrhizas (under these circumstances, the mycobiont can often entirely cover the root surface). Considering the root as a whole, the rhizoplane microbes are far from evenly distributed. There are relatively few microbes on the root cap and on the zone of elongation. It is the root hair zone that tends to be most heavily populated with microbes.

In addition to changes in microbial population densities in the rhizosphere, the nature and extent of cell adsorption to soil particles is also affected. Cells are particularly well attached in the rhizosphere, probably as a result of polysaccharide production by both the root and associated microflora. The strong attachment of rhizosphere microbes must be taken into account if extractive techniques for detection/enumeration are used.

Rhizodeposition of carbon provides a strong selection pressure so that microbial diversity is greatly reduced compared with the bulk soil. Of the microbes that colonise the rhizoplane and rhizosphere, the most common are the Gram-negative bacteria, whereas the coryneforms can become more important as roots develop (Campbell, 1985). Of the Gram-negative bacteria, it appears that fluorescent pseudomonads such as *Pseudomonas fluorescens* frequently dominate. Fungi tend to be relatively less important in the rhizosphere, probably because of the dense packing of the minimum void zone around the root, which effectively ensures that there are insufficient large channels for some fungi to approach the root. Any large channels tend to be the preferred routes for root hairs and the diffusion of root exudates and mucilages which provide a substrate for the rhizosphere bacteria.

Of course, of far greater ecological importance than microbial numbers is microbial activity. We know that microbial growth rates can be high in the rhizosphere and on the rhizoplane, the generation time of pseudomonads on pine roots being about five hours compared with three days for bulk soil (Bowen & Rovira, 1973). Rapid proliferation of microbes around and on the root surface, however, will continue only until the carbon supply from the root becomes limiting. In plant solution culture, the growth rate of bacteria in the rhizosphere decreases rapidly with time (Barber & Lynch, 1977).

The extent of the zone of stimulation of microbes in the rhizosphere is determined by the extent to which rhizodeposited carbon diffuses through the soil. This system has been modelled by Newman & Watson (1977) to show that the microbial status is controlled by the concentration of organic substrate, which, in turn, is determined by its production by the root and subsequent diffusion through soil, its production by the decomposition of insoluble organic matter, and its use by microbes. The model determined that the zone of root-associated, microbial enhancement could extend as far as 4 mm in a wet soil, with the zone becoming smaller in drier soil owing to greater exploitation of substrate at the root surface. Because of factors such as soil water potential, it is a mistake to assume that all of the soil around roots always provides stimulation to soil microbes.

The rhizosphere will be a zone of increased population density of a very wide range of soil microbes, particularly, of course, heterotrophs. Some parts of the nitrogen cycle that involve heterotrophs, therefore, will be driven by the rhizosphere C-flow. Non-symbiotic, aerobic, N_2-fixers such as *Azotobacter* will be active, although the ecological significance of this activity may not be great (see Figure 28, in Chapter 4). Even the denitrifying bacteria will be increased in the rhizosphere. This is because, although they are facultative anaerobes, the denitrifiers are more competitive as aerobic heterotrophs. The rhizosphere, therefore, represents a zone of high denitrification potential, although this will only be strongly expressed in terms of activity if the soil becomes water saturated periodically. The expression of this potential will depend on how well the soil is aggregated (anaerobic microsites readily develop inside aggregates) and whether the soil is subject to periodic saturation.

The presence of increased population densities of protozoa in rhizosphere soil may play an important role in releasing nutrients held in microbial tissue. Grazing of rhizosphere microbes by protozoa (and other soil animals such as nematodes) is probably particularly important in ensuring the efficient recycling of nutrients released by plants, rather than accessing additional, soil-derived nutrients for the plants.

Because of the wide range of microbes that is stimulated in the rhizosphere, it is difficult to assess the influence of rhizosphere microbial activity on plant growth. Rhizosphere microbes can both mobilise and immobilise plant nutrients, and can produce growth-promoting substances, such as gibberellins, as well as phytotoxins. Rhizosphere microbes, such as species of the fungi *Fusarium*, *Gaeumannomyces* and *Rhizoctonia* can also be plant pathogens, as well as antagonists against those pathogens. Clearly, the situation is complicated and we only see the net effect of the many growth-promoting and growth-inhibiting microbial processes. In general, the net effect is stimulatory to plant growth, although there is considerable potential for manipulation of the rhizosphere microbial community to further enhance plant growth (see Chapter 7).

The total volume of rhizosphere soil may be considerable, particularly where the vegetation has a dense root system. This is the case for grass and for many tree species. Root densities as high as about 200 cm cm^{-3} can be found in hardwood forests, and this translates to a situation where, if all the roots were parallel, there would be less than 1 mm between each root. Of course, not all of this will be actively producing root exudates, this activity being largely restricted to close to the root tips. In addition, mycorrhizal infection can considerably reduce the flow of available carbon from the root because the mycobiont represents such a considerable carbon sink. The 'mycorrhizosphere', therefore, generally has much lower microbial population densities than the rhizosphere adjacent to non-mycorrhizal root tips.

Many of the soil physicochemical parameters discussed in Chapter 1 control the distribution and activity of the plant/microbial interactions discussed. Soil pH, for example, is particularly detrimental to the development of the legume/rhizobial symbiosis, partly because of the rhizobial sensitivity to aluminium, which becomes increasingly soluble in more acid soils. The pH of the soil will also have an influence on the composition of the rhizosphere microbial population, although superimposed on this will be pH-regulating processes of the root itself. Also, water saturation of soils can be highly inhibitory to mycorrhizal development, and plants with their root systems in near-saturated soil tend not to have mycorrhizal fungal infection. Water stress in soil, on the other hand, reduces the diffusion of substrates and nutrients and creates an osmoregulatory stress for both plant and microbe.

ANIMAL/MICROBIAL INTERACTIONS

Soil animals have an indirect effect on the structure and activity of microbial communities through mechanisms such as inoculum dispersal, grazing (or predation), litter comminution, passage through guts and aggregate formation.

Many of the soil animals that process organic detritus in soil contain a diverse gut population of microorganisms that is involved in a variety of decomposition reactions. Earthworms, for example, contain a large population of cellulolytic and other bacteria, capitalising on the massive throughput of leaf litter in the worm gut. Passage of this material through the gut is associated with a considerable increase in microbial population density, particularly for spore-forming bacteria and actinomycetes. Even the earthworm cast material tends to have much higher microbial population densities than the bulk soil. It is uncertain what proportion of the worm's enzymatic activity (including cellulases, lipases, proteases, amylases, chitinases etc.) is caused by the worm itself and what proportion by the gut microflora, although the similarity in species diversity of microbes in the gut and in soil suggests that the earthworms simply use the microbes for food rather than use the microbes to digest food. Because of this, it is perhaps best to describe this association as commensal. This is not the only example of an association between a soil animal and cellulolytic microbes in soil. Many of the wood-attacking beetles (e.g. the ambrosia beetles) in forest soils actually culture cellulolytic fungi in their tunnels as a food source. The fungi, particularly the fruiting bodies, are regularly grazed by the beetles but only at a rate enabling the fungus to prosper. Because many of these fungi (such as *Ceratocystis ambrosia*) can only be found in association with the beetles, the association can be classified as mutualistic.

In addition to microbes forming commensal and mutualisitic associations with soil animals, many others are ingested by the animal and enter into the gut. Protozoa and nematodes graze on both soil bacteria (bacteriophagous) and fungi (mycophagous), whereas arthropods such as mites and springtails dominantly feed on the soil fungi. In many cases, the grazed microbes do not survive passage through the gut and are lysed. In other cases, however, the microbes pass through the gut and are returned in an active state to the soil environment. Microbial survival, after ingestion, may occur during grazing by components of the macro-, meso- and microfauna of the soil. If this egestion of living microbes is a significant soil process, then the guts of soil animals may be sites or 'hot spots' of intense microbial interaction in the soil.

ANIMAL/ANIMAL INTERACTIONS

Perhaps one of the most striking examples of an interaction between soil animals of considerable ecological significance is where the decomposition of organic matter in the soil is regulated by the predation of one soil animal by another. Mites can control the decomposition of buried leaf litter by consuming bacteriophagous nematodes. When mites are removed from the system through selective use of pesticides, there can be a sharp increase in the population of nematodes, causing a concomitant increase in the numbers of bacterial decomposers. The decomposition of the leaf litter is, therefore, retarded because of the interruption of this soil animal interaction.

An interaction of soil animals involving a component of the macrofauna is that involving moles and earthworms. Earthworm distribution and abundance largely controls that of the mole, not to mention that of a number of birds on the soil surface. It may well be, therefore, that a consequence of the trend towards low-input agriculture (particularly low inputs of pesticides, as well as the soil incorporation of crop residues) will be a large increase in both earthworm and mole activity.

PLANT/ANIMAL INTERACTIONS

Interactions between plant roots and soil animals can take a wide variety of forms, can be both beneficial and detrimental to the growth of the plant, and can often also involve interactions with soil microbes.

The dispersal of mycorrhizal fungal inocula by a number of soil animals is of benefit to many plants. This dispersal is particularly carried out by large, burrowing soil animals such as moles and rabbits, but also the meso- and microfauna. On the other hand, however, grazing of mycorrhizal fungal hyphae by soil animals, such as springtails and phytopathogenic nematodes can be detrimental to the growth of plants (Finlay, 1985). It appears that both ectomycorrhizal and VAM-forming fungi can be grazed in this way.

The ecological significance of grazing of mycorrhizal fungi in association with plant roots has yet to be assessed, but mycorrhizal fungal hyphae can comprise a very significant proportion of the total microbial biomass in some soils and, therefore, would appear to represent a major food resource for fungal-grazing soil animals.

A number of soil animals feed directly on plant roots. These animals include soil arthropods such as millipedes and springtails. It is not clear how much of the damage inflicted on plants by these soil animals is directly caused by the activity of root-grazing and how much by subsequent susceptibility of roots to soil-borne pathogens, particularly fungal pathogens.

MICROBE/MICROBE INTERACTIONS

Although these interactions are numerous in soil, one that stands out as being of particular ecological significance is that of the nitrifying bacteria, *Nitrosomonas* and *Nitrobacter*. These chemoautotrophs function in close association, because the product of one provides the substrate for the other.

$$NH_4^+ + \tfrac{3}{2}O_2 \xrightarrow{\text{\textit{Nitrosomonas}}} NO_2^- + H_2O + 2H^+$$

$$NO_2^- + \tfrac{1}{2}O_2 \xrightarrow{\text{\textit{Nitrobacter}}} NO_3^-$$

We know that these activities are tightly coupled because in aerobic soils we can rarely detect significant concentrations of nitrite (NO_2^-), which, in view of its phytotoxic nature, is just as well. Because of the substrate/product dependence between *Nitrosomonas* and *Nitrobacter*, their populations can be modelled in relation to substrate and product flow (e.g. Day, Doner & McLaren, 1978).

A substrate/product interaction similar to that operating for nitrifiers exists in the sulphur cycle where sulphur-oxidation reactions are largely carried out by a number of species of the genus *Thiobacillus*. Like the nitrifiers, the thiobacilli are chemoautotrophic bacteria and the population level and activity of any one species is, therefore, dependent on supply of a suitable form of reduced sulphur, often from the activity of another species. *Thiobacillus novellus*, for example, cannot oxidise elemental sulphur but freely oxidises both the substrates sulphite (SO_3^{2-}) and tetrathionate ($S_4O_6^{2-}$) through to sulphate.

Although sulphite can be produced through chemical reactions in the soil, the presence of substrates such as tetrathionate and, also, thiosulphate ($S_2O_3^{2-}$), necessitates microbial oxidation. The activity of *T. novellus*, therefore, is largely determined by the population and activity of the other species of the thiobacilli and, to a lesser extent, of other S-oxidising heterotrophs in the soil such as species of *Arthrobacter*, *Bacillus* and *Flavobacterium*, as well as a variety of soil fungi.

In addition to the interactions of the chemoautotrophic soil bacteria, many components of the soil's heterotrophic microbial community interact closely. An example of this can be found in the decomposition of lignin. Lignin degradation in soil is a very specialised process (see Chapter 4, pages 98–100), largely carried out by the Basidiomycotina in forest soils where lignin is most plentiful. Although lignin breakdown is specialised, its attack reveals cellulose microfibrils that are readily attacked not only by the lignin-decomposing Basidiomycotina, but also by many other cellulolytic microbes that are non-ligninolytic. Similarly, the breakdown of cellulose into cellobiose and glucose enables non-cellulolytic heterotrophs to live in association with the cellulolytic microflora.

COMPLEX INTERACTIONS

It is rare that biological interactions in the soil are as simple and clear-cut as some of those described in the preceding sections. Examination of earthworm cast material, for example, may often reveal a complex mixture of plant, microbial and animal fragments, but also intact protozoa (protected from enzymatic digestion by encystment), which in turn contain a variety of microbial cells. Much of the microarthropod grazing of the fungal component of forest mycorrhizas occurs in a matrix of decomposing faecal pellets of soil animals, particularly enchytraeid worms. Bacteriophagous nematodes and protozoa enable nutrients released from plants and immobilised by rhizosphere bacteria to be returned to the plant through excretion of surplus N from their digested prey. The activity of the nitrifying bacteria is readily regulated by a complex interaction of sources and sinks for substrate and product involving other microbes, soil animals and plant roots. Models are often helpful in providing a conceptual understanding of the behaviour of complex ecological interactions between different components of the soil biota.

SOIL BIOLOGICAL COMMUNITY DYNAMICS

Root population dynamics

Despite the often slow rate of change of above-ground biomass of many plants, the below-ground biomass of the roots is a highly dynamic system with formation of new roots, death of old roots, and decomposition of dead roots occurring on a continuous basis. Thus, the 1% of the soil volume that typically comprises plant root systems, and the associated rhizosphere soil, is a zone of intense change and activity in which the major part of soil nutrient cycling occurs.

In forests, between 30 and 90% of fine roots are lost and replaced annually and this 'turnover' of fine roots may represent a biomass of several thousand kilograms per hectare of forest (Fogel, 1985). The turnover time of fine (<1 mm) roots and mycorrhizas in unfertilised Sitka spruce can be as rapid as 16 weeks, with slightly larger roots (1–5 mm) having a turnover time of nearly four years (Alexander & Fairley, 1983). The equation for turnover time is given below.

$$\text{Root turnover time (y)} = \frac{\text{Root biomass (kg ha}^{-1}\text{)}}{\text{Mortality (kg ha}^{-1}\text{ y}^{-1}\text{)}}$$

The population dynamics for forest roots demonstrate the importance of the turnover of fine roots and mycorrhizas to the forest ecosystem, turnover of these components providing two to five times the amount of organic matter to the soil than provided by leaf and branch litter (Fogel, 1983).

The dynamic nature of root systems applies to herbaceous and grassland systems, as well as to forests. Indeed, even shorter turnover times can be realised. The roots of strawberry plants, for example, generally have turnover times between one and three weeks (Atkinson, 1985).

The turnover time of roots is not only determined by plant species. The nature of the soil environment will also be a critical factor, soils with low nutrient availability tending to support roots with longer turnover times than those in more nutrient-rich soils. Of course, the root systems of nutrient-poor soils will also tend to be more finely branched to exploit a greater soil volume. In addition, greater mycorrhizal infection of the roots will tend to occur in nutrient-poor systems.

Microbial population dynamics

Growth of microbes under closed and open conditions – relevance to soil

When there are no constraints on microbial growth in a closed, batch system, the rate of growth follows an exponential curve (Figure 18). In the context of the soil environment, this situation may briefly arise when there is a surplus of some microbial substrate and conditions for growth are favourable. The actual generation time of the organisms under study will depend on a whole spectrum of environmental parameters such as the nature of the substrate, temperature, pH and water potential. If all these parameters are optimal for

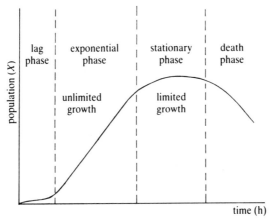

Figure 18. Population dynamics of soil microbes in a closed system.

growth, a condition only likely inside a growth vessel in the laboratory, then the generation time of the fastest-growing soil organisms such as a pseudomonad or a bacillus will be of the order of 20 to 30 minutes, with slower-growing soil fungi doubling every few hours or so. Cells growing under these optimal conditions are said to be growing at their 'maximum specific growth rate'.

The rate of change of population size (i.e. growth rate) = $\mathrm{d}x/\mathrm{d}t = \mu \cdot X_0$

where μ = specific growth rate
   X_0 = initial size of population.

Under optimal conditions

$$\mathrm{d}x/\mathrm{d}t = \mu_{\mathrm{max}} \cdot X_0$$

where μ_{max} = maximum specific growth rate.

If we use very high growth rates (particularly maximum specific growth rates) to describe microbial growth in the soil environment, some fantastic extrapolations can be made. For example, in less than three days, the mass of cells of a fast-growing soil bacterium, in exponential growth, will exceed the mass of the earth (Postgate, 1975)! Because this has clearly not happened, then the growth of microbes in soil must be under much tighter constraints than when growing exponentially in rich laboratory media.

The first difference between the soil population and an exponential culture is that the substrate for growth is usually limiting in the soil (Figure 18). Of course, the other major difference between the environments is that the soil is an 'open' system and the laboratory batch culture 'closed'. This means that we should more realistically study population dynamics under 'open' conditions of continuous culture, using the chemostat. Now, under these conditions, the population will achieve a steady state (i.e. the population is kept constant, with production of cells balanced by their washout, under a growth-limiting substrate concentration with a fixed dilution rate). Under these conditions, the growth yield of the cells (that is their use of substrate for growth) can be expressed in terms of the growth achieved from the amount of substrate used, over a certain time interval.

$$\text{Growth yield} = \frac{\text{Cell growth (g)}}{\text{Substrate used (g)}}$$

$$\text{or } Y = \frac{dX}{ds}$$

Of course, at steady state in a chemostat, the growth of cells is matched by their washout. In the soil environment, this washout will only occur to a limited extent, as most cells are retained by the soil. Cells will die and the population balance in the soil will be between cell growth and cell death, rather than through dilution/washout in the chemostat. The dead cells will themselves provide a source of substrate for the soil microbial population and contribute, therefore, to the total substrate available.

Utilisation of substrate carbon from dead cells can be an important strategy for microbial survival in soils. In a starved microbial population in the soil, it may be that few survivors are supported by the lysis products of the dead cells and, as a result, the survivors may multiply. This phenomenon is referred to as cryptic growth. It is still a poorly understood process in soils and is rarely considered in the population dynamics of soil microbes, but it may be that cryptic growth as well as oligotrophy (see Chapter 1, pages 19–20) are important strategies when soil microbial populations are under conditions of substrate/nutrient starvation.

Under optimal growth conditions, almost all of the substrate taken up by a cell or population of cells can be used for growth, with little diversion of this substrate for maintenance of the cell's integrity. In the soil, however, the environmental stresses may be great and this diversion of substrate into maintenance of cell integrity may become very considerable and even dominate the partitioning of substrate (Figure 19). Under these circumstances, the equation for growth yield must be modified to take into account this

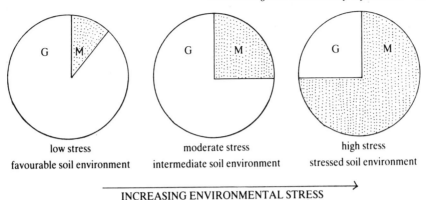

| low stress | moderate stress | high stress |
| favourable soil environment | intermediate soil environment | stressed soil environment |

INCREASING ENVIRONMENTAL STRESS →

Figure 19. The relation between the partitioning of substrate carbon/energy into growth (G) and maintenance (M) and the degree of environmental stress.

additional demand for 'maintenance' on substrate C-flow.

$$\text{Growth yield} = \frac{\text{Cell growth}}{\underset{\text{for growth}}{\text{Substrate used}} + \underset{\text{for maintenance}}{\text{Substrate used}}}$$

$$\text{or } Y = \frac{\mathrm{d}X}{(\mathrm{d}s_g + \mathrm{d}s_m)}$$

Competition between organisms in soil

Microbial competition

So far, we have only considered the simple case of one population of organisms growing in the soil. In reality, of course, different populations of soil organisms interact with one another. Two examples of these interactions are competition and predation, and these will be explained in some detail.

Competition between soil organisms occurs where two or more different populations (or individual organisms) have an active demand for the same resource or substrate. The most competitive population will be that which is able to sustain the highest growth rate under the prevailing soil conditions. This will largely depend on two factors. These are the maximum specific growth rate (μ_{max}) and the Michaelis constant (k) of the organisms/ populations. The latter refers to the substrate concentration at which half of

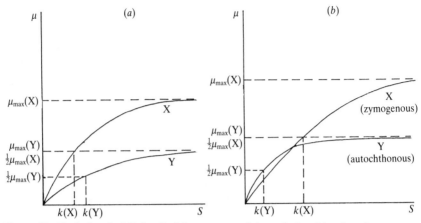

Figure 20. Variation in Michaelis–Menten growth/population kinetics of two populations of soil organisms (X and Y) competing for substrate S. (a) $\mu_{max}(X) > \mu_{max}(Y)$ and $k(Y) < k(X)$; (b) $\mu_{max}(X) > \mu_{max}(Y)$ but $k(X) > k(Y)$. Here, k is the Michaelis constant, S is the concentration of substrate S, and μ is the specific growth rate, given by $\mu = \mu_{max} \cdot S/(k + S)$.

the maximum specific growth rate is achieved (Figure 20). In the graph of Figure 20a, population X has a higher specific growth rate than population Y, regardless of substrate concentration. In Figure 20b, population X also has a higher maximum specific growth rate than population Y. Population Y has a relatively low Michaelis constant compared with population X, however, and so, at low substrate concentrations, produces a higher specific growth rate than population X. This concept may be of fundamental importance in the microbial ecology of soils because there are rarely high substrate concentrations in the soil. It is far more likely that concentrations will often be at or below the Michaelis constant level. Results from laboratory culture studies using artificially high substrate concentrations may be very misleading if they are readily extrapolated to the soil system for all conditions.

Autochthonous and zymogenous microbial populations in soil

A microbial population in soil, being more competitive than another at low substrate concentrations, but less competitive at high substrate concentrations, introduces the concept of autochthonous and zymogenous populations. The autochthonous populations, those most competitive at low substrate concentrations, are the indigenous soil organisms that 'tick over' under these conditions and persist actively in the soil for long periods of time. In physiological terms, as expressed in Figure 20, the autochthonous population tends to have a fairly low maximum specific growth rate, but a very low Michaelis constant. The zymogenous populations are not a significant component of the soil community under normal conditions, but proliferate when considerable additions of substrates such as plant or animal residues are introduced into the soil. The zymogenous organisms are capable of rapid multiplication and then tend to revert to resistant spore structures once the substrate has been largely exhausted. Again, in physiological terms, the zymogenous population tends to have a high maximum specific growth rate, and a high Michaelis constant (Figure 20). It was Winogradsky (1924) who first introduced the concept of autochthonous and zymogenous populations, proposing that the autochthonous soil microbes largely comprised the coccoid soil bacteria, while the zymogenous largely consisted of bacilli and spore-forming bacteria.

Although Winogradsky's theory may not be entirely correct, the soil microbial population not always being so sharply divided, the basic concept is still valuable, providing us with a clear physiological distinction between a community in soil that responds to widely fluctuating, decomposable resources and one that receives much lower, but steadier substrate flow. This physiological distinction is based on the sort of Michaelis–Menten population growth curves of Figure 20.

It may well be that the autochthonous and zymogenous components of the soil microbial biomass are spatially compartmentalised as well as physiologically distinct. The autochthonous population appears best suited to the smaller pores and inner microhabitats of soil aggregates where substrate supply will be low, but protection from protozoal grazing greatest. The zymogenous population appears better suited to somewhat larger pores and the outer microhabitats of aggregates where there is ready access to brief flushes of substrate supply, even though there is little protection from protozoal and other grazing when these sites are water filled. Evidence is now growing (e.g. Killham, Amato & Ladd, 1993) to support the theory that spatial location, in terms of pore-size distribution of functionally distinct components of the microbial biomass, determines substrate turnover and nutrient flow in soil. Elliot & Coleman (1988) have even proposed a hierarchical series of aggregate habitats of different sizes to explain some nutrient fluxes in soil and ecological interactions between organisms involved in detrital food webs.

r- and K-strategies – microbes and higher soil organisms

In recent years, soil ecologists have popularised the use of the concept of r- and K-strategies as a means of describing the competitive strategies of higher soil organisms and, to some extent, soil microbes. The r- and K-strategies are somewhat analogous to Winogradsky's zymogenous and autochthonous categories. The K-strategists are populations or species living at or near the carrying capacity of the soil environment, and they are broadly analogous to the autochthonous populations. The r-strategists are populations or species that intrinsically provide for rapid proliferations in response to an abundance of resource/substrate and are analogous to the zymogenous population. The r- and K-selection continuum, however, is based on complex logistic models that fit data for population dynamics of predominantly higher organisms, whereas the autochthonous/zymogenous system is physiologically based, using microbial population growth curves (Michaelis–Menten relationships) such as in Figure 20. The r–K selection continuum has been used to describe the competitive interactions of soil fungi (e.g. Cooke & Rayner, 1984), although there is little or no reliable, confirmatory data of fungal population dynamics in soil.

There is a danger that all competitive strategies will be described by soil ecologists using a single selection pressure such as in the r- and K-continuum. Such a broad use of the theory has been criticised (e.g. Parry, 1981). Clearly, one cannot extrapolate the single r- and K-theory to all microbial population dynamics in soil, and, in many cases, good use can be made of the simple physiologically based equations. There are, however, situations, such as certain successions of decomposer communities, where invoking the r- and K-theory has considerable potential.

Prey/predator interactions and microbial population dynamics in soils

In the soil environment, the simple population dynamics introduced will be complicated, not only by competition for a resource, but also by the fact that microorganisms will be subject to predation. This predation will largely take the form of grazing by soil protozoa, but also by nematodes and other soil animals. Grazing is mainly of bacteria, but fungi also represent a food source. The population level of the protozoa in soil is usually closely linked to that of their microbial food source, assuming the pores in which prey and

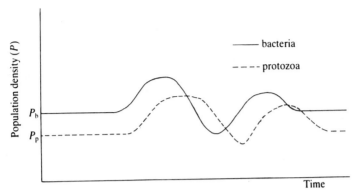

Figure 21. Soil bacterial population density as a function of soil protozoal density – an 'ideal' prey/predator relationship.

predator are located contain sufficient water. A pulse increase in the population level of soil bacteria (for example, because of a crop residue input), therefore, will generally be accompanied by a lagged pulse in protozoal numbers (Figure 21). This bloom of protozoa will then feed on the bacteria and the population levels of both groups of organisms will again gradually return to their previous 'equilibrium' status.

The rate of change of the bacterial population in soil will be equal to the growth rate of the prey, minus the death rate of the prey, minus the rate at which the prey are grazed by the protozoa:

$$\text{Rate of change of bacterial population} = \text{Growth rate of bacteria} - \text{Death rate of bacteria} - \text{Rate of protozoan grazing of bacteria}$$

If we are to succeed in the manipulation of soil microbial ecology for both agricultural and environmental benefits, we must first improve our understanding of the fundamental population kinetics of the soil microbiota. Only then can we realistically hope to understand the effects of any soil ecological manipulations.

Population dynamics of soil animals

In considering the population dynamics of most soil animals, an additional aspect to that considered for microbes must be included, that is the immigration and emigration of animals to and from the volume of soil under study:

$$X_T = X_0 + X_B - X_D + X_I - X_E$$

where X_T = the number of animals in a volume of soil at time T
X_0 = the number at time 0
X_B = the number born
X_D = the number that died
X_I = the number of immigrants
X_E = the number of emigrants.

The term X_B is partly determined by the fecundity of the soil animal species under study, which itself is related to a number of both environmental as well as species-related parameters. An example of a key environmental parameter affecting fecundity is the quality of substrate available to the animals. The fecundity of springtails, for example, is proportional to the nitrogen concentration of the fungal hyphae on which the springtails are grazing (Booth, 1983). The term X_B is also determined by the rate of reproduction, which, again, is influenced by a host of environmental parameters including water potential and temperature. The reproduction of some soil animals is strongly influenced by soil pH. Some protozoa, for example, have clear pH thresholds below which reproduction will not occur.

The term X_0, which expresses the mortality of the soil animals, has a 'continuous' component, but superimposed on this is an additional 'catastrophic' component. The latter may be caused by sudden and intense heating/desiccation of the soil or by freeze/thaw activity.

The rate of movement of animals in and out of the volume of soil under study is expressed by the terms X_I and X_E. There is considerable vertical migration due to seasonal effects of animals in the soil profile. The drying of the upper horizons of the profile in the summer, for example, causes a marked downward migration of animals such as earthworms, which are particularly sensitive to water stress. Freeze–thaw activity can also lead to these selective, vertical migrations of soil animals. Less extreme, diurnal temperature changes in soil also often result in the vertical movement of mites and other animals.

Horizontal movement of animals is often caused by a change in the physicochemical conditions of an adjacent soil volume. The addition of lime or manure to soil may encourage considerable immigration of animals from adjoining soil.

4 The ecology of soil nutrient cycling

INTRODUCTION

Many of the important nutrients in the life cycle of plants, animals and microorganisms are cycled in the soil between the soil organic matter and the inorganic nutrient pool. These so-called 'biological elements' such as carbon, nitrogen, sulphur and phosphorus form the main building blocks of cellular tissue and are initially absorbed by the lower forms of life as simple inorganic forms and are then converted to organic constituents within the cell. The death and decay of organisms and their tissues results in release of inorganic ions and, so, a cycle is established.

From the onset, it is essential to appreciate that nutrient cycling involves the activity of plants, microbes and animals. Many texts on nutrient cycling have tended to neglect one or two of these components, particularly the soil animals. This chapter attempts to provide a more balanced picture of the ecology of soil nutrient cycling.

THE CARBON CYCLE

Introduction – the global carbon cycle

Recent concern over the possible consequences of increasing concentrations of carbon dioxide in the atmosphere (part of the greenhouse effect), largely as a result of the burning of fossil fuels and the clearing/burning of large areas of forest, has created renewed interest in developing a full understanding of the global carbon cycle.

Apart from the burning of fossil fuels and forest fires, carbon dioxide is continually produced by all heterotrophs in the biosphere. On the other hand, carbon dioxide is fixed by autotrophs, particularly through the process of photosynthesis. Figure 5 in Chapter 1 illustrates this relationship between heterotrophy and autotrophy.

Although the total global reservoir of carbon is vast (more than 10^{16} t), only a small fraction of this carbon is actively involved in the fluxes of the carbon cycle, most of the earth's carbon being 'locked away' in sediments (mainly as carbonates), in carbonate in ocean waters, and in igneous rocks and fossil carbon. Putting the burning of fossil fuels to one side, the earth's active carbon fraction largely consists of carbon in living organisms, carbon in the organic matter of the soil and carbon in the atmosphere. The soil carbon pool is approximately five times the size of the atmospheric pool. The latter is approximately the same size as that in living organisms. These three pools together, however, amount to less than one thousandth of global carbon reserves.

This chapter will focus on the cycling of carbon in the soil/plant system. The total annual input of carbon into soil (from above and below ground sources) is estimated at 37.5×10^9 t (Schlesinger, 1984). At steady state, production of carbon dioxide through decomposition and respiration should release an equal amount of carbon back into the atmosphere. The amount of carbon in the atmosphere is so small in relation to the scale of the carbon flux, both into and out of this pool, that consumption of carbon by the plant/soil system would rapidly exhaust atmospheric resources if it were not for the continual respiratory return of carbon to the atmosphere. Estimates (Schlesinger, 1984) suggest, however, that the rate of release of carbon dioxide from world soils may be as much as twice that of the rate of input. This imbalance is largely the result of the clearing and cultivation of forests and other natural ecosystems, both reducing the capacity for primary production and accelerating the rate of decomposition of the soil's carbon reserves.

C-inputs to the soil carbon cycle

Figure 22 provides a diagram of the soil carbon cycle.

Carbon dioxide fixation

It is the autotrophs or primary producers that fix atmospheric carbon dixoide into more complex forms of organic carbon:

$$CO_2 + H_2O \rightarrow CH_2O + O_2$$

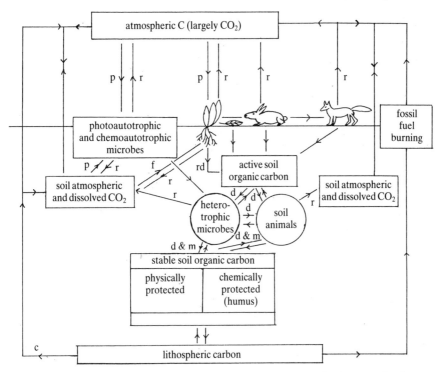

Figure 22. The soil carbon cycle. Abbreviations: p, photosynthesis; r, respiration; rd, rhizodeposition; f, fixation; d, decomposition; m, macromolecular synthesis; c, CO_2 from carbonates.

Primary production is an essential link in the soil carbon cycle as it is the main flux from the atmosphere to the soil biota and is defined as the rate at which energy is stored by photosynthetic and chemosynthetic activity of producer organisms in the form of organic substances. Net primary productivity is the rate of storage of organic carbon in these substances, in excess of respiration. In general, in the soil system, it is the plants (particularly the higher plants) that contribute most to primary productivity. There are also, however, photoautotrophic blue-green algae or cyanophyta as well as the eukaryotic algae which can contribute to carbon dioxide fixation. Photoautotrophic and chemoautotrophic bacteria may also make a very minor contribution. Net primary production varies greatly from one ecosystem to another. The highest rates of production are found in the tropical rain forests where 11 t ha^{-1} of atmospheric carbon are typically fixed annually as tree biomass (Table 11). Temperate forests fix about half of this, while temperate grasslands and arable systems fix about a quarter that of tropical forests. It is because of their high capacity for carbon dioxide fixation, as well as their widespread extent, that the current loss of tropical rain forest is thought to contribute so adversely to the greenhouse effect.

From Figure 22, it can be seen that the fixed carbon from the primary producers enters the soil either largely as plant litter (leaves, branches, roots etc.), as dead algal or bacterial cells, as exudates of roots and other organisms, and via various consumer organisms which form part of the food chain.

Other inputs to the soil carbon cycle

In addition to carbon inputs to the soil either directly from primary producers (Figure 22), or indirectly via the bodies and waste products of consumer animals, carbon also enters the soil as polycyclic aromatic hydrocarbons from the burning of fossil fuels and in industrial products such as pesticides. Some of these compounds, such as the insecticide DDT, are highly resistant to decomposition and may persist in the soil for many years.

Although primary production (and other sources) continually provides an input of carbon to the soil system, processes of decomposition and respiration continually return the carbon to the atmosphere as carbon dioxide. Soil organic carbon consists of material in various states of decomposition from recent inputs of plant litter to highly decomposed humus.

The turnover of carbon in soils

The ultimate end product of the aerobic decomposition of organic carbon in soils is carbon dioxide:

$$CH_2O + O_2 \rightarrow CO_2 + H_2O$$

Prior to the global increase in atmospheric carbon dioxide concentrations that have occurred in the past 100 years or so, production of carbon dioxide through decomposer activity was largely balanced by autotrophic fixation (Figure 5). The atmospheric concentration of carbon dioxide was, therefore, stable as a result of this equilibrium.

In productive ecosystems, the turnover of organic carbon in the soil is rapid. Tropical rain forests, for example, have a soil carbon pool about five times that of their annual net primary production and five times that of their standing biomass (Table 11). Less productive temperate forests, however, have a soil carbon pool more than ten times that of their annual net primary

Table 11. *Typical distribution of carbon in different ecosystems*

Ecosystem	Net primary production of C (t ha^{-1} y^{-1})	Standing biomass of C (t ha^{-1})	Soil organic carbon pool (t ha^{-1})
Tropical rain forests	11	11	80
Temperate forests	6	6	100
Temperate grasslands	3	0.4	150
Deserts	0.05	0.01	1

Some figures adapted from Whittaker, 1975.

production and standing biomass. Even less productive temperate grasslands have soil carbon reserves more than 30 times that of net primary production and more than 200 times that of the standing biomass. There is therefore a trend for a decreasing rate of carbon turnover in soil from productive to less productive ecosystems.

Forms of soil organic carbon

Approximately half of the organic carbon in soils is in aromatic forms, with a further 20% or so associated with nitrogen, and the remaining 30% roughly evenly divided into carbohydrate carbon and fatty acid as well as alkane carbon (Figure 23a). Although soil organic carbon exists in a great variety of forms, it can most simply be considered as three main pools – insoluble, soluble and biomass carbon. Insoluble soil organic carbon comprises well over 90% of total soil organic carbon and includes the main components of plant cell walls – cellulose and lignin – and the main component of many soil animal exoskeletons and fungal walls – chitin. The insoluble soil carbon pool also includes decomposed material in the form of soil humus. Soluble carbon provides an immediate substrate for a wide range of soil microbes and is largely produced by plant roots as root exudates, by other living soil organisms that produce exudates, and by the enzymatic decomposition of insoluble and biomass carbon. Because of its rapid assimilation as a substrate, concentrations of soluble carbon in the soil are very low, typically representing less than 1% of soil organic carbon. Excluding the primary

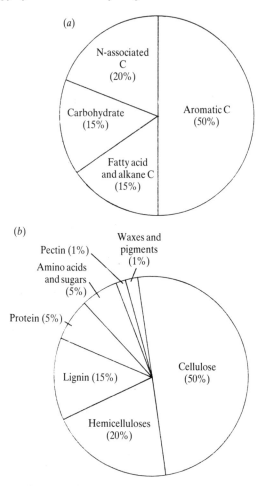

Figure 23. (*a*) Forms of organic carbon found in soil and their approximate relative amounts. (*b*) Some of the main forms of organic carbon entering the soil from plant residues.

producers, the biomass carbon pool of the soil consists of soil microbes and animals. It is the activity of the decomposer (saprophytic) soil microbes that is most responsible for the turnover of carbon in soils, even though the soil animals are intimately involved. All organic matter passes through the microbial pool before being redistributed to other pools (Figure 22). The biomass carbon pool, therefore, may only represent 1–2% of the total organic carbon in soil, but represents the driving force of the soil carbon cycle and, hence, of other soil nutrient cycles also (Paul & Voroney, 1980).

Decomposition of different forms of organic carbon in soil

Introduction

Plant residues, as litter, branches, root detritus and exudates, comprise by far the largest fraction of the carbon entering the soil, although microbes and animals also contribute to soil carbon supply. Figure 23b illustrates the main carbonaceous components of plants' residues.

When plant residues enter the soil, there is an initial flush of decomposition (two thirds of most plant residues generally decompose in one year), followed by a much slower, steady breakdown. This is because of two factors. The first is that some components of the residues are much more readily decomposed than others. The second is that the formation of stable substances, after the initial decomposition flush, prevents further rapid microbial attack. Humic substances are discussed more fully on pages 104 and 105.

The ultimate end product of organic matter breakdown in soil is carbon dioxide, assuming the soil is reasonably aerated. Because of this, production of carbon dioxide is often used as an indicator of decomposition rates. This is not always reliable as carbon dioxide can be produced in other ways, such as through root respiration. Respiration can, however, be related to individual substrates/residues if the latter are radiolabelled with ^{14}C. In the short-term, however, not all of the carbon from substrates produces carbon dioxide and more should be known about the fate of microbially processed carbon before evolution of carbon dioxide alone is used as a measure of decomposition rate.

Cellulose

Cellulose often represents more than half of plant residue carbon as well as being an important component of fungal and algal cell walls. Cellulose occurs in a semi-crystalline state in these residues with a molecular weight of approximately one million. The microbial decomposition of cellulose can be represented as follows.

Depolymerisation of cellulose is by specialised cellulolytic saprophytes, e.g. fungi such as species of *Fusarium*, *Aspergillus*, *Trichoderma* and *Penicillium*, or by bacteria such as species of *Bacillus*, *Pseudomonas* and *Clostridium*. Then:

Cellulose is a polymer of glucose units joined together by 1–4 linkages, and decomposition is catalysed by the enzyme system cellulase. Cellulase activity involves the loss of the crystalline structure of cellulose ('conditioning') as well as the subsequent depolymerisation. After depolymerisation, resulting short chains of glucose units are often referred to by specific names (two units, cellobiose; three units, cellotriose) and the enzymes involved in their hydrolysis to single glucose units are referred to as cellobiase and cellotriase. The decomposition of cellulose is representative of that of many large organic polymers in soil, with initial depolymerisation by specialised microbial enzyme systems, but subsequent release of simpler units serving as a substrate for a wider group of soil microbes. Ultimately, the release of low molecular weight compounds such as glucose into the soluble carbon pool provides a substrate for all heterotrophic soil microbes possessing glycosidase enzymes. Another common feature in the catabolism of polymeric substrates in soil is that there are two types of depolymerising activity that can occur:

endodepolymerase enzymes cleave the chains at random, whereas exodepoly-merases cleave only one or two units at a time from the non-reducing end of the polymer. The rate limiting step in terms of carbon turnover is the rate of depolymerisation, not the breakdown of the sub-units.

The breakdown of cellulose in soil involves soil animals as well as microbes. The physical comminution of plant litter by soil animals exposes greater surface area for microbial attack. In particular, because cellulose is often associated with lignin and hemicellulose, protected cellulose is often exposed by mechanical disruption from soil animals. The guts of soil animals such as earthworms often have high levels of cellulase activity and can digest completely, any partially decomposed plant material. In addition to this enzymatic activity of the gut, the cellulolytic activity of gut microbes also contributes to the role of earthworms and other soil animals in cellulose decomposition.

The decomposition of wood litter and fungal mats in forest soils involves considerable cellulolytic activity. Cellulose, often making up half of the dry weight of the wood and litter, occurs in filamentous microfibrils in a matrix of hemicelluloses and is sheathed in lignin. Most of the cellulolytic activity is caused by brown rot fungi, which are mainly Basidiomycotina. The activity of the brown rot fungi, removing the cellulose and hemicellulose, is relatively rapid, leaving the lignin to be decomposed much more slowly by white rot fungi. The ectomycorrhizal fungal mats of forest floors are also rich in cellulose and are grazed upon by soil microarthropods and other soil animals. Digestion of this substantial source of cellulose is facilitated by the interaction (in the gut and in the soil) of these animals with cellulolytic microbes.

Hemicelluloses

Hemicelluloses (polymers of hexoses, pentoses and uronic acids) can con-stitute up to one third of plant residue carbon. The hemicellulose pectin (about 1% or less of plant dry weight) is a polymer of galacturonic acid, with a molecular weight of about 400 000, and has an important structural role in plants, being a key component of the mid-lamella region of plant cell walls. The decomposition of pectin is illustrated below.

Pectin decomposition in soil

(*a*) Stage 1 – Pectin esterases

$$(RCOOCH_3)_n + nH_2O \rightarrow (RCOOH)_n + nCH_3OH$$

(b) Stage 2 – Depolymerases (exo- and endo-)

Carboxyl groups esterified in stage 1

(c) Stage 3

$$C_5H_{10}O_6 + 4O_2 \xrightarrow[\text{oxidase}]{\text{galacturonic acid}} 5CO_2 + 5H_2O + E$$

The enzyme system (including all three stages of decomposition) involved in catalysing pectin decomposition is pectinase and activity is repressed by high sugar levels in fresh plant residue. This repression is a key factor in determining the nature of microbial succession in plant litter breakdown. Pectinolytic bacteria in soil include species of *Arthrobacter*, *Pseudomonas* and *Bacillus*. Soil actinomycetes such as species of *Streptomyces* are also strongly pectinolytic, as are many soil fungi.

Pectinases have other important roles in soil ecology as well as the decomposition of pectin in plant residues. The penetration of plant roots by both mutualistic symbionts such as *Rhizobium* and mycorrhizal-forming fungi, as well as by pathogenic soil microbes, for example, is facilitated by pectinase activity.

Lignin

The most resistant component of plant residues entering the soil carbon pool is lignin. After cellulose and hemicellulose, lignin is the third most abundant component of plant residues. Lignin, with a molecular weight from ten thousand to over a million, is a complex non-uniform polymer of aromatic nuclei, with the basic building unit being a phenyl-propane (C_6–C_3) type structure.

$$
\begin{array}{c}
\text{R} \\
|\\
\text{C}-\text{C} \\
\text{HO}-\text{C} \qquad\quad \text{C}-\text{C}-\text{C} \\
\text{C}=\text{C} \\
|\\
\text{R}'
\end{array}
$$

The R and R' functional groups may be in three different forms:

(i) R and R' are H groups,
(ii) R is H and R' is OCH_3 (methoxyl),
(iii) R and R' are OCH_3 groups.

Different plant residues contain lignin with different functional group characteristics. Coniferous trees, for example, often tend to produce lignin with an abundance of type (ii) groups.

Lignin has a very disorderly, cross-linked structure because of the many permutations involved in bonding repeating units together. The units may be linked by strong ether groups (C–O–C) or by carbon (C–C). These links may be between two phenolic rings, between two propane side chains, or between a ring and a side chain. Bonds do not occur regularly as they do on polysaccharide structures such as cellulose.

The 'random' structure of lignin and the strong linkages make lignin very resistant to microbial and other soil biological decomposition processes. Because of this, the percentage of lignin carbon in decomposing plant residues tends to increase with time in the soil, and the residues most resistant to decomposition tend to be those that are rich in lignin.

The decomposition of lignin in soil can be considered as a three-stage process. Stage one involves the esterification of the exposed methoxyl groups. Stage two is a depolymerisation process, while stage three involves the splitting of the phenolic ring after initial side chain removal. The biochemical, microbiological and ecophysiological nature of stage two, the depolymerisation, is still the subject of considerable speculation, but must almost certainly involve the extracellular enzymatic cleavage of the inter-unit bonds.

In terms of the organisms in the soil responsible for lignin breakdown, many soil microbes are known to be able to degrade some of the individual aromatic molecules that occur in lignin polymers. Only a very limited number of soil microbes, however, can degrade the entire lignin structure, and these microbes are thought to be largely fungi of the Basidiomycotina and are collectively termed the white rots. White rot Basidiomycotina include such fungi as *Phanaerochaete chrysosporium* and *Coriolus versicolor*. These fungi must be capable of producing a vast range of specialised enzymes, such as esterases, phenolases and peroxidases for relatively small energy returns. Because lignin degradation by some of the white rot fungi is inhibited by high levels of nitrogen, it has been suggested that lignin degradation is a secondary metabolic function induced by nitrogen starvation rather than a function of primary metabolism (Kirk & Fenn, 1982). It is likely that the recent introduction of radiocarbon-labelled, model lignin structures will enable the decomposition of lignin in soil to be more effectively characterised.

Although soil animals do not possess lignase activity in their guts, they are nonetheless intimately involved in the breakdown process. Apart from increasing the surface area for microbial attack, the soil animals also tend to inoculate the substrate as they migrate through the soil. This is particularly true for forest floors, which are rich in lignin where the vertical movement of microarthropods, in particular, contributes to the inoculum of Basidiomycotina that attack the lignin substrate.

The lignin content of wood and litter represents a major control on palatability for the soil fauna, material rich in lignin providing low resource quality.

Despite the complexity of the molecule and its decomposition, lignin, like other organic polymers after initial depolymerisation, becomes a substrate for an increasing number of soil microbes. Ultimately, much of the lignin associated carbon, along with other forms of organic carbon, will be lost from the soil carbon cycle as carbon dioxide.

Rates of carbon turnover

The rate of turnover of organic carbon in soil will be determined by the resource quality (and quantity) of the substrate(s) in question, the inoculum potential of the decomposer organisms (both animal and microbial), inter-actions (both competitive and synergistic) between the decomposer organisms, and by the soil physicochemical environment (particularly temperature and water potential).

Simple sugars are broken down rapidly in the soil by most heterotrophic microbes. Over the concentration range likely to be encountered in soils, decomposition is likely to proceed according to first order kinetics. This means that the rate of decomposition is proportional to the substrate concentration.

$$D = dS/dt = dP/dt = kS$$

where D = velocity of reaction (decomposition)
       dS/dt = rate of disappearance of substrate with time
       dP/dt = rate of appearance of product with time
       S = substrate concentration at time t
       k = first-order rate constant.

Figure 24 shows normal and log plots of a decomposition reaction that follows first-order kinetics.

The time taken for a substrate to turnover according to first-order kinetics is referred to as the turnover time.

Turnover time = $1/k$

Simple sugars have large rate constants (k) of decomposition, as they are

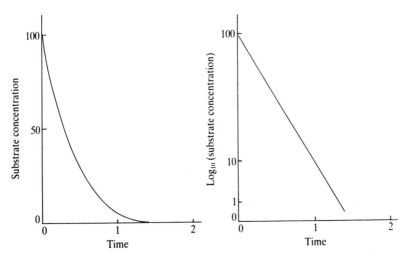

Figure 24. Normal and logarithmic plots of decomposition by first-order kinetics.

Table 12. *Typical first-order constants of decomposition and turnover times for some different forms of organic carbon in soil*

Form of C	Rate constant k (day^{-1})	Turnover time $1/k$ (days)
Glucose	1	1
Hemicellulose	0.07	14
Lignin	0.002	500

rapidly broken down in soil. At the other extreme, however, lignin has very small rate constants of decomposition and is, therefore, highly recalcitrant in soils. Indeed, it is unusual for more than half the lignin content of a plant residue to decompose in one year. Table 12 demonstrates some likely rate constants of decomposition for different forms of organic carbon in soil.

Of course, it must be remembered that if decomposition of a substrate is being determined by measurement of carbon dioxide evolution from the soil, then a correction factor for biosynthesis of cells must be included before rate constants and turnover times are calculated.

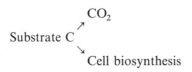

The correction factor for biosynthesis varies greatly. Fungi tend to be the most efficient utilisers of substrate carbon, with bacteria generally much less efficient. If half of the carbon from a sugar is used for biosynthesis by soil microbes, then the turnover time may be overestimated by a factor of one if a correction for biosynthetic diversion of carbon is not made.

Factors affecting the rate of carbon turnover in soil

A great many factors influence the turnover rate of organic carbon in soil. In general, warmer climates favour more rapid turnover and cooler climates favour a slower turnover. All soil factors (e.g. pH, Eh, temperature, water potential, structure, etc.), which in any way influence the nature and extent of heterotrophic activity in soil, will tend to influence the rate of carbon turnover, some more than others. The type of vegetation present also affects turnover time since it partly determines the resource quality of the decomposing organic matter (Swift, Heal & Anderson, 1979).

A number of indices are used to describe resource quality, the most commonly used being the C:N ratio. Generally, low C:N ratios are associated with high resource quality and rapid rates of decomposition, with high C:N ratios being associated with low resource quality and slow decomposition. The use of the C:N ratio as an index of resource quality is probably most reliable for broadly similar vegetation types.

Particular C:N ratios are sometimes quoted that indicate whether mineralisation or immobilisation will occur, although the picture is rarely that simple. Substrates of various C:N ratios are decomposed simultaneously, as well as there being factors other than C:N ratio determining decomposition rates. The lignin content, for example, also makes a critical contribution to resource quality and controls decomposition rates, as does the concentration of other polyphenolic molecules in organic residues such as melanin and tannin. Turnover times for carbon in different vegetation systems can be found in the literature (e.g. Jenkinson & Rayner, 1977), although times will vary depending on both climate and soil type, because all these factors are interactive. Leaf litter, for example, even from the same plant will be more decomposable if the plant is grown in a fertile soil with good nutrient supply than if the plant grows in nutrient-poor soil.

Decomposition of organic carbon in soil – production of stable soil organic matter

When carbon from plant, microbial and animal residues is processed by decomposer organisms (largely microbes) in the soil, the carbon is either lost as carbon dioxide, incorporated into the cells of the decomposer organisms, or enters a carbon pool that is relatively stable, either as a result of physical protection from attack by decomposers or as a result of chemical protection.

$$
\begin{array}{c}
\hspace{4cm} CO_2 \\
\hspace{4cm} \uparrow \\
\text{Residue C} \longrightarrow \text{Decomposer biomass C} \\
\hspace{4cm} \downarrow \\
\hspace{2cm} \text{Physically and chemically protected organic matter C}
\end{array}
$$

Physically protected organic matter

It seems that physically protected carbon is related to the structural characteristics of the soil. Part of this soil carbon pool can be rendered accessible to decomposition processes through physical disruption of the soil matrix. Some of this disruption may occur as a result of cultivation of the soil. It may well be that the reduction in structural integrity in some cultivated soils in many parts of the world is closely correlated with the loss of physically protected organic matter. Unfortunately, we are as yet unable to quantify and monitor this crucial component of soil organic matter and it remains largely a component of conceptual models.

Chemically protected organic matter

Chemically protected organic matter is often referred to as soil humus and the processes that contribute to its formation are collectively referred to as humification.

The humification processes are far from well understood, although we have become increasingly certain that the original theories of humification, based on humus originating from relatively small modifications to the resistant fractions of plant material, are no longer acceptable. The more modern view is that phenolic, lignin degradation products and some of the other products of residue decomposition are considerably modified by microbial reaction and/or through chemical, oxidative condensations to form the humic acids, fulvic acids and humin, which together make up the soil humus.

As with physically protected organic matter, we are unable to isolate and quantify the chemically protected fraction. The great age of much of the organic matter in soil, together with crude chemical fractionations, provides evidence of chemical protection, but separation of physical and chemical protection remains largely conceptual.

Even physically and chemically stabilised organic carbon is decomposed in the soil, but much more slowly than other carbon fractions. Turnover times involving hundreds or even thousands of years are more realistic for these carbon pools of the soil. The relatively rapid turnover of plant/microbial/animal residues is carried out largely by zymogenous soil microbes and the much slower turnover of 'stable' organic carbon largely involves the autochthonous soil microbes.

In recent years, attempts have been made to model the turnover of the various organic carbon pools of the soil. One of the first of these attempts was by Jenkinson & Rayner (1977). The model provided a simulation of carbon turnover in arable soil, and illustrates the relatively rapid turnover of plant residue-derived carbon and the microbial biomass carbon (carbon in the soil microbial biomass appears to turnover about every two years) as well as the very slow turnover of the microbially processed carbon that has been physically and chemically stabilised.

Decomposer communities in the soil

The decomposition of organic carbon in soil involves the complex interaction of microbes and animals. Most of the soil animals are not involved in primary decomposition, but are consumers of both the primary decomposing soil microbes as well as other soil animals. A decomposer food web of organisms, therefore, exists in the soil with a decreasing flow of carbon and other nutrients between progressively higher trophic levels of the food web. Figure 25 illustrates the type of detrital food web associated with a temperate grassland soil. The arrows represent the flow of carbon from one pool to another and do not include inputs (CO_2 fixation) and losses (CO_2 respiration).

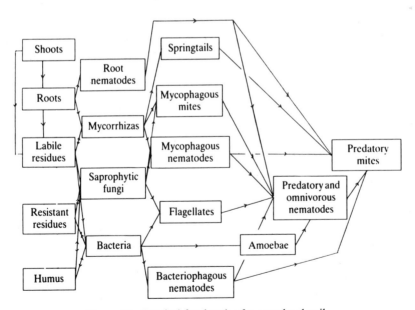

Figure 25. Detrital food web of a grassland soil.

The top of the web is represented by predatory mites and these are supplied with primary produced carbon via microbial decomposers, mycophagous and bacteriophagous soil animals, and secondary consumer soil animals. About 10% of the annual energy input to the soil from plant litter is used for growth and respiration by the soil animals of the detrital or decomposer food web (Richards, 1987). This is a misleading figure, however, as, although the soil animals contribute significantly less to total soil metabolism than the soil microbes, much of the activity of the microbes is facilitated by the functions of the animals.

Partitioning of the decomposer community

It is very difficult to effectively partition the functioning of the decomposer community in soil. This is largely because of the dependence of one component on another. One approach, however, has involved the use of litter bags of different mesh sizes to selectively exclude organisms of certain body size ranges from the decomposition process. Studies (e.g. Edwards & Heath, 1963; Anderson, 1973) using this approach have demonstrated the importance of soil animals and their contribution to observed differences in litter decomposition in soil between sites. Litter bags enable the contributions of the soil microflora (bacteria, fungi and actinomycetes), microfauna (including protozoa and nematodes), mesofauna (including springtails, mites and enchytraeid worms) and macrofauna (including large arthropods and earthworms) to litter decomposition to be assessed. The micro- and mesofauna are mainly secondary decomposers, although some primary decomposition of organic residues can be carried out. The macrofauna can carry out initial physical comminution and dispersion of the litter to provide a greater surface area for microbial attack. In addition, residues passing through the soil animal gut will be partly decomposed by the gut microbes as well as microbially inoculated for accelerated decomposition in the soil. Clearly, therefore, there is some general relationship between the size and function of the decomposer organisms in soil.

The interaction between the carbon cycle and other soil nutrient cycles

The carbon fraction of plant/microbial/animal residue-derived organic molecules such as cellulose, hemicelluloses and lignin are only associated with two other elements – hydrogen and oxygen. Many other organic molecules contain important plant nutrients such as nitrogen (found in proteins, peptides and amino acids, in nucleic acids, chitin, mucopeptides, amino sugars etc.), phosphorus (found in nucleic acids, phospholipids, phytin etc.) and sulphur (found in sulphur-containing amino acids – methionine and cysteine – and proteins), which remain unavailable for plant uptake until the 'parent' organic molecule undergoes decomposition processes in the soil. The release of organically bound nutrients into the plant-available, inorganic form (there are some cases when nutrients can be taken up in simple organic forms, but by far the most important plant-available forms are inorganic) is termed 'mineralisation'. Some examples of the release of nitrogen, phosphorus and sulphur in this way are provided in Chapter 1, page 4. A more detailed picture of nitrogen and sulphur mineralisation, however, can be found later in this chapter. These mineralisation reactions are of critical importance to the productivity of ecosystems because the major fraction of nutrients such as nitrogen, phosphorus and sulphur in most soils is in the organic form.

Of course it is not only the plants that require nutrients such as nitrogen, phosphorus and sulphur that are often locked up in organic molecules. The decomposer soil organisms (microbes and animals) themselves also require these nutrients to be incorporated into their bodies. Decomposition of the organic molecules such as cellulose, hemicellulose and lignin, which are free of bound nutrients, can only proceed if there is an adequate nutrient supply to the decomposer. If this supply is inadequate, then decomposition is said to be nutrient limited. The particular limiting nutrient will vary, not just from one ecosystem to another, but from one soil microsite to another and from one decomposer to another. Because of the dependence of decomposers on adequate nutrient flow in the soil, the decomposition of organic molecules must not be considered as a series of independent processes. It should instead be regarded as a complex of interdependent processes where nutrients from organic substrates that contain nutrients surplus to decomposer needs are supplied to decomposers of other substrates that contain insufficient bound nutrients. This use of nutrients by decomposers of nutrient-deficient substrates is termed 'immobilisation'. As decomposition proceeds, it is only the mineralised nutrients not immobilised that are available for plant uptake. A more detailed picture of the nature of mineralisation/immobilisation is provided in the discussion of the nitrogen cycle (pages 108–41).

Carbon cycling does not occur in isolation, but is intimately related to other forms of nutrient cycling in the soil. It is the need for the energy 'locked-up' in the carbon–hydrogen bond of organic molecules that drives the decomposition process, and hence the cycling of nutrients in soil. It is evident, therefore, that any change in the carbon cycle such as the greenhouse effect will inevitably bring about fundamental changes to other nutrient cycles of the soil/plant system.

THE NITROGEN CYCLE

Introduction

Nitrogen is essential for life. It is the cornerstone of the amino acids, the building blocks for the synthesis of cell peptides and protein, and is incorporated into such important biological components as chitin and mucopeptides, and is also an integral part of the genetic material of cells, the nucleic acids.

Plant growth in soils throughout the world is often restricted by the supply of available nitrogen and, as a result, it is nitrogen supply more than the supply of any other nutrient in the soil that limits UK and world crop production. Because of this, some 40×10^6 t of nitrogen are applied globally as fertiliser to increase crop productivity. In agricultural systems, the need to understand the nitrogen cycle is of paramount importance if maximum use is to be made of both fertiliser-derived nitrogen and the soil's own nitrogen reserves. In natural ecosystems, there are none of these additional, fertiliser nitrogen applications, but the need to understand the soil N-cycle is just as important. This is particularly because we must be able to assess how the N-cycle of these systems will respond to a disturbance, be it man-made or natural. Massive deafforestation, for example, may cause nitrate pollution of groundwaters because this soil N-pool is no longer being continually taken up by the trees.

Of course, it is not reasonable to consider the ecology of the soil nitrogen cycle in isolation. Although some microbial nitrogen transformations in soil, such as the nitrification reactions, make use of the energy within a nitrogenous molecule, most transformations of nitrogen depend on the associated supply of carbon (Paul, 1976). The flow of nitrogen in the soil, therefore, is intimately tied to the flow of carbon. In addition, the processes involved in the nitrogen cycle bring about changes to the soil environment that also affect other processes and cycles. All reactions of the nitrogen cycle, for example, can be associated with changes in soil pH because they involve a range of nitrogen

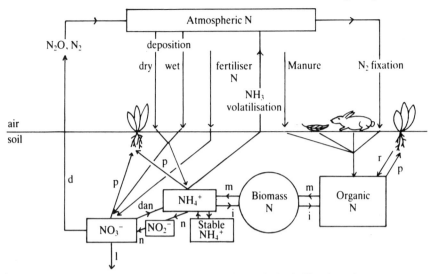

Figure 26. The soil nitrogen cycle. Abbreviations: d, denitrification; dan, dissimilatory and assimilatory nitrate reduction to ammonium; i, immobilisation; m, mineralisation; n, nitrification and subsequent leaching (l); p, plant uptake; r, root exudation and turnover.

species carrying from between one net positive charge per N-atom (e.g. ammonium, NH_4^+) through neutral charge (e.g. urea, $CO(NH_2)_2$, free nitrogen, N_2) to one net negative charge per N-atom (e.g. nitrite, NO_2^-; nitrate, NO_3^-).

N-inputs to the soil/plant system

Figure 26 provides a diagrammatic representation of the nitrogen cycle in soil. Obviously, the inputs of nitrogen (as dry and wet deposition, N_2 fixation, fertilisers, animal inputs etc.) will vary from place to place.

Atmospheric deposition

In some areas of Europe, atmospheric deposition of nitrogen from pollution sources can be as much as $40 \, kg \, N \, ha^{-1} \, y^{-1}$, in the form of both dry and wet deposition with global emissions representing over $100 \times 10^6 \, t \, y^{-1}$. This nitrogen is largely in the form of nitrous oxides and ammonia in the dry deposition, and in the form of nitrate and ammonium in the wet deposition. In polluted areas, therefore, a very significant contribution to plant N-uptake can potentially be made by atmospheric deposition. Of course, the acidity and other phytotoxic agents associated with atmospheric pollution may prevent the possible benefits of these additional N-inputs from being fully realised.

N_2-fixation

Although inputs of nitrogen to the soil are known to occur through fixation as one of the oxides of nitrogen by atmospheric electrical discharges, by far the largest amount of terrestrial nitrogen fixation is carried out biologically (about 140×10^6 t y^{-1}, globally).

N_2-fixing soil organisms   There are six main types of N_2-fixing organisms that can be found in soil: (i) free-living bacteria such as *Bacillus*, *Klebsiella* and *Clostridium* that fix N_2 anaerobically (*Bacillus* and *Klebsiella* are facultative anaerobes, which only fix nitrogen under reduced oxygen tensions, while *Clostridium* is an obligate anaerobe); (ii) bacteria of the genus *Rhizobium*, which fix N_2 mainly in the root nodules of leguminous plants (see Chapter 3, pages 62–6); (iii) actinomycetes of the genus *Frankia*, which fix N_2 in the root nodules of non-leguminous angiosperms such as alder (*Alnus glutinosa*) (these associations are often referred to as 'actinorhizas'); (iv) free-living cyanobacteria on the soil surface such as *Nostoc* and *Anabaena*; (v) symbiotic cyanobacteria such as are found in the lichen symbiosis; and (vi) N_2-fixing bacteria loosely associated with the roots of certain plants, sometimes referred to as 'rhizocoenoses' (the bacteria *Azotobacter*, *Beijerinckia* and *Azospirillum* are examples of this type of N_2-fixing soil microbe).

Soil N-inputs from biological fixation   Inputs of nitrogen to the soil from biological N_2-fixation vary widely from one ecosystem to another. At one end of the spectrum, tropical legumes such as alfalfa have been shown, on occasion, to fix at rates as high as over 400 kg N ha^{-1} y^{-1} (Tisdale, Nelson & Beaton, 1985). On the other hand, in soils of upland pastures in the UK, free-living (e.g. *Azotobacter*) and symbiotic (mainly clover) N_2-fixation may only account for an input of 5–30 kg N ha^{-1} y^{-1} (Figure 27).

It is fixation by grain and forage legumes that makes up by far the largest component of biologically fixed nitrogen in temperate agricultural soils. Despite the substantial contribution that this makes to the soil N-cycle of

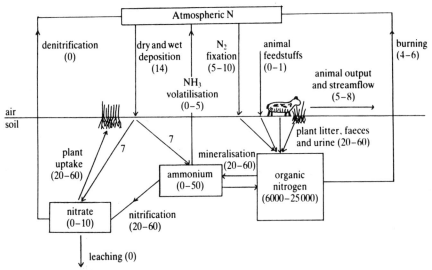

Figure 27. The nitrogen cycle of an upland UK pasture soil (pools in kg N ha^{-1}, fluxes in kg N ha^{-1} y^{-1}). Adapted from Batey, 1982.

these temperate systems, the input is relatively small compared with that added as fertiliser. In the UK, for example, about 0.4×10^6 t of nitrogen are fixed biologically, whereas fertilisers supply about 1.15×10^6 t (Royal Society, 1983). Globally, because of the many natural, unfertilised ecosystems, this picture is reversed, biological N$_2$-fixation supplying more nitrogen to the soil than fertilisers.

Soil ecology of biological N$_2$-fixation   The ecology of biological N$_2$-fixation is complex. One of the soil factors most influencing the form and rate of biological N$_2$-fixation, however, is soil pH. Many N$_2$-fixing organisms are acid sensitive. *Rhizobium trifolii*, for example, which forms the legume symbiosis with clover, cannot survive in the closer rhizosphere at pH 4.3 and below because of sensitivity to mobilised aluminium (Wood, Cooper & Holding, 1983). This is despite the fact that root elongation of clover is unaffected at this soil pH. *Azotobacter* is even more resistive to acidity, generally not being found in soil more acid than pH 6.0. *Beijerinckia*, however, is more acid tolerant than either *Rhizobium* or *Azotobacter*, although it is largely restricted to tropical soils.

A second major determinant of biological N$_2$-fixation in soil is the supply of available carbon because free-living N$_2$-fixers, with the exception of the cyanobacteria, are heterotrophs. Usually in soil, the rate of non-symbiotic

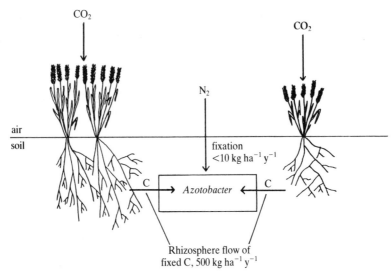

Figure 28. Maximum estimate for non-symbiotic nitrogen fixation in the cereal rhizosphere, assuming all rhizosphere carbon flow drives this fixation.

N_2-fixation is carbon limited. There is a very high demand for carbon from the inefficient nitrogenase system (one of the reasons for this inefficiency being that only about half of the electron flow to nitrogenase is transferred to N_2, the remainder being lost to H_2 evolution), such that for every gram of sucrose used as substrate by *Azotobacter*, less than 20 mg of N_2 is fixed. Because of this high demand for carbon, the rhizosphere has been selected as the main zone in the soil for aerobic, non-symbiotic N_2-fixation. Even here, however, the flow of carbon to the microbial N_2-fixer cannot generate an appreciable level of fixation. In a cereal crop, for example, there may be a rhizosphere carbon flow as high as $0.5\,t\,ha^{-1}\,y^{-1}$ in the soil. If all this carbon were available to an *Azotobacter* rhizosphere population, then this would probably only generate approximately $10\,kg\,ha^{-1}$ fixed N_2 (Figure 28). Of course, not all of this carbon would be available for N_2-fixation because other rhizosphere heterotrophs will compete for the carbon flow. It would seem, therefore, that there is little scope for exploiting non-symbiotic N_2-fixation for agronomic purposes, unless the roots of arable crops are designed to leak a great deal more carbon into the rhizosphere.

A third, key environmental determinant of N_2-fixation in soil is the oxygen status, because some of the non-symbiotic N_2-fixers are anaerobes, such as species of the genus *Clostridium*. These organisms will often be particularly active in ecological niches in wet soil where there is a ready supply of carbohydrate. The addition of crop residues, for example, rich in carbohydrates, should provide this environment. Cellulolytic microbes will attack the residues and release soluble carbohydrates, which the clostridia may harness for N_2-fixation. In wet soils, diffusion of oxygen to these sites of N_2-fixation will often be sufficiently slow to sustain this form of anaerobism for considerable periods. The process, however, is even more inefficient than for aerobic N_2-fixers such as *Azotobacter*, with typically less than 10 mg of fixed N_2 being produced from every gram of carbohydrate that is broken down.

A fourth environmental factor that strongly controls biological N_2-fixation in soil is the supply of available nitrogen. A soil with a high supply of available nitrogen will not provide for a high rate of fixation, either symbiotic or non-symbiotic. The energy costs of fixation are so high that available soil nitrogen is more preferable to the legume root or *Azotobacter* cell than atmospheric nitrogen. Fertiliser nitrogen additions, therefore, will probably be more inhibitory to biological N_2-fixation than any other soil factor. In natural ecosystems, the input to the soil of nitrogenous animal and plant residues will be similarly inhibitory, but on a much more local scale.

Measurement of N_2-fixation   The nitrogenase enzyme system, which catalyses the fixation of atmospheric nitrogen, is unable to distinguish between N_2 and acetylene (C_2H_2) and will readily reduce the latter to ethylene

$$N\equiv N \xrightarrow{\text{nitrogenase}} NH_3$$
nitrogen gas   ammonia

$$HC\equiv CH \longrightarrow H_2C=CH_2$$
acetylene   ethylene

This inability to distinguish between N_2 and C_2H_2 provides a simple, rapid means of measuring fixation rates. Nitrogen-fixing systems can be incubated in the presence of acetylene, with the production of ethylene providing a quantitative determination of N_2-fixation. This is known as the 'acetylene reduction technique'. More modern approaches to the measurement of N_2-fixation, involving the use of the stable nitrogen isotope ^{15}N, are considered later in this chapter (pages 138–41).

Supply of biologically fixed nitrogen to the plant   Biologically fixed nitrogen forms an important N-source for uptake by plants. In the case of the legume or other N_2-fixing plant/microbial symbioses (e.g. *Alnus* with the actinomycete *Frankia*), the nitrogen is transferred from the microbe to the host through translocation. The fixed nitrogen is translocated in the legume in the form of amides where the nitrogen is intimately bound to organic carbon. The movements of nitrogen and carbon around the plant, therefore, are closely related. Plants other than legumes can only gain access to this nitrogen when the nitrogen-fixing organism dies and is broken down by microorganisms in the soil. Transfer of nitrogen via mineralisation in the soil will be far less efficient, of course, than translocation within a symbiotic association or translocation between a symbiotic association and another plant by direct mycorrhizal connections. This is because other components of the soil biota, particularly the microbial biomass, will also compete to immobilise the released, mineral nitrogen.

Immobilisation/mineralisation reactions and plant N-uptake

Definitions

Mineralisation refers to the soil processes by which organic nitrogen is converted to mineral nitrogen. Immobilisation is the opposite of mineralisation, being the conversion of soil mineral nitrogen into organic forms. The two processes operate simultaneously in the soil and are mutually dependent. The amount of available mineral nitrogen (usually as ammonium and nitrate), found in soil will largely depend on the difference between rates of immobilisation and mineralisation

$$\text{Available N (mineral)} \underset{\text{Immobilisation}}{\overset{\text{Mineralisation}}{\rightleftharpoons}} \text{Organic N}$$

Soil N-status in relation to immobilisation/mineralisation

The lack of available nitrogen generally found in forest soils, for example, suggests that the balance in forests is usually tipped towards immobilisation. This means that the biological uptake of nitrogen by the trees and by the soil biota (largely fungi in an acid forest soil) exceeds the rate at which microbes can release nitrogen through decomposition of organic matter. The uptake of nitrogen by the trees and the losses of nitrogen from the soil are often exceeded by the inputs of nitrogen to the soil such as via litterfall,

N_2-fixation and atmospheric deposition. Until the system reaches equilibrium, therefore, there will be a set annual increase in the soil N-reserve. This occurs when arable soils are planted with trees where the net annual accumulation of soil nitrogen can be more than $50 \, kg \, ha^{-1}$. The rate at which mineral nitrogen is immobilised will depend on both the N-requirements of the growing plant through root uptake and the N-requirements of the soil biota.

Plant N-uptake and relation to soil pH

Roots take up most of the plant's nitrogen requirements in the form of mineral nitrogen, largely ammonium and nitrate. Nitrate largely reaches the root by mass flow and ammonium by diffusion. Although most plant N-uptake requires mineral nitrogen, a feature of mycorrhizal roots is that they are able to also take up a wide range of organic nitrogen compounds, particularly amino acids (Stribley & Read, 1980). Although ammonium may often be the preferred source of mineral nitrogen, most plant roots tend to take up most of their nitrogen as nitrate largely because ammonium is held on negatively charged soil particles. The form of nitrogen taken up by plants has a strong influence on soil pH. Plants dominantly taking up nitrate (using the enzyme nitrate reductase) will release bicarbonate and/or hydroxyl ions to maintain an internal charge balance, thereby raising the soil pH. Plants mainly taking up ammonium will release protons to maintain their charge balance, and this will lead to soil acidification. Plant nitrogen nutrition, therefore, has a fundamental bearing on pH status of soil, particularly in the rhizosphere, although the extent of the pH response will be modified by the buffering capacity of the soil.

Plant N-uptake in relation to the total soil N-pool

Plant uptake of nitrogen can account for $100 \, kg \, ha^{-1} \, y^{-1}$ for high-yield arable crops, although a figure of half this value would be likely for coniferous forest trees. Grass swards in upland, moorland sites in the UK are thought to take up between 20 and $60 \, kg \, ha^{-1} \, y^{-1}$ (Figure 27). Regardless of the vegetation type, the annual uptake of nitrogen by the growing plant represents only a minute proportion of the soil's total nitrogen reserves which are largely in a variety of resistant organic forms. In upland moorland soil and in forest soil in the UK, this total N-reserve is of the order of $5000-25\,000 \, kg \, ha^{-1} \, y^{-1}$. In a UK lowland, arable soil, the figure

Table 13. *The approximate percentage of the total soil nitrogen pool taken up each year by the vegetation of contrasting ecosystems*

Ecosystem	Approx. % total soil N removed by vegetation annually[a]	Approx. total soil N (kg N ha^{-1})
Tundra	0.4%	10 000
Temperate, upland moorland	0.5%	10 000
Temperate, coniferous forest	0.75%	20 000
Temperate, deciduous forest	0.7%	7500
Tropical rainforest	1–2%[b]	9000
Temperate arable (high-yield cereal)	5%	1000

[a] Total offtake is greater because offtake is from fertiliser N + soil + litter.
[b] Calculated from data of Vitousek (1984).

will be around 2500 kg ha^{-1} y^{-1}. The amount of total soil nitrogen taken up annually by vegetation for these different ecosystems is shown in Table 13.

C:N ratios and immobilisation/mineralisation

Plant roots are not the only component of the soil biota competing for mineral nitrogen. The soil microbial biomass and the soil fauna will also make demands on this soil N-pool. This demand varies, largely depending on the C:N requirement of the organism (Figure 29) and the C:N ratio of the substrates (i.e. plant and animal residues/waste products) that the organism is processing. If the substrate is cereal straw, for example, with a C:N ratio typically of 100:1–150:1, then extra, mineral nitrogen will be required to process the straw, i.e. net immobilisation will occur. A C:N ratio of about 20:1 for arable soils is generally regarded as the approximate threshold between net mineralisation and net immobilisation. Although the C:N ratio of the decomposing substrate plays a fundamental role in determining whether or not mineral nitrogen will be released, the picture is not always simple. Substrates of differing C:N ratios are decomposed simultaneously. Also, sometimes, release of nitrogen from decomposing residues occurs at the onset of decomposition. Sometimes, however, release only occurs after

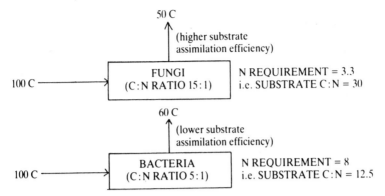

Figure 29. A model of the relationship between the type of decomposer soil microorganism and the minimum C:N ratio for the decomposition of organic matter in soil.

an initial period of accumulation and when a critical nitrogen level is reached (Berg & Staaf, 1981).

Immobilisation/mineralisation balances and the environment

Understanding the balance between mineralisation and immobilisation is critical both for agronomic and environmental reasons. Massive deafforestation provides an example where a serious imbalance of mineralisation/immobilisation can have significant ecological ramifications (Figure 30). If the trees typically take up 50 kg N ha^{-1} y^{-1}, then removal of the trees will tend to lead to much of this mineralised nitrogen being washed or leached out of the soil profile in the form of nitrate. This is very much an oversimplification, however, as deafforestation brings about changes to the nitrogen cycle, other than mineralisation and immobilisation. High nitrate concentrations in drainage waters are associated with eutrophication, causing algal blooms, which, as a result of their subsequent breakdown by heterotrophic microbes, can cause oxygen-depletion of the waters with the consequent death of many freshwater fish and other aquatic organisms.

Measurement of nitrogen immobilisation/mineralisation in soil

Because of the importance of immobilisation/mineralisation in regulating the productivity of ecosystems, considerable effort has been made to develop reasonable means of measuring net mineralisation in the field. All the

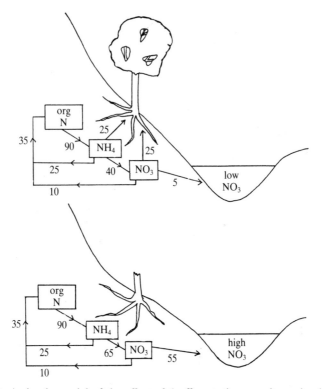

Figure 30. A simple model of the effect of deafforestation on nitrate levels in drainage waters (all values have units of kg N ha^{-1} y^{-1}).

methods developed rely on measurement of the accumulation of mineral nitrogen in the absence of actively growing roots. This typically involves *in situ* incubation of soil cores or samples in sealed containers of some kind. The great problem of this approach is the soil disturbance involved. The physical structure of the soil is disturbed and the moisture regime held artificially. In addition, any effect on N-mineralisation of rhizosphere microbial processes will be precluded.

Attempts have been made to measure net mineralisation through the use of laboratory assays, although such assays can only provide information on the sizes of the pool of mineralisable nitrogen at the time of sampling and may be an unreliable index of net mineralisation in the field (Hart & Binkley, 1985). The use of ^{15}N pool dilution techniques has become increasingly accepted as a powerful means of estimating the size of the mineralisation on flux (see pages 138 and 141).

Immobilisation/mineralisation – soil organisms (and enzymes) involved and their ecology

The entire soil biota is involved in the N-mineralisation/immobilisation process. Immobilisation of nitrogen is carried out by the plant roots, the soil animals and the soil microbial biomass. Mineralisation, however, is restricted to the soil microbes and animals. In the case of much of the N-containing organic matter in soil, mineralisation is non-specialised, being carried out by a very wide range of soil microbes (the soil animals, although involved in primary decomposition, are most important in comminuting, priming and dispersing the residues prior to microbial attack). A good general rule is that the more complex the substrate, then the more specialised the microbial mineralisers processing it, although most N-containing molecules in plant and animal residues are reasonably easily broken down compared with some of the N-free residue components such as cellulose, pectin and particularly lignin. Urea, the most readily decomposable form of organic nitrogen, is often completely mineralised in a matter of hours or a few days, and, in some soils, well over half of the microbial plate count possess the enzyme urease which catalyses urea hydrolysis.

Urease and other N-mineralising activities in soil tend to raise pH, creating zones and microsites of higher pH in the soil – in extreme cases, such as in the vicinity of urea and animal wastes, the soil may be several pH units higher than the bulk soil. These sites provide an interesting niche in the soil in terms of microbial pH relations.

The involvement of soil animals in the mineralisation process is particularly important. The roles of different components (micro-, meso- and macrofauna) of the soil animal decomposer community are discussed on pages 105–6. Soil animals not only comminute plant and animal fragments, thereby accelerating the mineralisation process, but also carry out mineralisation processes within their guts. These mineralisations are catalysed by a wide range of digestive enzymes including proteases, nucleases and chitinases. In addition to mineralisation in the gut, passage through the soil animal gut can also inoculate the residue fragments and prime them for subsequent, accelerated mineralisation in the soil. In temperate forest soils, mineralisation of nitrogen by soil fauna is thought to equal or exceed that of the microbial decomposers (Anderson *et al.*, 1985). In acid, forest and moorland soils, acid-tolerant soil animals such as enchytraeid worms, springtails and mites are mainly responsible for the faunal contribution to decomposer activity.

Soil animals play an important role in movement and concentration of nitrogen through the soil profile. The cast and mound material of a number of soil animals is highly enriched in nitrogen (and other nutrients). The termite mounds of tropical and sub-tropical soils, for example, receive continual inputs of organic nitrogen in the form of plant litter. Subsequent decomposition of these residues and of the faecal pellets of the termites leads to a concentration of nitrogen in the mound and concomitant lowering of the C:N ratio.

Statements regarding the relative contributions of microbes and animals to mineralisation processes are misleading because the involvement of soil animals should not be considered in isolation, but in terms of a complex interaction with the decomposer microbes. Grazing of bacterial and fungal biomass is a major mechanism enabling the mineralisation/release of nitrogen for uptake by the plant. In the absence of this grazing, (involving protozoa, nematodes, microarthropods etc.), release of plant-available nitrogen in soil can be reduced by nearly 50% (Clarholm, 1985). The interaction of soil microfauna and microbial biomass in releasing mineral nitrogen is of particular importance in the rhizosphere where the release of carbon by the plant root can cause the rhizosphere microbial populations to expand and immobilise any available nitrogen. In the short term, this may outcompete the plant in nutrient acquisition. This phase will be short lived, however, and a bloom of microbial grazers (largely protozoa) should release the microbial nitrogen back to the soil solution for plant uptake.

Of particular importance in the nitrogen mineralisation process in less acid soils are the earthworms and their interaction with soil microbes. Lumbricid worms significantly increase the mineral nitrogen content of soil (Syers & Springett, 1984), and current research is focusing on their possible value as a soil inoculum to help unlock the massive reserves of nitrogen held in organic matter in forest soils. In deciduous woodland soils with a high base status, favourable to earthworm activity, the annual nitrogen flux through the earthworms may be several times the 30–70 kg ha^{-1} contained in the leaf fall. Because of earthworm susceptibility to low pH, many forest soils, however, would require liming before providing a suitable growth environment for the earthworms.

Although plants, microbes and animals are all involved in cycling of nitrogen in soil, some of the N-transformations can occur in the absence of any of these components of the soil biota. This is because a number of enzymes that catalyse N-transformations are produced extracellularly as well as intracellularly. Because enzymes in soil solution represent ready substrates for attack by proteolytic microbes, they tend to persist in the soil by adsorption to soil particles. These adsorbed, largely hydrolytic enzymes such as urease, can be responsible for nitrogen cycling in sites in the soil, such as micropores, where no organisms are present or where activity of organisms is severely restricted.

N-forms in the soil – mineralisation pathways and the fate of mineralised nitrogen

Figure 31 illustrates some of the main forms of nitrogen (and their pathways of mineralisation) entering the soil in plant residues that provide the dominant input of fresh organic matter to the soil. Of course, most of the plant residue comprises compounds that do not contain nitrogen, such as cellulose, hemicellulose and lignin. Much of the nitrogen mineralised from N-rich compounds of plant residues such as proteins, peptides, amino acids and nucleic acids will therefore be immobilised in the processing of the more carbonaceous substrates. In addition to the forms of plant residue nitrogen shown in Figure 31, lesser amounts of nitrogen are also mineralised in the soil from the various microbes (containing nitrogen in mucopeptides, chitin and nucleic acids) and animals (containing nitrogen in protein, chitin, nucleic acids, and waste products such as urea).

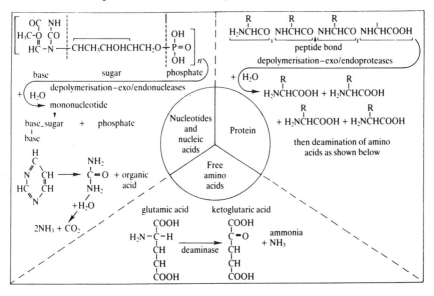

Figure 31. Some of the main forms of organic nitrogen entering the soil through plant residue inputs, and their likely pathways of mineralisation.

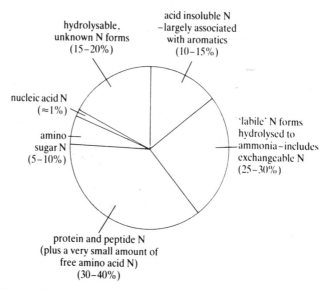

Figure 32. Forms of nitrogen found in soil and their approximate relative amounts. Note that the amino sugar N will include almost all microbial biomass N, which itself accounts for about 5% of total soil N-pool.

Of the main forms of nitrogen typically found in soil, over 90% is organic, and much of this is associated with very resistant organic matter (Figure 32). Ammonium mineralised from fresh inputs of organic matter does not remain in the soil for long and is rapidly transferred to other N-pools in the soil/plant system.

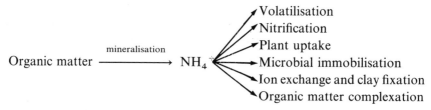

Competition for mineral nitrogen in soil

The available, mineral nitrogen (largely ammonium, NH_4^+, and nitrate, NO_3^-) pool of the soil (in solution and on exchange sites) is competed for by most components of the soil biota, but particularly by plant roots and free-living soil microbes.

Competition for soil mineral nitrogen between roots, microbes and animals depends on a number of factors. The rooting density will be of critical importance, this factor perhaps explaining competition between plant types as well as between roots, microbes and animals or whether or not the root is mycorrhizal will be important because absorption of mineral nitrogen is much higher for mycorrhizal roots compared to non-mycorrhizal (Bowen, 1973). The effective C:N ratios of the organic matter being decomposed by the microbial biomass will largely determine whether mineral nitrogen, either added as fertiliser (or through atmospheric deposition) or mineralised from the organic matter, will be immobilised by the microbial cells, or released for plant uptake because it exceeds microbial demand.

The concentration and form of the mineral nitrogen pool will also be critical in controlling competition for this pool. The effect of concentration will largely be a function of the comparative Michaelis–Menten kinetics for absorption for both the roots and the soil microbes. Michaelis–Menten kinetics, of course, represent a considerable simplification of the nature of ion uptake by plant roots. The kinetics of N-uptake for the root will vary depending on the mycorrhizal properties of the root and on the extent of suberisation, absorption being highest at or near the apical tips of young, unsuberised roots (Bowen, 1973). Superimposed on this, however, is the form of the mineral nitrogen in the soil. Most plant roots and microbes will readily take up ammonium and nitrate, but in some cases, the nitrate reductase enzyme is either absent or only slowly induced. Competition for mineral nitrogen between plant roots and microbes may, therefore, be influenced by the level of nitrification in the soil.

Much evidence to date on the nature of competition for mineral nitrogen between roots and microbes comes from studies involving trenched plots where growing roots are effectively excluded. In forest soils, these plots accumulate significant concentrations of mineral nitrogen, although insufficient to account for the typical uptake of nitrogen by the tree roots (Harmer & Alexander, 1985). Increased turnover of dead roots or prolonged activity of excised live roots may both have contributed to this shortfall.

The involvement of soil animals in competition for mineral nitrogen in soil occurs in a number of ways, but probably most importantly through their role as grazers of microbes, leading to release of immobilised nitrogen into a plant-available form. Because the soil microfauna require adequate moisture for activity and movement, the soil water potential will be the major determinant on this aspect of soil nitrogen dynamics.

Increasing use is being made of ^{15}N as a means of characterising nitrogen flow in soil/plant systems, although ^{15}N methodology has still to be developed to investigate competition for mineral nitrogen. The use of ^{15}N pool dilution and tracer techniques, however, offers by far the most promise for the study of competition for mineral nitrogen in soil because other approaches involving the selective suppression or removal of components of demand for mineral nitrogen prevent competitive interactions and fundamentally change the nature of the soil system.

Although mineralised ammonium may often be the preferred N-source to plants (and to soil microbes and animals), nitrate tends to be the form most taken up. This is because the cation ammonium (NH_4^+) is attracted to sites of negative charge (e.g. on clay and organic matter particles), whereas the anion nitrate (NO_3^-) is highly mobile and moves easily to the plant root by mass flow. The soil process by which ammonium is converted to nitrate is nitrification.

Nitrification

Definition and occurrence in soil

As can be seen from the nitrogen cycle in Figure 26, nitrification in soil involves the oxidation of ammonium, via nitrite, to nitrate. This is an over-simplification, however, and, more recently, the definition of nitrification has been extended to include 'the biological oxidation of any reduced form of nitrogen to a more oxidised form'. Nitrification occurs throughout the soil, although it can often mistakenly be presumed not to occur because of the absence of nitrate in the soil. This is particularly true of the rhizosphere, where the lack of nitrification is often attributed to allelopathy. Although allelopathy may occur (pages 129–30), nitrifiers are readily isolated from most rhizosphere soil and it seems likely that the lack of net nitrification may often be caused by uptake and immobilisation of nitrate by the plant root and the rhizosphere heterotrophic microflora, respectively.

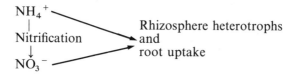

Autotrophic nitrification in soil

It is generally accepted that the dominant form of nitrification in most soils is chemoautotrophic, largely carried out by the Gram-negative bacteria *Nitrosomonas* and *Nitrobacter*. The reactions carried out are summarised below.

Nitrosomonas

$$NH_4^+ + O_2 + H^+ + 2e^- \rightarrow NH_2OH + H_2O$$

ammonium   hydroxylamine

and

$$NH_2OH + H_2O \rightarrow NO_2^- + 5H^+ + 4e^-$$

hydroxylamine   nitrite

Nitrobacter

$$NO_2^- + H_2O \rightarrow H_2O \cdot NO_2^- \rightarrow NO_3^- + 2H$$

nitrite   nitrate

In the case of *Nitrosomonas*, the oxidation state of nitrogen is changed from -3 to $+3$, and in the cases of *Nitrobacter*, from $+3$ to $+5$. The energy yields to the chemoautotrophs are approximately 65 kcal (or 8.8 ATP molecules) per mole for *Nitrosomonas* and 18 kcal (or 2.5 ATP molecules) per mole for *Nitrobacter*. These energy yields are rather low compared with most heterotrophic metabolism. A mole of glucose may, for example, under optimal conditions, yield an aerobic microbe 280 kcal (or 38 ATP molecules). This partly explains why autotrophic nitrifier growth is relatively slow in the soil and even in laboratory culture where conditions for growth can be made much closer to optimal. Natural generation times for nitrifying bacteria of the order of 20–40 h, coupled with their small numbers in most soils, can give a very misleading impression of their vital contribution to nitrogen cycling and to soil ecology.

Nitrification and soil pH

Nitrification is associated with the production of hydrogen ions (H^+) and these protons are a source of acidification, particularly in weakly buffered soils. Sustained use of ammonium-based fertilisers on arable soils can cause sufficient increase in acidity that lime applications are made to restore the balance. In some soils of the world where lime has not been used to restore pH after prolonged nitrification of fertiliser-derived ammonium, declining productivity due to soil acidity has occurred. Much of this may be a result of the loss of acid-sensitive soil organisms such as earthworms, which are vital to maintenance of soil fertility.

Measurement of nitrification in soil

Most measurement of soil nitrification is carried out in the laboratory where ammonium is added to the soil and its rate of oxidation to nitrite and nitrate measured. Because substrate is added, we refer to the rates observed as 'potential', rather than real, rates. The soil is often made into a slurry to aid diffusion of substrate to sites of nitrifier activity in these assays. The danger of slurry incubation is that the system may become anaerobic and denitrification may occur, removing nitrate from the system before it can be measured. An alternative approach is to use a perfusion column where the soil is continually being oxygenated by a fresh perfusing solution that contains the ammonium substrate. These perfusion systems have considerable advantages and can be used to partition different forms of nitrification in the soil (Killham, 1987).

Environmental consequences of nitrification

The ecological significance of nitrification is profound, the process not only supplying nitrogen to plants in its most available form, but also producing an N-pool that is particularly susceptible to loss from the soil system. This loss, through leaching and denitrification, can often mediate serious and damaging environmental pollution, as well as remove a valuable soil resource.

Nitrate, the end product of nitrification, is a highly mobile anion in soil and is readily leached, through the soil profile, into drainage waters. Leaching of nitrate nitrogen at annual rates as high as 100 kg ha^{-1} from arable land is not uncommon in parts of the UK (Foster, Cripps and Smith-Carrington, 1982), representing a considerable economic loss as well as being of environmental concern.

One possible adverse environmental consequence of high nitrate leaching is eutrophication, a process briefly discussed on pages 117 and 118. In addition, nitrate is considered to be hazardous to human health when present in high concentrations in drinking water (the EEC legal limit for drinking water is 50 ppm NO_3). In exceptional cases, the drinking of water containing significant concentrations of nitrite, a transient intermediate of nitrification, has led to infants contracting 'blue-baby' disease or methaemoglobinaemia where the bloodstream supply of oxygen is restricted by the competitive complexation of the haemoglobin with nitrite in place of oxygen.

A third potential hazard of nitrification is that nitrite can react with secondary amines in the soil to produce nitrosamines, which can be assimilated by plants and are thought to be associated with cancer in humans. Environmental pollution resulting from denitrification of nitrate is considered on page 135. Possible formation of cancer-related nitrosamines in soil is shown below.

$$\begin{array}{c} R \\ \diagdown \\ \diagup \\ R' \end{array} NH + NO_2{}^- \rightarrow \begin{array}{c} R \\ \diagdown \\ \diagup \\ R' \end{array} N\!-\!NO + OH^-$$

secondary amine + nitrite → nitrosamine

Because nitrification is fundamentally involved both in terms of crop productivity and environmental pollution, increasing effort is being paid to controlling and managing the rate of nitrification in arable systems in order to marry this rate closely with that of crop uptake, to prevent nitrate loss from the soil system. This effort has partly been through the development of chemical inhibitors of nitrification such as N-serve (Nitrapyrin) and didin (Dicyandiamide). These inhibitors restrict the activity of *Nitrosomonas* rather than *Nitrobacter*, enabling the accumulation of ammonium rather than phytotoxic nitrite in the soil. An inhibitor can hopefully be found that will not only inhibit nitrification, but will also control the rate of hydrolysis of urea because this is often the nitrogen fertiliser applied. Without coupling the rate of urea hydrolysis to the nitrification rate, considerable amounts of ammonia may be volatilised from the soil.

Ecology of soil nitrification and the role of heterotrophs

In recent years, understanding of the ecology of soil nitrification has changed. Two new aspects have become particularly evident. The first has been the realisation that nitrification is not as restricted by soil pH as was traditionally thought. Indeed, through mechanisms such as surface attachment, slime production, and location close to sites of mineralisation, nitrifier cells may be protected from the bulk pH of the soil that is measured with 'crude' pH electrodes. In addition to this 'micro-habitat' theory of nitrification at low pH, it may be that some nitrifiers in the soil are acid adapted and behave entirely differently from the laboratory cultures on whose ecophysiological behaviour our earlier misunderstandings were based. This is linked with the possibility that *Nitrosospira* may replace *Nitrosomonas* in some autotrophic nitrifier communities at low pH. Perhaps only with the development of appropriate isolation and enrichment techniques can an acid-adapted nitrifier community be effectively investigated. The second aspect of a changing understanding of nitrifier ecology is that the exclusive involvement of chemoautotrophic bacteria in nitrification in all soil types has been questioned. Certain fungi and heterotrophic bacteria have a role to play in nitrification also, particularly in acid forest soils (Killham, 1990), although the significance of heterotrophic nitrification is the subject of considerable speculation and controversy. The selection of fungal nitrifiers in these soils is not simply pH related, despite the extreme acidity (often below pH 4.0) that can be encountered, but also substrate related (Killham, 1987). The nitrifying fungi can nitrify organic nitrogen directly without the appearance of ammonium as an intermediate, suggesting that the chemo-autotrophs may be competitively excluded from involvement (Killham, 1987).

Other ecological factors may also determine the rate and nature of the microbial nitrification process in soil. Soil water potential and soil temperature, for example, are involved. Autotrophic nitrifiers are amongst the soil microbes most sensitive to water stress, whereas fungal nitrifiers are generally much more tolerant of water stress. Because soils such as those beneath coniferous forest are often subject to extremes of water stress, it may be that fungal nitrification in these systems is also selected for by the regime of water potential. Low temperatures often limit the rates of nitrification in temperate soils. Despite this, soil nitrification can proceed in forest soils at 0 °C (Martikainen, 1984), although it is not clear whether this is of autotrophic or heterotrophic origin – nitrifying bacteria can adapt to low temperatures (Malhi & McGill, 1982), but there are also low-temperature adaptations in soil fungi.

Soil animals and nitrification

It has always been assumed that nitrification in soil is a purely microbial phenomenon. A range of higher animals, however, can also nitrify in environments of low nitrate supply (Wood, 1988). It is possible, therefore, that certain soil animals may be able to nitrify and that this is not necessarily a feature of their gut microflora. Although there is no reliable information, it seems unlikely that nitrification by soil animals is of ecological significance.

The involvement of free radicals in soil nitrification

The possible involvement of free radicals in nitrification by soil microbes has recently been suggested (Wood, 1988), and such a theory has particular attractions in terms of fungal nitrification. Firstly, fungal attack of lignin in acid forest soils (an environment thought to favour fungal nitrification) can generate hydrogen peroxide.

$$\text{Lignin} \xrightarrow{\text{Basidiomycotina}} H_2O_2$$

Also, aromatic radicals, intermediates of lignin degradation, can be oxidised to produce protonated superoxide radicals, which then dissociate to produce superoxide radicals.

$$\text{Aromatic radicals} + O_2 \rightarrow HO_2 \rightarrow O_2^- + H^+$$

Superoxide radicals will react with hydrogen peroxide to generate hydroxyl radicals.

$$H_2O_2 + O_2^- \rightarrow {}^\cdot OH + O_2 + OH^-$$

It is these hydroxyl radicals that may be involved in driving the nitrification process. It is thermodynamically unlikely that these radicals will react directly with ammonia in the cell.

$$NH_4OH + 2^\cdot OH \rightarrow NH_2OH + 2H_2O$$

It seems more likely that, if there is involvement of free radicals in fungal nitrification, that the hydroxyl radicals react with an organic intermediate rather than directly with ammonia.

Allelopathy and soil nitrification

Allelopathy can be defined as any direct or indirect harmful effect by one organism on another through the production of chemical compounds released into the environment. The term is generally used when the deleterious effect is caused by a higher plant or its residues.

It may be that the lack of nitrification in soils such as some coniferous forest soils, and the form of nitrification in others, are the result of total or selective allelopathic inhibition, respectively.

For many coniferous forest soils, most of what little available nitrogen is present is usually in the form of ammonium, with little or no nitrate present (although low nitrate levels are not necessarily indicative of low nitrification). It may be that different forest tree species cause different degrees of allelopathic inhibition on the nitrifier microbial community and that this inhibition has important ecological implications because it maintains nitrogen as ammonium in the ecosystem and thereby conserves energy. Nitrification is generally low in forests where there is a mor type of litter mulch (particularly under spruce and several other conifers). Considerable losses of nitrate can occur after clear-cutting forests, however, with associated proliferation of autotrophic nitrifiers. Stimulation of nitrification on clear-felling cannot, however, be directly related to removal of allelopathic inhibition because of the many other concomitant changes that occur in the soil on clear-felling. The water potential and temperature of a soil, for example, change dramatically on clear-felling, and there are fundamental changes to the whole nitrogen dynamics of the soil.

If allelopathic inhibition of nitrification can occur in coniferous forest soils, it may be subject to seasonal fluctuations and be dependent on the growth stage and successional stage of the forest.

If allelopathy is an inhibitory mechanism of nitrification in soils, then it is likely that the allelopathic agents are various types of polyphenolic compounds, including tannins, flavonoids and a variety of other polyphenols. The relative activities of these compounds will depend on their mobility in the soil solution and on their production under different plant species (Rice, 1974).

It may always remain uncertain as to what extent allelopathy inhibits nitrification in coniferous forest, grassland, or any other soil systems. This is because single allelopathic effects cannot be factored out in real systems, and results of *in vitro* experiments where single potential allelopathic agents are tested cannot be extrapolated to field situations.

It is all too easy to invoke allelopathy as a theory for a lack of net nitrification without detailed assessment of the many other soil ecological factors which must be taken into consideration.

Conclusions

In future years, with modern techniques such as selective physiological blocking, ^{15}N-tracer characterisation of N-pools and fluxes, and the use of nucleic acid probes, the true ecology of nitrification will be understood and many out-dated concepts revised.

The presence and accumulation of nitrate in soil can lead, under conditions of high heterotrophic activity and low oxygen diffusion, to loss of nitrogen through the process of denitrification.

Denitrification

Introduction and definition

Denitrification is the process where nitrate replaces oxygen as the electron acceptor in soil microbial respiration. Denitrification is often referred to as dissimilatory nitrate reduction. It should not be confused with assimilatory nitrate reduction (where nitrate is immobilised by cells and reduced for synthesis of cell constituents) and dissimilatory reduction of nitrate to ammonium, which is discussed on page 136. Denitrification is carried out by facultative anaerobes, dominantly heterotrophic bacteria, the most common being species of the genera *Pseudomonas* and *Alcaligenes*.

Occurrence in soil

Denitrification occurs when oxygen diffusion rates in soil are insufficient to supply the demand from microbial respiration. This situation is particularly likely when soil is at or near water saturation and oxygen diffusion is slowest (see Chapter 1, pages 16–24), and when a recent addition of available carbon (e.g. a crop or animal residue) to the soil has stimulated heterotrophic microbial activity. Denitrification will also occur in microsites in aerated soils as long as there are water-saturated aggregates large enough to restrict sufficiently the diffusion of oxygen to the zone of denitrification potential (Chapter 1, pages 18–19). Under these conditions, and where nitrate is present in the soil (as a result of nitrification), nitrate will replace oxygen as the dominant electron acceptor (this tends to occur at an oxygen concentration of about 1 μM) and the soil nitrate pool will undergo dissimilatory reduction.

$$NO_3 \rightarrow NO_2 \rightarrow NO \rightarrow N_2O \rightarrow N_2$$

As a result of denitrification, nitrogen is mainly lost from the soil as both N_2O and N_2. In most soils, N_2 is the dominant gaseous product of denitrification, although N_2O evolution becomes increasingly important in more acid soils, such as coniferous forest and heather moorland systems.

Table 14. *Examples of denitrifying bacteria in soil, and their metabolism/energy source*

Denitrifier	Metabolism	Energy source
Pseudomonas aeruginosa	Heterotroph	Soil organic matter
Pseudomonas fluorescens	Heterotroph	Soil organic matter
Alcaligenes denitrificans	Heterotroph	Soil organic matter
Bacillus licheniformis	Heterotroph	Soil organic matter
Paracoccus denitrificans	Chemoautotroph	H_2
Alcaligenes eutrophus	Chemoautotroph	H_2
Thiobacillus denitrificans	Chemoautotroph	Reduced S
Rhodopseudomonas sphaeroides	Photoautotroph	Sun

Denitrification and soil pH

Unlike nitrification, which is a source of acidification in the soil, denitrification causes an increase in soil pH. Nitrogen loss through denitrification, in the form of nitrogen (N_2), nitrous oxide (N_2O) or nitric oxide (NO), is a base-forming reaction because of the production of hydroxyl ions (OH^-) equivalent to the amount of nitrate that has been denitrified. The optimum pH for denitrification is slightly above neutrality, although the process will proceed more slowly under acid conditions.

Denitrifying microbes in soil – anaerobic and aerobic denitrification

Most denitrifiers in soil are heterotrophic bacteria requiring preformed organic carbon as their energy source, although a number are autotrophic (both chemoautotrophic and photoautotrophic) (Table 14). The variety of energy sources and the variety of forms of organic matter (from simple sugars to complex aromatics) that can be used by denitrifiers contribute to make the soil ecology of denitrification far from simple. All of the above microbes carry out denitrification anaerobically. It has generally been assumed that this is the only way that denitrification could proceed, although it has been shown that *Thiosphaera pantotropha* can heterotrophically nitrify and denitrify simultaneously (Robertson, van Kleef & Kuener, 1986). Evidence of aerobic denitrification suggests that denitrification may not only be restricted to anaerobic microsites in aerobic soils, although the ecological significance of aerobic denitrification in soil is unknown.

Denitrification in the rhizosphere

Denitrifying bacteria are generally more competitive as aerobic heterotrophs in soil than they are as denitrifiers. This means that sites of intense heterotrophic activity in soil will also tend to be sites of high denitrification potential. The rhizosphere, for example, although it may rarely experience reducing conditions for some soil/plant systems, is a natural zone of proliferation for heterotrophs and, hence, numbers of denitrifiers (denitrification potential) will tend to be higher than in the bulk soil (Figure 33). This means that, when anaerobic conditions do prevail in the soil, high rates of denitrification will occur in the rhizosphere, assuming adequate concentrations of nitrate in the soil solution. In addition, denitrification may occur in soil aggregates in the rhizosphere, even when this system is well aerated, if the aggregate pores are water filled and oxygen diffusion restricted. Enhanced denitrification in the rhizosphere has important implications for sampling, because effective measurement of denitrification potential and activity in soil must take into consideration the root architecture of the vegetation present. Because this measurement of denitrification usually involves a sealed soil core, the placement of cores in relation to plant root systems will be critical in interpreting the N-flux data obtained.

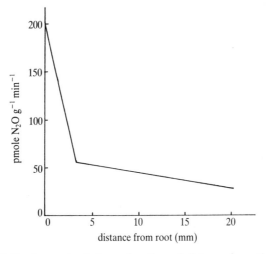

Figure 33. Denitrification potential as a function of distance from the plant root. Modified from Smith & Tiedje, 1979.

Measurements of soil denitrification

Estimates of denitrification from the plant/soil system have often been based on what is generally referred to as 'the difference method'. Any amount of nitrogen that cannot be accounted for in a budget study of applied nitrogen is considered to be caused by denitrification. This approach, however, is far less satisfactory than direct measurement.

Measurement of soil denitrification often involves the use of sealed soil cores and the addition of acetylene gas to the cores. The acetylene rapidly diffuses through the soil to the sites of denitrification where it acts as a block of the terminal reductase, ensuring that N_2O is the sole product of denitrification (Ryden *et al.*, 1979).

$$NO_3 \rightarrow NO_2 \rightarrow NO \rightarrow N_2O \nearrow \xrightarrow[\substack{\text{C}_2\text{H}_2 \\ \text{block}}]{\substack{\text{measured by} \\ \text{gas chromatography}}} N_2$$

One of the main drawbacks to this 'acetylene-block' technique seems to be that acetylene will also block the primary oxidase of autotrophic nitrification. Because autotrophic nitrification is usually supplying the nitrate pool (both nitrification and denitrification can be spatially separated and so go on simultaneously in soil), then the acetylene-block technique may underestimate the true denitrification flux. In acid, forest soils, however, where nitrification often seems to be fungal in origin, acetylene should not affect nitrification and hence the acetylene-block technique should provide a good estimate of denitrification. The technique has shown that in acid forest soils, even under conditions of prolonged field waterlogging and with application of N-fertiliser, denitrification is not generally important. A further drawback of the acetylene-block technique is that nitrous oxide can be generated by means other than denitrification in soil, although production of N_2O by autotrophic nitrification should not be a problem if the acetylene is blocking the primary oxidase. Nitrous oxide produced during assimilatory reduction of nitrate to ammonium by both fungi and bacteria may, however, cause overestimation of the denitrification flux.

Significance of denitrification in soil

Even with the limitations of the acetylene-block technique, it still provides a reasonable indication of the likely significance of the denitrification process. The technique has shown that 5–10% of added fertiliser may be lost by denitrification from loam and clay soils under grass in the UK (Ryden, 1981). Rates of denitrification as high as $1 \text{ kg N ha}^{-1} \text{ day}^{-1}$ can occur when high nitrate concentrations in soil coincide with warm temperatures, high soil water content and a reduced oxygen concentration due to microbial respiration. Because of the obvious relation between denitrification and heavy rainfall, the best means of minimising fertiliser loss, both through denitrification and, of course, through leaching, is to have a reliable weather forecast before fertiliser application. Improved soil drainage, to prevent soils becoming waterlogged, will also minimise denitrification-mediated fertiliser nitrogen loss.

The use of ^{15}N is increasingly providing the most reliable determinations of the denitrification flux (see pages 140–1).

Environmental consequences of denitrification

Like the process of nitrification, denitrification is strongly implicated with environmental pollution. Nitrous oxide, produced by denitrification, particularly under acid conditions, is oxidised, in the stratosphere to nitric oxide, which is thought to destroy ozone.

$$N_2O + O \rightarrow 2NO$$

(O is formed by photodissociation of ozone), then

$$NO + O_3 \rightarrow NO_2 + O_2$$

A second possible adverse effect of denitrification occurs when phytotoxic nitrite briefly accumulates in soil. This is because of a lag in the establishment of nitrite reduction compared with that of the nitrate reduction.

Because of the potential importance of denitrification both in terms of economic loss and environmental pollution, better estimates are required of the significance of the process at the ecosystem and global level. At present, denitrification is often calculated by difference in nitrogen budgets rather than by direct determination, although field measurements of the flux involving the acetylene block as well as ^{15}N methodology are becoming increasingly reliable and widespread.

Not all of the consequences of denitrification are adverse. If denitrification did not occur, then anaerobic soils might emit products such as hydrogen sulphide and methane, which can cause even greater agronomic and environmental problems than the products of denitrification. Denitrification may also act as a 'safety-valve' by releasing nitrogen from soils that are receiving heavy, pollutant loads of nitrogen such as in acid rain.

Dissimilatory reduction of nitrate to ammonium

In addition to the denitrifying bacteria, which can use nitrate as an alternative electron acceptor and reduce it ultimately either to nitrous oxide or free nitrogen, there is also a group of fermentative soil bacteria that can carry out dissimilatory reduction of nitrate to ammonium. The relative importance of denitrification and dissimilatory reduction of nitrate to ammonium in the soil environment is far from certain. Denitrification may be the dominant process in environments rich in nitrate but poor in carbon, whereas the dissimilatory reduction of nitrate and nitrite to ammonium tends to dominate in carbon-rich environments, which are preferentially colonised by fermentative bacteria (Tiedje *et al.*, 1982). For many of the bacteria responsible for dissimilation to ammonium, formate is a major electron donor both for nitrate and nitrite, although most of the research on the nitrate reductase activity has been restricted to enteric bacteria such as *Escherichia coli*. Only through experiments with soil bacteria will the ecological significance of dissimilatory reduction of nitrate to ammonium be assessed.

Ammonia volatilisation

Definition and occurrence

The gaseous loss of ammonia from soil can, under certain circumstances, represent a significant loss of nitrogen from the soil/plant system. The partial pressure of ammonia is high and so, if present in the unadsorbed state such as in decomposing manures or in a patch of hydrolysing urea fertiliser, then ammonia will be volatilised from the soil surface.

$$CO(NH_2)_2 + H_2O \xrightarrow{\text{urease}} 2NH_3\uparrow^{\text{volatilisation}} + CO_2$$

Manures and animal slurries on arable land can lose over half of their nitrogen owing to ammonia volatilisation (Royal Society, 1983). Future development of inhibitors of urease enzymes in soil may reduce the loss of volatilised ammonia from manures and urea-based fertilisers.

Soil factors affecting ammonia volatilisation

Volatilisation of ammonia is highest under dry conditions, when the temperature is high, when there is considerable air movement above the soil, and where the pH of the soil is alkaline. The strong effect of pH on volatilisation of ammonia is largely because the equilibrium between ammonium (NH_4^+) and ammonia (NH_3) in the soil solution is strongly towards ammonium at acid or near-neutral pH. Because of this, loss of nitrogen through NH_3 volatilisation tends to be considerably higher in arable systems compared with forests where the pH of the forest floor is generally much lower (Hulm & Killham, 1988). The clay and organic matter contents of a soil will also be vital in influencing the degree of ammonia volatilisation, because both these soil components provide exchange sites for ammonium.

Ammonia volatilisation and the plant

The presence of a vegetation cover has a marked effect on the net loss of ammonia from the soil/plant system, not only because the plant root will compete for ammonium in the soil, but also because most plants have a considerable capacity for direct foliar absorption of volatilised ammonia. This source of nitrogen to plants is often completely ignored, although cereal plants can contribute as much as 10% of their nitrogen requirements from ammonia present at normal atmospheric concentrations (Tisdale *et al.*, 1985). When ammonia is present at higher atmospheric concentrations, such as in parts of Holland with a very high population of grazing livestock, then this contribution of atmospheric ammonia to the plants' nitrogen budget will be much higher. Clearly also, systems where foliage is particularly dense, such as grass swards of pasture land, will tend to have the potential for very high rates of ammonia absorption. Many trees are also important sinks for volatilised ammonia, although the typical contribution of atmospheric ammonia to a tree's nitrogen budget is uncertain.

Environmental consequences of ammonia volatilisation

Apart from the obvious waste of a potential plant nutrient, volatilisation can also lead to direct damage of plants, microbes and soil animals because cell membranes are highly permeable to ammonia and the local pH rise in the cell is too rapid for normal compensation mechanisms to operate. Generally, reduction of soil microbial populations due to the toxicity of volatilised ammonia will be short lived, but ammonia damage to plants may be irreversible.

Measurement of ammonia volatilisation

Because of its potential importance in N-cycling and as a possible agent of crop damage, considerable attention has been given to the measurement of ammonium volatilisation. A simple static trapping system for monitoring volatilisation is often used. The ammonia is trapped in acid beneath a canopy that covers the soil. Although simple and cheap to make, this system has the weaknesses that it prevents air movement over the soil (which tends to increase volatilisation) and that it usually prevents foliar uptake of ammonia (which reduces volatilisation).

Minimisation of ammonia volatilisation may well be achieved in future through the use of mechanistic models (e.g. Rachhpal-Singh & Nye, 1986), which should facilitate avoidance of fertiliser/manure application under conditions of potentially high volatilisation.

The use of ^{15}N in the study of soil N-cycling

In recent years, there has been a marked increase in the use of the heavy, stable isotope of nitrogen, ^{15}N, as a means of characterising and quantifying individual nitrogen fluxes in the soil/plant system. An enrichment of 0.3 atom % in excess of background ^{15}N (0.3663 atom %) is considered to be sufficient for monitoring transformations of applied nitrogen in a soil/plant system (Olson, 1979). In this way, then, ^{15}N is being used as a 'tracer' to follow applied nitrogen through the system. A second approach is to pulse label an individual N-pool in the soil with ^{15}N and monitor the ^{15}N dilution of that pool as subsequent N-transformations occur. This 'pool-dilution' approach generally involves high ^{15}N enrichments and fairly short periods whereas the tracer approach can often involve much more considerable periods of investigation.

A stage is rapidly being reached where almost all microbial N-fluxes can be characterised and quantified through the use of ^{15}N methodology.

Measurement of N_2-fixation with ^{15}N

Quantification of N_2-fixation rates in legumes and other N_2-fixing plant/ microbial symbioses can be achieved by ^{15}N, by two broad approaches. One involves growing the plant in an atmosphere containing $^{15}N_2$ and then, at the end of the experiment, digesting the plant material prior to mass spectrometric determination of the fixed ^{15}N. Although most satisfactory, this approach is expensive ($^{15}N_2$ is expensive to generate at high enrichments and a purpose-built sealed plant/soil microcosm is required), and so a second approach using a $^{15}NH_4$ addition to soil has sometimes been adopted. Here, uptake of ^{15}N by an N_2-fixing (i.e. inoculated with the appropriate N_2-fixing microbe, e.g. *Rhizobium*, *Frankia* etc.) plant is compared with a non-inoculated, non-fixing plant of similar growth stage. The difference in ^{15}N between the two plant/soil systems should provide a reasonable measure of the fixation rate.

Fixation of N_2 can be estimated by determining the natural abundance of ^{15}N in plant tissues because the fixation process leads to a natural depletion of ^{15}N. Because of variability in natural abundance in soil and plants, large numbers of samples are needed and inter-specific comparisons are difficult.

Measurement of immobilisation/mineralisation with ^{15}N

Determination of microbial nitrogen immobilisation/mineralisation rates requires the measurement with time of microbial biomass ^{15}N and mineral ^{15}N after the soil addition of ^{15}N, either as mineral nitrogen or as organic nitrogen (e.g. a labelled plant residue), in the absence of growing plant roots. The technique necessitates a reliable means for determining ^{15}N held in microbial biomass. This is currently thought to be best achieved by the use of chloroform fumigation to kill microbial cells, followed by a direct extraction (K_2SO_4 and KCl are found suitable) of the nitrogen released (Brookes *et al.*, 1985). Because this flush of nitrogen is both organic and inorganic, then a digestion is used prior to mass spectrometric analysis, to convert all the biomass-N released to ammonium. A conversion factor is required to convert the fumigation N-flush to biomass-N as not all cell-N is released by fumigation (typically, only 40% or so of this nitrogen is released). Determination of net mineralisation rates requires the exclusion of plant roots from the ^{15}N-labelled soil, usually achieved either through the use of a plastic bag or a cylindrical cover inserted into the soil. Mineral nitrogen is usually extracted with 1 or 2 M KCl, as this ensures removal of ammonium from most exchange sites in the soil.

One of the greatest difficulties encountered in using ^{15}N to determine the mineralisation flux is that ^{15}N in the soil mineral N-pool not only undergoes isotope dilution due to mineralisation, but is also subject to re-immobilisation due to continuous turnover by the microbial biomass. This complexity cannot easily be resolved because it is not possible to determine from the ^{15}N enrichment of the mineral N-pool, how many cycles of turnover have occurred.

Measurement and characterisation of nitrification using ^{15}N

Determination of nitrification rates using ^{15}N is probably best achieved through pool dilution of ^{15}N-labelled soil nitrate. The power of ^{15}N in the study of soil nitrification also extends, however, to characterising the nature of the process. For example, the operation of a heterotrophic nitrification pathway that bypasses the soil ammonium pool, accessing organic nitrogen directly and converting it through to nitrate, can be investigated.

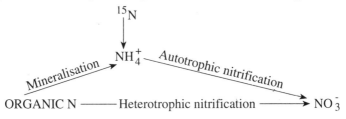

With the soil ammonium pool ^{15}N-labelled, the appearance of ^{15}N in the nitrate pool will indicate whether nitrification is proceeding via the classical autotrophic pathway or via an alternative heterotrophic pathway, which may enable organic nitrogen to be nitrified directly to nitrate, bypassing the soil ammonium pool.

Measurement of denitrification and ammonia volatilisation with ^{15}N

Measurement of gaseous N-loss from soil through denitrification is readily facilitated through ^{15}N tracer methodology. Applying ^{15}N labelled fertiliser nitrogen to the soil/plant system, monitoring the appearance of $^{15}N_2O$ (in the presence of the acetylene block) or $^{15}N_2O$ and $^{15}N_2$ (in the absence of the C_2H_2 block) can, by Gas Chromatographic Mass Spectrometry (GCMS), enable the denitrification flux to be related to the initial fertiliser application. Gaseous N-loss through ammonia volatilisation can similarly be related to fertiliser applications through ^{15}N tracer methodology, by mass spectrometric determination of $^{15}NH_4$ in an acid trap above the soil after ^{15}N-labelled fertiliser addition. Although these gaseous fluxes of denitrification and ammonia volatilisation can be determined without ^{15}N, it is only with ^{15}N methodology that the importance of the fluxes in terms of fertiliser loss can be established.

Problems in using ^{15}N to study soil nitrogen cycling

It would first appear that ^{15}N methodology will provide all the answers to the soil ecologist studying N-cycling. Although ^{15}N can provide many answers that more traditional approaches cannot, there are many situations where its use is unnecessary and there are also many potential pitfalls to be wary of. One potential problem is that the natural ^{15}N abundance of individual N-pools is not necessarily that of the total soil ^{15}N level. Labelled ^{15}N-molecules tend to react more slowly in biological systems than do ^{14}N molecules. There is a tendency, therefore, for substrates to become enriched with ^{15}N. For example, in the denitrification pathway, approximately 2% more ^{14}N-molecules will react in a given time compared with ^{15}N-molecules:

$$NO_3 \rightarrow NO_2 \rightarrow NO \rightarrow N_2O \rightarrow N_2$$

^{15}N depletion along
$\longrightarrow$
denitrification pathway

Because of these complexities of natural abundance of various soil N pools, and because any addition of ^{15}N to the soil N-pool can change the natural enrichment/depletion kinetics of the soil system, great care must be taken in the design and interpretation of ^{15}N experiments.

THE SULPHUR CYCLE

Introduction

Sulphur is one of the essential elements required by all forms of life. In plants, it is an important component of certain amino acids (methionine and cysteine) and of a large number of organic compounds that comprise enzyme systems. Although plants contain as much sulphur as phosphorus, and sulphur is as important as nitrogen in the formation of protein, sulphur has traditionally been regarded as a nutrient of secondary importance to nitrogen, phosphorus and potassium in most soil/plant systems. In more recent years, with the importance of sulphur in atmospheric pollution and also with the increasing worldwide identification of crop S-deficiencies, much more attention has been given to studying the cycling of sulphur in the soil/plant system.

S-inputs to the soil/plant system

Figure 34 illustrates the soil sulphur cycle. As is the case for nitrogen, sulphur inputs from the atmosphere vary widely from place to place, largely as a consequence of variation in atmospheric pollution from the burning of fossil fuels. These inputs, like those of nitrogen, can be through deposition in rain and snow, in dry particulates and through direct gaseous absorption and may vary from up to $100\,kg\,S\,ha^{-1}\,y^{-1}$ in areas close to industrial pollution sources to less than $5\,kg\,S\,ha^{-1}\,y^{-1}$ in rural areas distant from these sources (UNEP, 1991). The most important mechanism of input of atmospherically derived soil sulphur is direct absorption of gaseous SO_2. The most important soil property governing the rate of direct absorption is the moisture status of the soil, the process being enhanced by increasing soil moisture.

In farming systems, compound fertilisers have traditionally been the largest

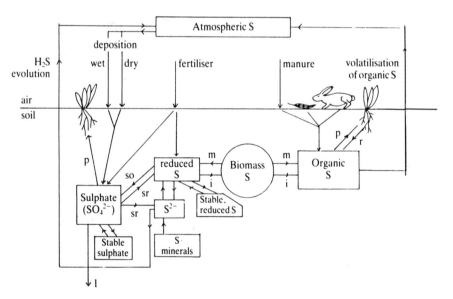

Figure 34. Soil sulphur cycle. Abbreviations: i, immobilisation; m, mineralisation; p, plant uptake; r, root exudation and turnover; so, oxidation and subsequent leaching (l); sr, reduction.

S-inputs to the soil/plant system. Most modern fertilisers, however, do not contain significant concentrations of sulphur. Any agricultural inputs of sulphur are now mainly provided by pesticide applications. It is the reduction in farm inputs coupled with the growth of high S-demanding crops and some reductions in levels of atmospheric S-pollution that has led to soil/crop S-deficiencies (Stevenson, 1986).

Sulphur mineralisation/immobilisation reactions in soil

By far the dominant form of sulphur taken up by plants and soil microbes is sulphate (SO_4^{2-}). The sulphur may originate from the weathering of soil minerals, from the atmosphere, and from organically bound sulphur. The transfer of sulphur between the inorganic and organic pool is entirely caused by the activity of the soil biota, particularly the soil microbial biomass, which has the greatest potential for both mineralisation and also for subsequent transformation of the oxidation state of sulphur.

Forms of sulphur in soil

It is generally accepted that well over 90% of the sulphur in most non-calcareous, non-tropical, surface soils is in organic forms, about half in the form of sulphate esters and esters with C—O—S linkage (Tisdale, Nelson & Beaton, 1985), about 20% in the form of sulphur directly bonded to carbon such as S-containing amino acids (Biederbeck, 1978), and the remainder in a variety of largely inert organic forms.

Biological and biochemical mineralisation

Mineralisation of organic sulphur in soil takes place by two main processes, biological and biochemical. Carbon-bonded sulphur is mineralised biologically during oxidation of carbon by soil organisms for provision of energy whereas non-carbon-bonded organic sulphur is mineralised through enzymatic catalysis external to the cell membrane. An example of this latter biochemical release of sulphur, in the form of sulphatase-catalysed cleavage of sulphate esters, has already been provided in Chapter 1 on page 4.

Sulphur is released into the inorganic pool in a variety of oxidation states from sulphide (oxidation state -2) to sulphate (oxidation state $+6$).

Soil ecology of S-mineralisation

Rates of S-mineralisation in soil are influenced by similar environmental factors to those controlling N-mineralisation. Soil factors that most affect microbial growth and production/activity of enzymes such as water potential, temperature, pH, the presence of plants, drying/heating cycles and the form and quantity of organic sulphur will have the most significant influence on rates of S-mineralisation in soil.

In most soils, the inorganic S-pool is very small and biological uptake, both as microbial immobilisation and plant uptake, is dependent on an adequate rate of mineralisation. Some soils cannot meet the sulphur demands of all crops in this way, and this S-deficiency is often not offset by fertiliser, pesticide and atmospheric S-inputs (Hoque & Killham, 1987).

Ecological studies of soil S-mineralisation have focused exclusively on the role of the microbial biomass and have paid little or no attention to the involvement of soil animals. The great similarities between the cycling of sulphur and nitrogen (particularly with regard to mineralisation from organic matter) suggest, however, a fundamental involvement of soil animals in S-mineralisation. Until further information becomes available, it can be assumed that the quantitative involvement of soil animals in the cycling of sulphur is approximately similar to that for nitrogen (pages 119–21).

Immobilisation and plant uptake

The conversion of sulphur into microbial protoplasm renders it unavailable for uptake by plants, and the sulphur is, therefore, regarded as being immobilised. The process of assimilatory sulphate reduction occurs in microbes and plants, but not in animals, the latter not having the necessary enzyme machinery.

$$ATP + SO_4^{2-} \xrightarrow{\text{ATP-sulphurylase}} APS + PPi$$

$$APS + ATP \xrightarrow{\text{APS-kinase}} PAPS + ADP$$

The assimilation process, therefore, involves the activation of the sulphate ion by a two-stage process leading to the production of energy-rich sulphate nucleotides (esters) APS (adenosine 5'-sulphato-phosphate) and PAPS (adenosine 3'-phosphate, 5'-sulphato-phosphate). The overall reaction, therefore, involves the use of two molecules of ATP for every molecule of

PAPS formed and approximately 6 kcal mole^{-1}.

$$2ATP + SO_4^{2-} \rightarrow ADP + PAPS + PPi$$

This reaction is the only known route of organic sulphate formation and the nucleotides are then used in the synthesis of the S-containing amino acids. The overall reaction scheme is represented below.

$$SO_4^{2-} \rightarrow APS \rightarrow PAPS \rightarrow [\text{active sulphite}] \rightarrow \text{sulphide}$$
$$\swarrow\nwarrow \text{serine}$$
$$\text{cysteine}$$

Cysteine is then used as the building block for the other S-containing amino acids, which are then combined into proteins.

The balance between S-mineralisation and immobilisation in soil will largely depend on the concentration of readily utilisable sulphur in organic residues relative to the utilisable concentrations of carbon and nitrogen.

C:S and N:S ratios

The critical C:S ratio in carbonaceous materials, above which immobilisation exceeds mineralisation, appears to be in the range of 200:1 to 400:1 (Stewart, Porter & Viets, 1966), although superimposed on this is the concentration of nitrogen, immobilisation being encouraged by a widening of the N:S ratio.

Oxidation of inorganic S-compounds in soil

The oxidation process is of fundamental importance because the ultimate source of sulphur in soils is the S-bearing minerals, and many S-fertilisers are also based on reduced forms of sulphur. Elemental sulphur, sulphides and several other inorganic S-compounds can be oxidised in soil by purely chemical processes but these are generally less important than microbial S-oxidation.

Autotrophic S-oxidation

Generally, microbial S-oxidation proceeds rapidly and almost all of the inorganic S-pool in soils is in the sulphate form. In most soils, oxidation is dominated by the thiobacilli, by far the most studied group of soil S-oxidisers.

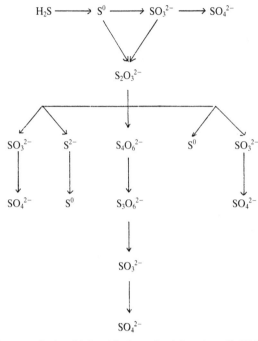

Figure 35. Pathways of microbial oxidation of sulphur in soil. H_2S, hydrogen sulphide; S^{2-}, sulphide; S^0, elemental sulphur; $S_2O_3^{2-}$, thiosulphate; $S_4O_6^{2-}$, tetrathionate; $S_3O_6^{2-}$, trithionate; SO_3^{2-}, sulphite; SO_4^{2-}, sulphate. Adapted from Goldhaber & Kaplan, 1974.

Figure 35 illustrates the pathways of oxidation of reduced S-compounds to sulphate by thiobacilli. Of the nine species of thiobacilli, five have been studied in detail and their substrate-specificity found to vary greatly (Table 15). Oxidation of soil sulphur by thiobacilli can therefore be seen as involving a community of species, many of which are dependent for substrate on the product of others.

Autotrophic S-oxidation and pH

The extreme acid tolerance of certain species of the thiobacilli represents an adaptation to one of the greatest environmental extremes that can be experienced in the natural environment, and results from the production of protons in the oxidation of sulphur in a similar manner to acidification by autotrophic nitrifiers. *Thiobacillus ferrooxidans* and *T. thiooxidans* grow best

Table 15. *Oxidation reactions of the thiobacilli*

Oxidation reactions

(1) $2S + 3O_2 + 2H_2O \rightarrow 2H_2SO_4$

(2) $Na_2S_2O_3 + 2O_2 + H_2O \rightarrow Na_2SO_4 + H_2SO_4$

(3) $2Na_2S_4O_6 + 7O_2 + 6H_2O \rightarrow 2Na_2SO_4 + 6H_2SO_4$

(4) $2KSCN + 4O_2 + 4H_2O \rightarrow (NH_4)_2SO_4 + K_2SO_4 + 2CO_2$

(5) $5S + 6KNO_3 + 2H_2O \rightarrow 3K_2SO_4 + 2H_2SO_4 + 3N_2$

(6) $5Na_2S_2O_3 + 8NaNO_3 + H_2O \rightarrow 9Na_2SO_4 + H_2SO_4 + 4N_2$

(7) $12FeSO_4 + 3O_2 + 6H_2O \rightarrow 4Fe_2(SO_4)_3 + 4Fe(OH)_3$

(8) $5Na_2S_2O_3 + 4O_2 + H_2O \rightarrow 5Na_2SO_4 + H_2SO_4 + 4S$

(9) $Na_2S_4O_6 + Na_2CO_3 + \frac{1}{2}O_2 \rightarrow 2NaSO_4 + 2S + CO_2$

Thiobacilli involved	Reactions
T. thiooxidans	1–3
T. denitrificans	1–6
T. ferrooxidans	1, 2 and 7
T. novellus	2 and 3
T. thioparus	1–4, 8 and 9

at around pH 2–3; even more acid tolerant is *T. acidophilus*, which is routinely cultured at pH 1.4 (Tuovinen & Kelly, 1973). This pH is more than one hundred thousand times more acid than many arable soils!

Ecology of soil microbial S-oxidation – autotrophy v. heterotrophy

Although some thiobacilli can grow as heterotrophs, oxidation of sulphur by the thiobacilli is chemoautotrophic and this has traditionally been considered to be the only significant form of S-oxidation in soil. The involvement of heterotrophs in S-oxidation in soil, however, has become increasingly recognised. A wide range of heterotrophic bacteria (Friedrich & Mitrenga, 1981), fungi (Killham, Lindley & Wainwright, 1981) and actinomycetes (Yagi, Kitai & Kimura, 1971) can oxidise various forms of reduced sulphur *in vitro*. Heterotrophic S-oxidation appears very analogous to heterotrophic nitrification for several reasons. (*a*) Neither process has been shown to be energy linked. Certainly, if energy production is involved, yields are insignificant compared to those of their autotrophic counterparts (S-oxidising *Thiobacillus*, nitrifying *Nitrosomonas* and *Nitrobacter*). (*b*) S- and N-oxidising heterotrophs can utilise both inorganic and organic forms of sulphur and nitrogen, respectively, unlike their autotrophic counterparts. (c) Although their exact role and significance in soil is uncertain, it seems that heterotrophic S-oxidisers and nitrifiers only dominate certain specific soil environments that favour their growth/activity at the expense of the autotrophs. Below pH 5, *T. thioparus* dominates, and *T. thiooxidans* dominates below pH 5. In acid forest soils, as is the case for nitrification, it is perhaps most likely that the fungi may dominate the S-oxidation process. It is almost certainly, however, a gross oversimplification to consider pH as the only determinant of the composition of the soil S-oxidiser and nitrifier, microbial communities. It may also be that because of their very different growth requirements, S-oxidising and nitrifying chemolithotrophs can live in a mutualistic association with the heterotrophs.

It is probably because of the variety of microbes responsible for S-oxidation that the factors controlling soil S-oxidation vary from one soil to another. Generally, the amount of available sulphur, soil moisture and temperature will most markedly affect S-oxidation rates. Because of the variety of S-oxidisers, however, the effect of the form of sulphur (organic v. inorganic) and soil pH on soil S-oxidation will not be a straightforward relationship.

With very few exceptions, the rate of supply of plant-available sulphate in soils is not limited by the rate of S-oxidation, but by the rate at which organic sulphur is mineralised into the inorganic S-pool.

Reduction of oxidised sulphur-compounds in soil

Dissimilatory or respiratory sulphate reduction is carried out largely by certain heterotrophic bacteria, which use sulphate as the terminal electron acceptor in their anaerobic respiration. Because these bacteria are heterotrophs, organic matter enhances the reduction of sulphate. Various organic compounds serve as hydrogen donors, including lactate, maleate, pyruvate, formate, choline and simple primary alcohols.

The sulphate-reducing bacteria in soil are obligate anaerobes and the main genera are *Desulfotomaculum*, *Desulfovibrio* and *Desulfobacter*. Other heterotrophic soil microbes are involved, although their ecological significance and biochemistry of reduction are uncertain. These heterotrophs include bacteria, as well as fungi and actinomycetes.

Soil ecology of sulphate reduction

The soil ecology of the sulphate reducers is dominated by three main factors. (*a*) Sulphate reduction is generally restricted to water-saturated soils because strongly anaerobic conditions must pre-dominate (a redox potential of approximately $-220\,mV$ prevails when SO_4^{2-} is the dominant electron acceptor at neutral pH). (*b*) Being heterotrophs, sulphate reducers are controlled by the supply of organic matter as their energy source. (*c*) Sulphate reduction necessitates an adequate supply of sulphate in the soil solution. Because concentrations of sulphate in soil are generally low, only a limited number of sites (e.g. soils/sediments affected by sea water, sulphate-fertilised soils, S-polluted soils and soils affected by weathering of S-minerals) are likely to express high rates of sulphate reduction.

Soils amended with sewage or animal slurry can be sites of intense sulphide production. A great deal will depend on the levels of nitrate in the soil because under water-saturated conditions, respiratory demand will soon deplete dissolved oxygen. A high nitrate concentration, however, will buffer the redox potential from falling to electron acceptance by sulphate. Production of H_2S in soil may have serious agronomic implications because the roots of many plants are sensitive to high H_2S concentrations.

An interesting ecological niche for sulphate reduction is in the outer rhizosphere of paddy rice plants (Kimura, Wada & Takai, 1979). This zone is an ideal situation for sulphate reduction, being maintained at water saturation and with a constant supply of available carbon in the form of exudates from the roots of the rice plants. Ordinarily, the H_2S produced would be toxic to the roots of the rice plant, but this potential phytotoxicity is avoided because firstly, most of the sulphide is bound by the iron present in the paddy soil, and secondly, because the inner rhizosphere is aerobic (being continually supplied with O_2 by the aerenchyma of the plant) and any H_2S will be rapidly re-oxidised by the thiobacilli.

Volatilisation of sulphur from soil

A number of volatile organic sulphur compounds can be released from the soil, particularly when the soil is rich in decaying plant/animal residues, and particularly when the soil is under waterlogged, reducing conditions. Sulphur is released in the form of mercaptans, methyl and ethyl sulphides, thiols and a variety of other volatile organics (Table 16).

Table 16. *Some volatile, sulphur-containing organic compounds released from soil because of the decomposition of organic matter*

CS_2	Carbon disulphide
COS	Carbonyl sulphide
CH_3SH	Methane thiol
CH_3CH_2SH	Ethane thiol
$(CH_3)_2S_2$	Dimethyl disulphide
$(CH_3CH_2)_2S_2$	Diethyl disulphide
CH_3SCOCH_3	Methyl thioacetate

The significance of volatilisation of organic sulphur compounds compared with H_2S evolution is uncertain, as is the biochemistry of volatilisation, although H_2S and dimethyl sulphide are the major forms of gaseous sulphur emitted from soil and together they contribute a very major input to the global, atmospheric sulphur cycle.

5 Ecology of extreme soil environments – soil water stress

INTRODUCTION

Adaptation of plant, microbial and animal communities (and their inter-actions) to prevailing conditions can readily be observed across a wide range of environmental gradients. Environmental conditions need not be extreme for adaptation to occur, although some of the most striking adaptations at both the population and organism level tend to be found in extreme, and often isolated, environments.

The forces of natural selection that determine the nature of communities under different environmental conditions were first documented by Darwin and the principles remain applicable today. Where modern techniques have been particularly of value is in identification of many of the subtle genetic changes that continually proceed and that may confer a competitive ecological advantage. The changes may be small, but with time may lead to the development of new and unique species, much better adapted to the prevailing conditions.

A variety of soil conditions can be considered extreme in terms of a habitat for the soil biota, either because of extremes in temperature, water regime, salinity, acidity or some other environmental stress. If the environmental stress is periodic, some changes to the plant, microbial and animal community may occur. Periodic water stress, for example, may prevent the establishment of an algal component to the soil microbial community. If, however, the environmental stress is maintained for a considerable period, the biota will tend to differ more strongly in terms of species composition, form and activity compared with the biota of less extreme environments. Because of the specialised nature of many of the adaptations to extreme environments, adapted organisms are often poor competitors under more moderate con-ditions.

One of the most interesting and widespread of extreme soil conditions occurs under water stress, matric and osmotic. Extreme soil conditions in terms of water stress do not necessarily imply an extreme soil environment in the long term. Soil water stress can occur in all soils, even in climates with plentiful and well-distributed rainfall. In fact, water availability can period-ically limit plant growth in temperate, maritime climates such as the UK, although clearly, it is in the more arid regions of the earth that the effects of water stress are of most interest. In particular, because of the need to improve and extend agriculture on arid and saline soils, because of large-scale crop failures due to drought and because of concerns over global climate change, the ecology of water-stressed soils has received considerable research attention in recent years. Great advances are also being made to genetically improve the tolerance of important crop cultivars to water/salt stress. It is impossible, however, to realise the full benefits of this technology unless a better understanding is developed of the ecology of the soil environment into which these genetically modified cultivars are to be introduced.

To understand the ecology of water-stressed soils and the related adapt-ations of plants, microbes and animals, it is first necessary to develop an understanding of the basic responses to water stress at the organism level.

SOIL WATER/SALT STRESS AND THE PLANT

The concept of soil water stress and its matric and osmotic components has been introduced in Chapter 1 (pages 12–16). The relation between matric water potential, the thickness of water films around soil particles, and the wilting point of most plants, was also discussed. Permanent wilting point is the moisture status of soils that causes irreversible wilting of the foliage, and occurs around -15 bar or -1.5 MPa water tension in many soil/plant systems. Water is available to plants from this permanent wilting point to a maximum upper level termed field capacity. This latter term requires further explanation: water tends to move from an area of high potential to one of lower potential, so that soil water draining from a saturated zone to an unsaturated zone is replaced by air from the atmosphere. Some time after a soil has been saturated with water, drainage can be seen practically to cease, with the field capacity being the percentage of water remaining in the soil at this stage. Between these two states of field capacity and permanent wilting point, soil water is available to plants. This has considerable ecological significance because, from the point of view of plant/crop growth, it is not the total water-holding capacity that is significant, but the available water-holding capacity. Soil particle distribution in terms of different size and shape will affect the relation between matric potential and the percentage of water in the soil. In simple terms, light, sandy soils, which have a low field capacity, will tend to release a large proportion of this water to the plant, whereas heavier soils with finer particulate composition and a much higher field capacity will release a smaller proportion of this water. The net result is that, although the two soil types have greatly contrasting field capacities, their available water supply may be really rather similar.

Superimposed upon the matric potential stress in soils is the osmotic stress due to the presence of dissolved salts in the soil water. A 0.1M solution of potassium chloride will produce a negative water potential of nearly 5 bar or 0.5 MPa. In areas of saline and arid soils, the plant must continually combat a variable combination of matric and osmotic stress.

Some plants escape the effects of soil water stress by flowering and setting seed before the onset of drought. Most plants, however, respond to soil water stress through adjustment of cell turgor pressure and cell osmotic potential.

$$\Psi_c = \Psi_E = P_T - \Pi_c$$

where Ψ_c = cell water potential

Ψ_E = environmental water potential (soil matric potential + soil osmotic potential)

P_T = cell turgor pressure

Π_c = cell osmotic potential

Water stress involves a decrease in Ψ_E and hence Ψ_c. To prevent a loss in cell turgor (P_T), the plant may increase the cell solute concentration (i.e. Π_c). This osmotic adjustment as a means of maintaining cell turgor under water stress is termed dehydration avoidance (i.e. drought tolerance at high tissue water potential). Amongst the main solutes synthesised by plants for this purpose are betaine, a quaternary ammonium compound, and malic acid. One of the adaptative mechanisms of some plants that are particularly tolerant to extremes of water stress involves the selective synthesis and accumulation of these solutes. Manipulation of plant genetics to produce higher concentrations of intracellular solutes that are compatible with the enzyme machinery of the plant cell appears to be one of the most promising ways of engineering plants to be more suitable for arid and saline soils.

There is a vast range of adaptive, physiological (e.g. increases in membrane permeability to facilitate solute flux reductions in the activity of the

Table 17. *Response mechanisms of plants to soil water stress*

Response category	Representative response mechanisms
Drought escape	Ephemeral growth – rapid flower and seed production
Drought avoidance	Increased hydraulic conductivity
	More effective root development – depth, branching etc.
	Reduced leaf surface area for evaporation
	Reduced conductivity of epidermis
Drought tolerance	Increased cell elasticity
	Compatible solute accumulation

photosynthetic enzyme ribulose diphosphate carboxylase and other indices of photosynthetic activity) and morphological (e.g. reduction in intercellular space, reduction in cell size, reduced size of meristematic cell vacuoles, contraction or thickening of cell protoplasm, increased production of waxy cuticle on the leaf surface, reduction in leaf surface area, stomatal closure, increased mesophyll resistance) response mechanisms of the plant to water stress.

Plant response mechanisms to water stress are summarised in Table 17. Plants best adapted to extreme soil water stress can employ a considerable number of these mechanisms in their overall response strategy and have often developed particular mechanisms to a highly specialised degree.

THE PLANT ROOT AND SOIL WATER STRESS

It is the region of the root hairs that absorbs most of the water to supply the needs of a growing plant. The root hairs have a very large surface area to ensure optimum contact with soil water and, with a turnover time of only a few days, are continually replaced by new root hairs closer to the extending root tip.

The driving force behind water absorption by roots is the gradient of water potential between the sap of the xylem and the soil. Movement will therefore only occur when the xylem sap has a more negative water potential (comprising a matric and osmotic component) than the soil pores into which the root has extended.

In terms of the plant root itself, one of the major factors in determining plant survival under conditions of soil water stress is whether the root is able to extend quickly enough to maintain contact with zones of soil where water potential remains adequate under dry conditions (Scott Russell, 1977). This is exemplified by the considerably greater tolerance to soil water stress of a deep-rooting grass such as *Festuca* compared with a more shallow-rooting grass such as *Phleum*. In desert environments in which soil conditions of water stress are most extreme, there are two root system strategies for acquisition of water. Rapid growth of ephemeral species is facilitated by shallow root systems that opportunistically exploit rainfall events. In contrast, the growth of perennials is facilitated by deep (up to 30 m for *Acacia* trees) root systems that exploit groundwater reserves.

As well as rooting depth, the size and density of the root system (i.e. the degrees of branching) will also play an important part in determining plant resistance to soil water stress because the quantity of water that enters a plant can depend upon the amount of root present per unit volume of soil in which water is available.

One of the main consequences of water stress on the root can be the increased efflux of carbon into the soil (Barber & Martin, 1976). Carbon flow from roots includes carbon secreted as mucilage and carbon released by lysis of root tissue, and both of these components of carbon flow are increased in zones of localised soil water stress, even though other sections of the root have adequate water (Martin, 1977). A broadly similar picture of root carbon flow under water stress seems to occur in tree seedlings where a drop in matric soil water potential from about 0 to -12 bar (0 to -1.2 MPa) is associated with a considerable (about five-fold) increase in carbon flow from the roots (Patrick-Reid, 1974). The ecological significance of increased diversion of carbon as exudation from plant roots under soil water stress may be considerable, both as a factor involved in reducing plant growth as well as providing substrate for microorganisms. Whether increased diversion of root carbon exudation translates to a net increase in rhizosphere carbon flow will depend on how much the total carbon budget of the plant (i.e. net photosynthesis) will be affected by the water stress, and this will vary from one plant to another.

In addition to changes in quantity of root carbon exudation, the nature of the exudate may also change in response to water stress, affecting substrate quality.

Root exuded carbon as a supply of substrate, assuming sufficient soil water is available for movement to the microbe, is being provided at a time when

Table 18. *The effects of water stress on plant cell water potential*

Stress level	Soil water potential (bar)	Dehydration below saturation (%)
mild	−4 to −5 (−400 to −500 kPa)	8 to 10
moderate	−12 to −15 (−1200 to −1500 kPa)	10 to 20
severe	> −15 (> −1.5 MPa)	> 20

(Modified from Hsaio, 1973.)

the microbe needs to synthesise organic cell solutes for osmoregulatory control. Perhaps, then, the plant can contribute to the survival of rhizosphere soil microbes under soil water stress either through enhanced substrate supply or because many of the organic solutes (particularly the amino acids) can be transported directly into microbial cells (Killham & Firestone, 1984*b*). Carbon flow from plants under water stress, therefore, may well serve as both a microbial substrate and directly as a microbial osmoticum. Restricting carbon flux from root to microbe will be the more negative water potential at the root surface compared to the bulk soil. Because of this water potential gradient, there is a mass flow of water towards the root (Foster & Bowen, 1982). This may lead to an accumulation of carbon at the root surface, limiting the extent to which rhizosphere microbes can benefit from root-derived substrate supply for osmoregulatory needs.

After a period of water stress in the soil, rainfall may quickly return conditions to those of plentiful available water. A key strategy of plant survival will, therefore, be how quickly new root growth can take advantage of the improved growth conditions. Many grasses, for example, are extremely adept at producing new root biomass when a soil is rewetted.

Although the types of plant response to soil water/salt stress are applicable to most plant species, there is of course tremendous variation between different plants in terms of their adaptation and tolerance to water stress. The effects of water stress on plants can be classified on the basis of severity (Table 18).

Some plants suffer considerably reduced growth under even mild stress whereas, in others, growth may continue to a soil water potential as low as -50 bar (-5 MPa). Most higher plants, however, are killed by a loss of 40–90% of their normal water content and this tends to occur around -15 bar (-1.5 MPa). In addition to variation in tolerance to soil water stress between plant types, response to water stress will tend to vary with plant age. More mature plants tend to continue growth at water potentials that prevent growth of seedlings (Tesche & Gomell, 1973). It also seems that growth of plants is more adversely affected by soil water stress during early flower initiation than at later stages of development (Levitt, 1972).

Under conditions of soil water stress, the plant is not only suffering from reduced availability of water to the roots, but also from reduced supply of nutrients. This will be particularly true for nutrients such as calcium and nitrate, which move to the root predominantly by mass flow, which requires a movement of soil water. It will also be true, although to a slightly lesser extent, for nutrients such as phosphate that are dominantly moved to the root through diffusion where a continuous film of soil water is required.

MYCORRHIZAL RESPONSE TO SOIL WATER STRESS

The earliest terrestrial plants may well have evolved from their aquatic ancestors partly by developing associations with microorganisms. These associations may have reduced the difficulties encountered by the plant in adjusting to water stresses for the first time. Because of the almost ubiquitous occurrence of mycorrhizal associations, and their capacity for dense coverage of the root system, these associations may have developed as a fundamental regulator in plant water relations.

There is increasing evidence to show that the mycorrhizal symbiosis has a very important role to play in plant water relations. This seems to be particularly true for the ectomycorrhizal symbiosis, which is largely between fungi of the Basidiomycotina (a number of Ascomycotina are also involved) and tree hosts. Mycorrhizal tree seedlings, for example, can often resist drought better than non-mycorrhizal seedlings (Bowen, 1973), and ectomycorrhizal fungi can grow in solutions of higher osmotic stress than that which plasmolyses non-mycorrhizal root hairs (Mexal & Reid, 1973). Mycorrhizal fungal mycelia may also enhance water transport to trees, although there is no direct evidence for this.

Little information is available concerning the effect of VAM fungal infection on the water relations of the many herbaceous plants that are readily infected, although there appears to be greater drought tolerance in certain VAM seedlings compared with corresponding non-mycorrhizal seedlings (Mosse & Hayman, 1971). Enhancement of water-stress tolerance of *Citrus* by VAM (Levy & Krikun, 1980) also points to an important role of VAM in the water relations of plants growing under extremes of soil water stress.

MECHANISMS OF MYCORRHIZAL MEDIATION OF PLANT DROUGHT TOLERANCE

In considering mechanisms, the first to be considered is whether mycorrhizal fungal hyphae can directly increase the transport of water (and nutrients) due to greater exploitation of soil water resources. Transport of water by the hyphae of the mycobiont will be most important for plants with limited root penetration, but less so for plants that extend much deeper root systems.

It has been proposed that VAM infection strongly increases water transport from soil, through roots, to host plant leaves (Safir, Boyer & Gerdemann, 1971) and similar proposals have been made with regard to the ectomycorrhizal symbiosis. Considering a possible 'direct transport' mechanism for mycorrhizal mediation of drought tolerance, the development of the ectomycorrhizal fungal mycelium well away from the root itself suggests that this system is most suited for the operation of such a mechanism. Theoretical calculations have been made (e.g. Sanders, Mosse & Tinker, 1975), however, which conclude that VAM fungal infection can only lead to trivial increases in direct water flow.

An important feature of possible mycorrhizal mediation of drought tolerance not generally considered in theoretical calculations of VAM-mediated water flow is the number of hyphal entry points per unit of plant root length. The more entry points, the greater the potential for water inflow into plants, and estimates dismissing VAM-enhanced plant water flow may have underestimated this factor because hundreds of hyphal entry points may exist for every centimetre of root.

In addition to hyphal entry points into the plant, the hyphal length and surface area linking the root with the soil will be fundamental to VAM-mediated plant water relations. Up to 50 m of hyphal length may be present per gram of grassland soil (Tisdall & Oades, 1979). It has been speculated that a hyphal diameter of 5 μm and a root diameter of 500 μm will lead to 1 m of hyphae having a surface area equivalent to 1 cm of root length (Read & Boyd, 1986). On the basis of this it can be estimated that each gram of grassland soil may have hyphae equivalent to 50 cm of fine roots. Perhaps, then, fungal mycelium can extend outward from the root surface and exploit water resources beyond the depletion zones around the root. Again, the ectomycorrhizal fungi that can produce rhizomorphs (fascicled strands of fungal hyphae in the soil that may be found over considerable distances from the tree root) seem the most likely mycorrhizal system to function in this way.

A number of alternative mechanisms can be postulated to explain mycorrhizal mediation of drought stress. The better recovery of VAM seedlings of *Citrus* from drought stress compared to non-mycorrhizal has been linked to effects on stomatal regulation (Levy & Krikun, 1980). Stomatal regulation is known to be stimulated by cytokinin levels in the plant. Increased cytokinin levels can occur in response to mycorrhizal infection and this has been tentatively linked with the improved water relations of the host plant (Allen *et al.*, 1981). Sterols are also present at higher concentrations in mycorrhizal roots than in non-mycorrhizal roots, and this could enhance plant growth under water stress, because sterols can influence membrane permeability and hence the water relations of the plant (Powell & Bagyaraj, 1986).

Because plant roots tend to lose more carbon when subjected to water stress (Martin, 1977) and because the mycorrhizal mycobiont is a sink for root released carbon, a feature of mycorrhizal mediation of tolerance to water stress may well be the more efficient carbon economy of the root system.

PHOSPHORUS NUTRITION AND MYCORRHIZAL RESPONSE TO WATER STRESS

Although enhanced growth of mycorrhizal plants in soils with plentiful moisture supply has often been attributed to improved phosphorus nutrition, the drought tolerance of mycorrhizal plants can also be attributed to the ability of VAM fungi to maintain adequate phosphorus nutrition when low soil moisture decreases the mobility of phosphate ions (Nelson & Safir, 1982). Increased hydraulic conductivity in mycorrhizal plants appears to be associated with the improved phosphorus status of the drought-resistant, infected plants (Read & Boyd, 1986).

In understanding the mechanisms of mycorrhizal mediation of drought tolerance, it is difficult (and probably invalid) to distinguish between nutritional advantages and those conferred by water uptake alone. In mycorrhizal plants under conditions of low available soil phosphorus, for example, higher hydraulic conductivity may be associated with changes such as higher leaf water potential, higher transpiration rates and lower stomatal resistances than in non-mycorrhizal plants (Nelson & Safir, 1982). At higher levels of available soil phosphorus, however, these parameters may be similar in infected and uninfected plants, whereas under some circumstances, hydraulic conductivities and water flow rates can be higher in mycorrhizal compared to non-mycorrhizal plants, even with the addition of phosphorus to the non-mycorrhizal plants (Hardie & Leyton, 1981).

WATER STRESS AND THE MYCORRHIZAL INFECTION PROCESS

In addition to established mycorrhizal symbioses, the mycorrhizal infection process itself may have to operate under water-stressed conditions. Under these circumstances, the osmoregulatory properties of the fungus itself will be a key factor in determining the speed and success of root colonisation.

The main mycorrhizal forming fungi are not among the most tolerant to soil water stress. The Basidiomycotina, which are involved in most of the ectomycorrhizal symbioses, appear to have a tolerance to water stress, based solely on the salt concentration of a liquid culture medium, of up to about -70 bar (-7 MPa) (Harris, 1980). Growth rate, and hence root colonisation potential, will, however, be substantially reduced at much lower water stresses. Further, matric stress will tend to have a stronger adverse effect than the corresponding osmotic stress. There is no direct information available on the water stress tolerance of the endomycorrhizal-forming zygomycotina because these fungi cannot be grown *in vitro*, although the tolerance of other, related fungi such as members of the Mucorales suggest a similar tolerance to the Basidiomycotina (Harris, 1980). Although this tolerance is low compared with many other soil fungi, it is considerably greater than the water potential at which most host plants wilt from water stress.

WATER STRESS AND SOIL MICROBES

Water stress affects the soil microbial community in two different ways. Firstly, as the soil dries, the thickness of water films around soil particles and the neck diameter of water-filled pores becomes progressively less

(Table 1 in Chapter 1). All soil bacteria must live in this water and many require to move through it. Motile bacteria, although only 1 μm or so in dimension, generally require a water film of at least 5 μm for adequate movement. The second way in which soil microbes are affected by water stress is that the free energy of the soil water remaining becomes progressively less as the soil dries out. This is a function of both matric tension, and osmotic tension due to the dissolved salts in the soil solution that become more concentrated as less and less water is present.

Table 3 in Chapter 1 provides a rough guide to the relative tolerance to water stress of the different components of the soil microbial community. Filamentous fungi (particularly the Ascomycotina) and actinomycetes tend to be amongst the most tolerant microbes to water stress, sometimes able to grow at water potential stresses of -200 bar (-20 MPa) or greater. Filamentous fungi can bridge the air gap (i.e. soil pore space) between water films. This air should be at the same potential as the water around it but, when the soil is drying, the equilibrium is often not reached and the potential of the air is much lower than the water. Adaptation by fungi to conditions such as these may explain why many fungal soil processes can proceed, albeit at a slower rate, at soil water potential stresses exceeding -100 bar (or -10 MPa).

Because the microbial cell must maintain an internal water potential similar to that of its environment (microbial cells have minimal turgor), solutes must be accumulated within the cell. There are two types of solute that can be accumulated by microbial cells. (i) 'Stress' solutes (e.g. NaCl, KCl etc.) may be taken up from the soil environment, either by passive diffusion or by selective ion pumping. Accumulation of stress solutes does not involve the 'expensive' energy costs of organic solute synthesis but, because these stress solutes can become, as their name suggests, inhibitory to intracellular enzyme machinery, their accumulation may become detrimental to the cell. This can be minimised by selective ion pumping (Figure 3 in Chapter 1) so that inhibitory ions such as Na^+ are effectively excluded from the cell and less inhibitory ions such as K^+ are accumulated instead. Of course, there is an energy cost to the cell for this ion pumping but the cost is still minimal compared to solute synthesis. (ii) Solutes may be synthesised by the cell in order to obtain compatibility with intracellular enzymes. These compatible organic solutes include a range of amino acids (favoured by procaryotes) and carbohydrates (favoured by eucaryotes). Soil microbes have been classified on the basis of their pattern of cell solute accumulation under water stress (Table 19).

Table 19. *Strategies of solute accumulation in soil microbes*

Tolerance to water stress and representative members	Solute accumulation strategy
LOW Osmoregulatory class not found in soil – only in fresh water habitats owing to sensitivity to matric stress.	**CLASS 1** Accumulation of inorganic salts (e.g. NaCl, KCl) only.
LOW/MEDIUM e.g. Most Gram −ve soil bacteria, some yeasts and algae. Most Mastigomycotina and Zygomycotina.	**CLASS 2** Intracellular accumulation of inducible compatible solutes (e.g. glutamate, proline, gamma-amino butyrate for bacteria; polyols such as glycerol for fungi; mannitol for algae etc.).
MEDIUM e.g. Few Gram +ve soil bacteria; most lichens.	**CLASS 3** Intracellular accumulation of constitutive compatible solutes (e.g. glutamate for bacteria; arabitol for fungi).
HIGH e.g. Most Gram +ve soil bacteria.	**CLASS 4** Intracellular accumulation of inducible and constitutive compatible solutes.

(Adapted from Harris, 1980.)

Class 1 microbes are not likely to be found in soil, being most sensitive to water stress. Their response to water stress will be through loss of turgor (up to above -5 bar or -500 kPa) and then through water loss and passive accumulation of the stress solute (e.g. NaCl). Growth of these cells will cease at -5 bar. Class 2 microbes can accumulate amino acids (for bacteria) and polyols (for fungi and other eucaryotes – algae, protozoa etc.) with production induced by water stress. Class 3 microbes accumulate compatible solutes such as glutamate (procaryotes) and arabitol, erythritol and mannitol (eucaryotes) under water stress, but are not able to supplement this with production of inducible compatible solutes. These microbes are much less sensitive than Class 1 and 2 microbes to the potential plasmolytic effect of cell dehydration under water stress because water loss to achieve water potential equilibrium by intracellular solute concentration is markedly decreased by the presence of constitutive compatible solutes. Class 4 microbes have the best of both worlds, being able to accumulate compatible solutes constitutively, and also able to induce production of compatible solutes. These microbes are the most resistant to soil water stress and include almost all of the Gram-positive soil bacteria, particularly the actinomycetes, which are amongst the most water-stress tolerant of all soil microbes. Microbes in this osmoregulatory class tend to have a very strong cell wall and restricted membrane permeability to enable them to resist the influx of stress solutes as well as to retain intracellularly produced constitutive and inducible compatible solutes.

It is important to distinguish between water/salt-stress tolerant soil microbes and halophiles. Unlike the tolerant microbes, halophiles actually require high salt concentrations. In soils, halophilic activity is restricted to procaryotes and these bacteria have a salt requirement for maintenance of cell membrane and intracellular enzyme stability (Brown, 1978).

One of the most tolerant groups of non-halophilic soil microbes, the actinomycetes, are Gram-positive, filamentous, heterotrophic bacteria and often totally dominate the processing of organic matter in saline and arid soils. They fit into the Class 4 of Table 19 with regard to osmoregulatory strategy, producing both constitutive and inducible compatible solutes. The dominant inducible compatible solute in actinomycetes appears to be proline (Killham & Firestone, 1984a). This is a neutral amino acid and so does not require an additional charged species to enable the cell to maintain charge balance. Figure 36 demonstrates the pattern of compatible solute accumulation in streptomycetes with increasing salt stress of the liquid growth medium.

Synthesis of amino acids, particularly of ring structures such as proline, requires a substantial carbon/energy input to the cell, and osmoregulatory strategies such as that in Figure 36 require a carbon-rich growth medium. To operate this strategy in the soil, the carbon (if indeed, sufficient is available) must either come from other microbial cells, the plant root (see pages 155 and 156) or from the non-biomass soil organic matter. The plant root may be a likely source if there is vegetation present. Not only will plant roots increasingly divert carbon to the soil under water stress, but also exude a considerable proportion of this carbon in the form of amino acids. Perhaps these free amino acids are taken up directly by the soil microbes such

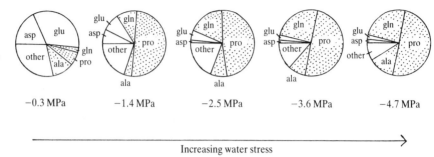

-0.3 MPa   -1.4 MPa   -2.5 MPa   -3.6 MPa   -4.7 MPa

Increasing water stress

Figure 36. Pattern of amino acid accumulation in a soil streptomycete in response to salt/water stress. Abbreviations: ala, alanine; asp, aspartic acid; gln, glutamine; glu, glutamic acid; pro, proline. The shading indicates major accumulating amino acids. Modified from Killham & Firestone, 1984*a*.

as the proline, glutamine and alanine-accumulating soil streptomycetes illustrated in Figure 36. This would increase the specific growth yield of the cell, because uptake of exogenous amino acids will reduce the need for their synthesis as compatible cell solutes (Killham & Firestone, 1984*b*). The plant root may, therefore, not only contribute carbon for synthesis of compatible cell solutes, but also, to some extent, provide the solutes themselves.

WATER STRESS AND SOIL ANIMALS

As with the soil microbial biomass, water stress also influences the size and activity of the soil animal community both because of reduction in water-filled pores and thickness of soil water films (which controls soil aeration, and the mobility of some animals), and because of the reduction in free energy of the water, making water uptake increasingly difficult.

There are very few soil animals that can survive in the soil for prolonged periods of drought although some components of the soil/animal community are particularly sensitive to water stress. Earthworm numbers and activity correlate closely with soil moisture levels (Lee, 1985), and shallow soils that tend to dry readily discourage earthworms. It has long been known that the production of earthworm casts, an excellent indicator of earthworm activity, is directly related to rainfall and soil moisture status. Enchytraeid worms are more tolerant to soil water stress than earthworms, although their numbers too have been correlated with extremes of soil moisture. Heavy mortality of enchytraeids during the summer months in pasture soils can almost certainly be attributed to soil water stress.

Soil animals with protective chitinous exoskeletons such as many of the soil arthropods (e.g. ants, myriapods and mites) tend to be much more resistant to soil water stress than the soil animals with exposed soft tissue such as the earthworms and the soil gastropods (slugs and snails), which tend to desiccate readily under dry conditions. Another feature of many drought-resistant soil animals is the development of a thick lipid layer in the cuticle.

Soil protozoa are generally sensitive to water stress and their numbers tend to decline with increasingly negative soil water potentials. There is, however, considerable variation among the different protozoa in terms of susceptibility to water stress. Ciliates, for example, are particularly sensitive to soil water stress. It appears that active growth of ciliates, such as *Colpoda steinii*, ceases when pores with neck diameter of 6 μm or greater become air filled (Darbyshire, 1976). Flagellates, however, tend to be much more tolerant of dry soil conditions.

Most soil protozoa require a continuous water film, considerably exceeding the thickness of their body, to facilitate their movement in the soil. Because some protozoa are greater than 80 μm across, even small reductions in soil moisture can have a marked effect on protozoa, with significant rates of protozoal activity (movement and grazing) being largely restricted to periods shortly after rainfall or irrigation when the soil is at or near field capacity.

Under conditions of soil water stress, protozoa may encyst. In this condition, they can survive periods of prolonged drought, only returning to the active trophozoite form when the soil is significantly rewetted. Nematodes can also encyst as a means of avoidance of soil water stress. The degree of tolerance of many of the soil microfauna to water stress is related to the effectiveness of their mechanism for encystment, and excystment, when favourable moisture levels are restored.

Another strategy of avoidance of soil water stress by soil animals is through movement down the soil profile to wetter soil conditions, a mechanism well known for earthworms.

The soil animals best adapted to water stress are, not surprisingly, those that are found in the most extreme conditions of water stress, the deserts. These organisms have phenomenally low transpiration rates and are able to take up water against massive, negative potential gradients.

CONCLUSIONS

Understanding the ecology of soil water stress, particularly with regard to adaptation of organisms and their associations, has never been more important. The problem of soil drought and salinity presents one of the greatest obstacles to enabling agriculture to meet the needs of the world's growing population and to predicting effects of climate change.

Although this chapter has detailed the response to water stress of each component of the soil biota, there is considerable interaction between these responses. The response of the microbe to soil water stress, for example, is intimately associated with those of plants and soil animals. In addition, water stress is rarely the only environmental stress affecting the soil biota in times of drought. Extremes of soil temperature may also be involved and it is difficult to factor out effects of temperature from those of water stress.

6 *Ecology of polluted soils*

INTRODUCTION

In 1985, the first international meeting on contaminated/polluted soil was held in the Netherlands, recognising the need to understand causal processes of soil pollution and to explore possible remedial procedures (Assink & van den Brink, 1986). Some of the chief pollutants of soils are detailed in Table 20, along with the main sources of these pollutants.

Soil pollution due to acid deposition and due to radionuclide deposition is of intense current interest and this chapter focuses on the ecology of these two forms of soil pollution.

ECOLOGY OF SOILS POLLUTED FROM ACID DEPOSITION

Introduction

A great deal of literature is available concerning the effects of acid rain on the biology and chemistry of soils. Many of the biological and chemical responses are interrelated and cannot realistically be considered separately. The most valuable research into the effects of acid deposition (and, indeed, most forms of soil pollution) on soils, therefore, is where an interdisciplinary approach is taken.

Effects of acid deposition on soil processes

The rates of a whole range of key soil biological processes can be affected (increased or decreased) as a result of acid deposition. These processes

Table 20. *Some agents of soil pollution and their main sources*

Agent of soil pollution	Main source
Heavy metals	Vehicle exhausts, sewage sludge, smelter and industrial effluents
Acid deposition	Emissions from burning fossil fuels
Oil	Oil transport and storage
Pesticides and associated residues	Farm-applied chemicals
Fluoride	Aluminium smelting
Gases such as methane, hydrogen sulphide, ethylene	Landfill degradation
Nitrate	Fertilisers and atmospheric inputs
Radionuclides	Nuclear waste and atmospheric inputs from reactor accidents
Polychlorinated biphenyls (PCBs)	Electrical insulators

include plant growth (Firestone *et al.*, 1984), soil respiration (Strayer & Alexander, 1981), leaf litter and cellulose breakdown (Hovland, 1981), degradation of pesticides (Francis, Olson & Bernatsky, 1980), soil urease activities (Pancholy, Rice & Turner, 1975), non-symbiotic N_2-fixation (Francis *et al.*, 1980), N-mineralisation (Strayer, Lin & Alexander, 1981), nitrification (Tamm, 1976), and denitrification (Firestone *et al.*, 1984). In addition, the degree of interaction in a number of plant/microbial associations in soil can be reduced by acid deposition. These include mycorrhizal associations (Ulrich & Pankrath, 1983), legume/rhizobial associations (Shriner & Johnston, 1981), and a range of host/parasite interactions involved in plant diseases (Shriner, 1978).

Factors controlling the extent of acid deposition effects

The extent of the effects of acid deposition will depend on the scale and anionic composition of the deposition, and on the physicochemical properties of the recipient soil environment, particularly the soil's buffering capacity.

(*a*) The scale of the acid deposition and its effect on soil biological activity will largely depend on proximity to sources of SO_2 and NO_x emissions and

Table 21. *Relationship between rainfall pH and the hydrogen ion loading per unit area of soil*

pH of rainfall	H^+ ion loading of soil $(kg\ ha^{-1})$
2	100.0
3	10.0
4	1.0
5	0.1

Modified from Likens, Bormann & Johnson, 1972.

on the physical nature (dry or wet, magnitude and duration of rain event etc.) of the deposition. Table 21 illustrates the logarithmic relationship between the pH of rainfall and the amount of protons incident on the soil.

Because of the massive increase in proton flux with increasing rain acidity, extrapolations from any experiments that greatly accelerate acid deposition to soil must be treated with extreme caution.

(b) The anionic composition of acid deposition (either dissolved in rainfall or in the soil solution) will greatly influence the effects on soil biological activity. The main anions, SO_4^{2-} and NO_3^- may vary greatly in their relative proportions and this must be considered when assessing potential effects of acid deposition on N-limited and, to a lesser extent, S-limited ecosystems. Tree uptake can often account for most of the N-input due to acid rain in sensitive areas, for example, although rarely accounts for much of the S-input because many of the soils have little available nitrogen, but can often be saturated with respect to sulphate.

(c) The soil's buffering capacity will largely depend on the parent material and the 'stage of evolution' of the soil. The buffering capacity of a soil comes from the nature and amount of sites for cation exchange in the soil. Exchange between protons (H^+), largely in the form of hydronium ions (H_3O^+), from the acidic deposition, and base cations on the surface of soil particles, leads to acidification when the base cations are subsequently leached away. Acid soils with organic and mineral colloids that have surface exchangeable cations (other than protons) with several positive charges (e.g. Al^{3+}, Fe^{3+}, Mn^{4+}) tend to allow only slow exchange (i.e. they are well buffered against further acidification) compared with soil colloids with surface cations of

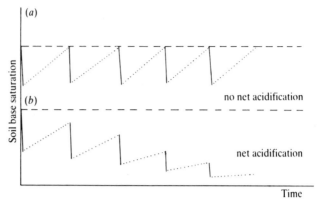

Figure 37. The soil's base saturation is reduced by inputs of acidity (such as through acid deposition) but may be wholly (*a*) or partly (*b*) replenished by mineral weathering. The solid line indicates the loss of base cations owing to acid input; the dotted line indicates replacement of base cations from mineral weathering.

predominantly only single or double charge (e.g. K^+, Na^+, Ca^{2+}), which have a much lower buffering capacity.

The base saturation (the percentage of the cation exchange capacity occupied by bases) of soil is being continually renewed by mineral weathering releasing more base cations to compete with the incoming protons for the exchange sites (Figure 37).

In time, if the overall buffering action of the soil is insufficient to enable neutralisation of the acids deposited (as acid rain or as dry deposition) or produced in the soil (carbonic acid from dissolution of carbon dioxide from biological respiration, acid mineral cations such as $Al(OH)_n^{(3-n)+}$, protons exchanged by plants and microbes in uptake of nutrient cations, oxidation of reduced nitrogen and sulphur, biological production of organic acids from decomposition etc.), then soil acidification will take place. This will be particularly evident in non-calcareous, coarse-textured (i.e. sandy) soils such as most podzols and dystric cambisols where there is little or no base-saturation/renewable input from mineral weathering to buffer against acidification.

Acid deposition and soil ecology–mechanisms of effects

Acid depositions to soil appear both to increase and reduce the rate of many biological processes. This is partly owing to varying sensitivities and susceptibilities of different processes, but also to the fact that acid depositions can have both (i), a 'stimulatory' and (ii), an 'inhibitory' effect on the soil biota. (i) Acid depositions provide an input of biologically available nutrients, particularly nitrogen (mainly in the form of both ammonium and nitrate) and sulphur (mainly in the form of sulphate). In soil systems where biological activity (plant, microbe, animal) is limited by either of these nutrients, therefore, an enhancement of soil biological activity may well result from the acid deposition (Killham, Firestone & McColl, 1983). (ii*a*) An input of protons to the soil is unlikely to inhibit directly the activity of most of the soil biota. Sometimes, components of the acid deposition may, however, be directly inhibitory. The bisulphite anion (HSO_3^-), for example, a solubility product of SO_2, may be present in acid rain and is highly toxic to soil bacteria and fungi (Babich & Stotzky, 1978). (ii*b*) Generally, most acid depositions, although unlikely to inhibit directly soil biological activity, may have a number of indirect, inhibitory effects. Acid depositions may, for example, be sufficient to mobilise toxic metal species in soil solution. Soil aluminium, and to a lesser extent manganese, can be mobilised in this way, both as free metal ions and as organic chelates, and a great many soil biological processes are highly sensitive to these mobilised metals. Fungal spore germination, for example, is particularly susceptible to inhibition by mobilised soil aluminium resulting from extreme acid depositions (Firestone, Killham & McColl, 1983). It does not require a change in bulk soil pH for mobilisation to occur. A localised, short-lived drop in soil pH, such as might occur in the surface layers of soil subjected to acid deposition, may be sufficient to cause transient mobilisation. The rhizosphere of some plants can be more acid than the bulk soil because of uptake of soil ammonium in exchange for protons. Transient pulses of pollutant-derived acidity in the rhizosphere, therefore, may be sufficient to cause mobilisation that would not occur in the bulk soil. Because the rhizosphere and surface layers of the soil are zones of high microbial, animal and root (particularly in some forest soils) activity, transient metal mobilisation may be sufficient to cause marked changes in a range of soil biological processes. It is still uncertain, however, whether acid-induced aluminium or manganese toxicity is the causal agent of reduced soil biological activity under field conditions and which metal species (organic chelates or metal ions) are the most biotoxic forms of the mobilised metals. Sometimes a range of heavy metals is deposited in association with acid deposition. This will be particularly true of pollution downwind of metal smelters where lead, copper, zinc and cadmium are often deposited. In general, low pH increases the bio-availability of heavy metals. The effects of mobilised heavy metal ions on different components of the soil biota are complex. Soil microorganisms, for example, show considerable variation in terms of heavy-metal tolerance (Gadd & Griffiths, 1978), with some soil bacteria such as the acidophilic thiobacilli having phenomenal tolerance to heavy metals such as copper and zinc (Tuovinen, Niemela & Gyttenberg, 1971). Mechanisms of tolerance vary from one metal to another and from one microbe to another. Sometimes, tolerant microbes exclude the toxic metal, whereas others have developed special means of detoxifying the metal once inside the cell. This may involve formation of a stable complex or the complete removal of the metal from the cell. (ii*c*) A second possible indirect, inhibitory effect of acid depositions to soil biological activity may result from acid-induced changes to soil organic matter availability, affecting the release of substrate for many soil heterotrophs. Soil acidification will be associated with reduced solubility of organic matter and with flocculation of many organic colloids. Acid deposition, therefore, may reduce substrate availability to heterophs, thereby inhibiting their activity in the soil.

Changes in the soil biota due to acid deposition

When soil biological processes are changed by acid deposition, this may be because of either a change in the size and composition of the soil biotic community, or because of a change in the activity of the soil biota or of the enzymes catalysing the process in question.

Increasing soil acidity is associated with a declining species composition of the soil microbial community (Francis *et al.*, 1980). Soil acidification tends to lead to an increase in the ratio of fungal biomass:bacterial biomass in soil, although this does not necessarily also apply to relative activities (Lohm, 1980). The autotrophic nitrifier community in soil has often been assumed to be particularly sensitive to acid deposition, although the evidence to support this is based only on experiments involving liquid cultures. Many of the fungi involved in interactions with growing plants are also thought to be acid sensitive, although evidence, again, however, comes from observations under soil-free conditions. More investigations are needed where the buffering effect of the soil is included.

Acid deposition has been correlated with changes to the activity of soil enzymes including dehydrogenase (catalysing total, terminal electron acceptance), urease (catalysing urea hydrolysis), phosphatase (catalysing the cleavage of phosphate from phosphate esters) and arylsulphatase (catalysing the cleavage of ester sulphate) (Killham *et al.*, 1983). A change in soil biological activity, rather than community size, due to acid deposition may result from increasing environmental stress causing an increase in the maintenance energy requirement of the soil organisms. Partitioning of carbon/energy into maintenance and into biosynthesis provides a very sensitive indicator of the short-term ecophysiological impact of acid deposition (or any other environmental stress) on the soil microbial community (Killham, 1985).

Changes to soil processes can occur as a result of acid deposition causing perturbations to components of the soil biota. It is probably more likely, however, that little net change to soil processes will have resulted from the replacement of the activity of sensitive species with that of species more tolerant to the acid deposition. This concept will probably hold true for all components of the soil biota including microbes, animals and plants.

Acid deposition and effects in the rhizosphere

In terms of effects on plant growth, the most important zone of the soil in response to acid deposition will be the rhizosphere. Unfortunately, because the nature of the rhizosphere varies considerably (in terms of pH relations, carbon flow, allelopathic effects etc.) from one plant to another, there can be few general rules concerning rhizosphere response to acid deposition. A number of effects on particular groups of plants have, however, been identified. This is particularly true for legumes where acid deposition can decrease nodulation (Shriner & Johnston, 1981). Reductions in non-symbiotic N_2-fixation due to acid deposition also occur when soils are pre-amended with glucose (Francis *et al.*, 1980), a situation analogous to the rhizosphere where the plant root supplies carbon to energy-demanding, free-living N_2-fixers such as *Azotobacter*.

Of considerable ecological importance are the effects of acid deposition on the mycorrhizal symbiosis and on rhizosphere pathogen activity because almost all terrestrial plants are involved in these types of association and their role in plant growth and ecosystem productivity is of paramount importance. There have been some suggestions that acid deposition may have a deleterious effect on the mycorrhizal symbiosis (Ulrich & Pankrath, 1983). Firm evidence of the effects of acid deposition on mycorrhizal associations, however, is scarce and particularly difficult to interpret because of other complicating factors such as the level of available phosphorus in the soil and the heavy-metal status of both the acid deposition and the soil itself (Killham & Firestone, 1983). Because of the host promiscuity of many mycorrhizal-forming fungi, it may often be that, where acid deposition inhibits colonisation of a root by one fungus, another can take over and occupy that niche. In some circumstances, the fungal mycobiont (especially septate fungi) of the association may even provide the plant with tolerance to soil acidity by complexing heavy metals in the fungal mycelium and preventing them reaching the host plant (Bradley, Burt & Read, 1981). In terms of pathogenic activity in the rhizosphere, acid deposition is thought to be an important factor. Simulated acid rain appears to reduce the incidence of soil-borne plant disease caused by fungi, bacteria and nematodes (Shriner, 1978). Acid rain, therefore is of relevance to almost every facet of microbial ecology.

Acid deposition and soil animals

Probably the most neglected aspect of studying the effects of acid deposition on soil ecology is the impact on the soil animals. The species composition of soil animals, however, can be greatly affected by high rates of acid deposition. Numbers of enchytraeid worms in forest-floor material are particularly reduced by acid deposition, whereas numbers of springtails tend to increase (Lohm, 1980). In one detailed study of the effects of simulated acid rain on the composition of the soil animal community, where numbers of enchytraeids were severely depleted by the acid treatments, concomitant increases in springtail numbers were entirely the result of an increase in abundance of one species, *Tullbergia krausbaueri* (Baath et al., 1980). Because of the importance of soil animals in the turnover of plant debris, any change in the population structure and activity of soil animals may have a marked effect on ecosystem productivity.

Conclusions

Probably more misleading information is available on the effects on acid deposition than on any other aspect of soil ecology. This is largely because of the difficulties in designing experiments and monitoring programmes which can predict the consequences of long-term, field exposure of soil to acid deposition. Greatest confidence should be placed in results obtained from long-term field studies that involve realistic rates of acid deposition and where an interdisciplinary (involving soil chemistry and soil biology – soil animals, microbes and plants) approach is taken to investigate effects.

ECOLOGY OF SOILS POLLUTED WITH RADIONUCLIDES

Introduction

The accidental release at Chernobyl, in April 1986, of long-lived radio-nuclides into the environment focused research interest on the behaviour of these radio-isotopes in the soil/plant system. An understanding of this behaviour is essential if we are to be able to predict the food chain, and ultimately, the human health impact of radionuclide deposition, accidental or otherwise.

As with acid deposition studies, research on the effects of radionuclide deposition requires an interdisciplinary approach, involving an under-standing of both the physicochemical and biological properties of the soil environment.

Dynamics of radionuclides in soil

The movement of pollutant radionuclides in soil will depend both on the isotopes involved and their concentration as well as on the physico-chemical nature of the recipient soil. Of particular concern after Chernobyl were the radionuclides ^{137}Cs and ^{90}Sr. Caesium-137 is a beta and gamma radiation emitter with a half-life of 30 years (^{134}Cs was also released as a result of Chernobyl but has a much shorter half life – 2 years). Strontium-90 is a beta emitter with a half-life of 28 years. Both ^{137}Cs and ^{90}Sr are products of nuclear fission reactions and are therefore regularly released into the environ-ment as a result of weapons testing, nuclear power production and nuclear fuel reprocessing (Haury & Schikarski, 1977). In April 1986, however, a massive release of these and other radionuclides occurred as a result of the reactor accident at Chernobyl. Parts of the UK received a total radionuclide deposition of more than 200 kBq m^{-2}, with levels of ^{137}Cs and ^{90}Sr being particularly high (Clark, 1986).

Caesium-137, a monovalent, alkali metal cation, behaves quite similarly to potassium in the soil/plant system, although its atomic radius is slightly greater than potassium. Strontium-90, a divalent cation, behaves similarly to calcium. Movement of these radionuclides through the soil will largely depend on the cation exchange capacity (CEC), the base composition/saturation of the cation exchange sites, and on the charge and hydrated ion radius of the radionuclide. Divalent radionuclides such as strontium, therefore, will tend to be more tightly held on exchange sites than monovalent radionuclides such as caesium.

Much of the radionuclide deposition of the UK from Chernobyl fell on upland areas where peat soils predominate. These soils, with very high CECs (often over 100 meq 100 g^{-1}) and generally low base saturation, will tend to favour exchange between protons and the radionuclides, particularly ^{90}Sr. Field surveys of organic forest soils (e.g. Carbol, Ittner & Skalberg, 1987) show that ^{137}Cs, which should be less strongly adsorbed to soil particles than ^{90}Sr, remains quite tightly held in the surface horizons with a 'half value' depth (i.e. the depth above which more than half of the isotope remains) after nearly 6 months of about 3 cm! Inputs of competing cations will tend to cause mobilisation of the radionuclides and render them available for biological uptake and cycling. Inputs of ammonium from animal wastes and inputs of calcium from liming, for example, will tend to desorb the radionuclides (particularly ^{137}Cs) from their exchange sites. Both these forms of input of competing cations commonly result from farming activities and will have a major bearing on radionuclide dynamics of soils under either pastoral or arable farming. Of course, in the case of arable farming, the physical disturbance of the soil through processes such as ploughing, may have an even greater effect on radionuclide movement in the profile.

In peats and other soils where the CEC is dominantly of organic origin, radionuclides will be held as insoluble organic chelates as well as simply by charge. In more mineral soils where CEC is clay based, radionuclides will be held by charge only. Clays can, however, hold radionuclides, particularly caesium, with great strength. This is because the caesium becomes trapped within the clay lattice preventing subsequent ion exchange with the soil solution. This type of interlayer fixation will be particularly strong in illitic clay minerals, micas, and biotites with vermiculites and montmorillonites being less effective.

Prediction of the fate of radionuclides in soils is essential ultimately to predict the behaviour of radionuclides at the food-chain and ecosystem level. Most modelling of radionuclide dynamics in soil relies on a weak empirical approach, based on measurement of solid–liquid distribution coefficients (K_0 values) and transfer factors between soil and vegetation. Values of these coefficients obtained under laboratory conditions, however, have little or no field value and progress must be made towards obtaining *in situ* values for these coefficients based on predictions from soil properties that are much more readily and reliably measured in the laboratory (Cremers *et al.*, 1988).

Cycling of radionuclides by the soil biota

Plants

Both caesium and strontium, being analogues of potassium and calcium, are highly 'bioactive' and are readily taken up by components of the soil biota, particularly if they are limited by these nutrients. Uptake will tend to be greater in peaty rather than mineral soils, partly because of the greater exposure of the exchange sites in the peat soils. Uptake will also tend to decrease as the clay content of the soil increases, as the capacity for clay fixation of radionuclides increases.

In the uplands of the UK where much of the Chernobyl deposition occurred, growth of the moorland vegetation on the widespread acid, peaty soils responds well to potassium. This would therefore suggest that radionuclides that are analogues of potassium such as caesium (and rubidium) will be readily taken up by moorland species such as heather (*Calluna vulgaris*).

Even vegetation types that are not so responsive to potassium will still require it as a macronutrient and so will take up significant levels of radionuclide analogues. Caesium-137, for example, was present in grass pasture in N.E. Scotland at levels of 10 to 20 Bq kg^{-1} four months after Chernobyl (Martin, Heaton & Robb, 1988). Transfer factors (these refer to the ratio of the specific activity of the radionuclide in the vegetation to the specific activity of that radionuclide in soil – both activities usually being measured in becquerels per kilogram) for caesium between 1.5 and 5 are likely for unimproved upland pastures, post-Chernobyl (Livens & Loveland, 1988).

As with plant uptake of soil nutrients, uptake and translocation (and hence release into above-ground food chains) of radionuclides is seasonal, being greatest in the spring and early summer. Of course uptake is also dependent upon plant species as well as on a whole variety of other plant variables, particularly the stage of development of the plant (Bell, Minski & Grogan, 1988).

Because of the high biological activity of radionuclides such as ^{137}Cs and ^{90}Sr, plant roots will almost certainly provide a major pathway for radio-nuclide movement in the soil profile. Uptake, translocation and then root decomposition/turnover will ensure a ready cycling of radionuclides within the rooting depth of most soils. As the rooting depth migrates through the soil profile during the growing season, so too will the zone of cycling of the radionuclides. How 'tightly' the radionuclides are cycled in the soil/plant system will largely depend on how cation retentive the soil is in terms of exchange/chelation and on the root system itself (Figure 38). Dense root systems such as under grassland vegetation will tend to be particularly effective in mediating this radionuclide cycling.

The period over which radionuclide cycling may be maintained in the soil/plant system will depend on a number of factors, but particularly on

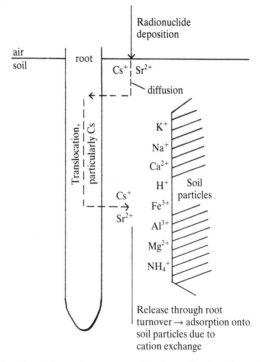

Figure 38. The root is an important vector for the soil migration of highly bioactive radionuclides such as caesium.

soil type. Peaty soils, which facilitate removal of the radionuclides from exchange sites more readily than many clay soils, may have active cycling for many years after initial deposition. Uptake and cycling of ^{137}Cs by *Calluna vulgaris*, for example, continued 20 years after deposition on moorland soils (Bunzl & Kracke, 1986).

The cycling of radionuclides by plants will, to some extent, be a function of the climatic conditions under which the plants are growing. For example, plants at a higher altitude will tend to take up greater amounts of radionuclides than those at lower altitudes and this is probably more related to the greater rainfall experienced by the plants than any differences in plant physiology.

Radionuclides in herbage grazed by higher animals will partly be retained by the animal but the bulk will be returned to the soil in animal wastes. The rapid breakdown of these wastes will further encourage the ready cycling of the radionuclides in the soil/plant system.

Because of the high rates of radionuclide uptake by some plants, the growth and removal of above-ground parts of such plants may have potential as part of a future strategy to rehabilitate contaminated soil after radionuclide deposition.

Mycorrhizas

We know that mycorrhizal fungal infection, particularly of the VAM type, can stimulate plant metal uptake in soils where phosphorus and the metals in question are sparingly available. Infection by VAM can enhance plant uptake of a vast range of trace and minor elements (Killham, 1985) as well as calcium (Tinker, 1978) and potassium (Bowen, 1984). The uptake of ^{90}Sr, a tracer analogue for calcium, is enhanced by VAM infection (Bowen, 1984). There is very strong circumstantial evidence, therefore, that VAM (and probably ectomycorrhizal) infection will enhance plant uptake and cycling of radionuclides, particularly ^{137}Cs and ^{90}Sr if they are deposited on an ecosystem as a result of accidental release. On this basis, the high phosphate status of fertilised arable soils may well minimise radionuclide uptake by crops from contaminated soil because high phosphate levels inhibit mycorrhizal development.

Soil microbes

Free-living microbes in the soil may be important agents of both movement and retention of radionuclides. Microbial cells will immobilise the radionuclides by both uptake and simple surface adsorption. Uptake of caesium may be particularly marked if the cells are potassium limited, because the radionuclide is an analogue of potassium. Surface adsorption will reflect the surface chemistry of the cells, but may be quite high because of the net negative charge on most cell walls. Microbial cells will also release immobilised radionuclides back into the soil through cation exchange of surface-adsorbed radionuclides and by osmoregulatory efflux of those in the cell cytoplasm, as well as by mineralisation reactions of organically complexed nuclides, on death of the cell. Microbes will also be involved in mobilisation of radionuclides in the soil itself through the breakdown of insoluble organic chelates holding the radionuclides.

As with plants, the potential for uptake and cycling of radionuclides by soil microbes, and by animals, will vary greatly from one organism to another. Free-living saprophytic fungi are strong accumulators of ^{137}Cs. Presumably, this accumulation is the result of mobilisation of the radionuclide during decomposition of organic matter and subsequent uptake is analogous to that of mineralised potassium. Ectomycorrhizal-forming Basidiomycotina fungi are also known to be good accumulators of ^{137}Cs (Haselwandter, 1978). Fruiting bodies of species of *Cortinarius*, *Rozites* and *Agaricus* can strongly accumulate this isotope. Radionuclide accumulation in the mycelium and fruiting bodies of Basidiomycotina has important ecological ramifications in terms of food-chain transport, because of the fundamental involvement of the ectomycorrhizal Basidiomycotina in the nutrition of their tree host, and also because the fruiting bodies represent a major food source for a number of soil animals and microbes, as well as above-ground animals such as deer.

Fungi, in association with blue-green algae in the lichen symbiosis, are strong accumulators of radionuclides such as ^{137}Cs on the soil surface and, as with fungal fruiting bodies, food-chain transport of radionuclides results because lichens are an important source of food for above-ground animals, particularly deer.

Soil animals

The contribution of the soil fauna is a key aspect of radionuclide cycling in the environment. The presence of soil animals can double the loss of caesium from contaminated litter, even though the fauna are expending only 1% of the total decomposer energy budget of the soil (Crossley & Witkamp, 1966). The presence of soil animals can also markedly change the time sequence of mineralisation/immobilisation of radionuclides from contaminated plant residues, particularly through temporary immobilisation (Malone & Reickle, 1973).

Probably the main role of the soil animals, particularly earthworms, in terms of radionuclide dynamics, is through their major contribution to the vertical and lateral mixing of soil. Because soil animals such as springtails graze fungal hyphae, particularly those associated with mycorrhizas, redistribution of grazed material with potentially high concentrations of radionuclides must play an important role in the cycling of these pollutants. Soil animals are also prey to many higher animals and so have a key function in the food chain transport of radionuclides.

Modelling of radionuclide movement in the soil/ plant system

Research on the movement and cycling of pollutant radionuclides in the soil/plant system will eventually lead to the construction of reliable models to enable effective prediction of the ecosystem fate of radionuclides. A simple mechanistic model predicting the fate of caesium in soil beneath grassland has been developed by Kirk & Staunton (1989), and is intended to expose areas where we lack the fundamental knowledge of caesium dynamics, rather than predict movement in real situations, largely because of the current scarcity of available data.

Conclusions

Much of the cycling of radionuclides in ecosystems is centred in the soil where plant roots, microbes and animals are all actively involved in the 'bio-mobilisation' and translocation of the radionuclides. The cycling of radionuclides in the soil/plant system must be understood to assess fully the impact of pollutant radionuclides on human health.

7 Manipulation of soil ecology – 'soil biotechnology'

INTRODUCTION

In recent years, a greater understanding of soil ecology has facilitated the emergence of a soil biotechnological revolution where biological components (plants, microbes and animals) of the soil/plant system are manipulated to increase plant (i.e. crop) productivity. These manipulations are increasingly involving genetic change although many can simply involve the selective introduction, control or removal of soil organisms.

The first microbial inoculum to be introduced into agricultural systems as a biofertiliser was almost certainly *Rhizobium*, the controlled use of rhizobial inocula dating back to the late nineteenth century.

BIOFERTILISATION BY RHIZOBIAL INOCULATION

Potential for inoculation – temperate and tropical agriculture

There are a variety of N_2-fixing legumes currently used in temperate agriculture. The 'grain legumes' include broad beans (*Vicia faba*), peas (*Pisum sativum*), runner and haricot beans (*Phaseolus* spp.) and lupins (*Lupinus* spp.). The 'forage legumes' include a variety of clovers (*Trifolium* spp.), lucerne or alfalfa, and medics (*Medicago* spp.), fenugreek or birdsfoot trefoil (*Trifolium ornithopodioides*), lotus (*Lotus*) and vetches (*Vicia* spp.). For most of these legumes, rhizobial inoculation is not required. Broad beans, for example, fix an average of 200 kg N ha^{-1} y^{-1} in the UK (Nutman, 1976) and the nodules generally function satisfactorily without inoculation (Cooper, Hill-Cottingham & Lloyd-Jones, 1976). Lucerne (or alfalfa) on the other hand, however, shows considerable potential for improved fixation/production from rhizobial inoculation.

In tropical agriculture, the potential for improved crop productivity from rhizobial inoculation is generally much higher than for temperate systems. Crops such as soybeans (*Glycine max.*), peanuts (*Arachis hypogea*) and mung beans (*Vigna radiata*) are good examples of tropical legumes that can benefit enormously from rhizobial inoculation.

In general, inoculation will be most effective when the soil's indigenous rhizobia are either ineffective or present in insufficient numbers to provide a reasonable inoculum. An extreme case of this latter problem can be found in Australia where native populations of rhizobia are often completely absent. Similar situations may also exist when previously barren soils, such as in arid areas, are brought into cultivation. These types of situation contrast sharply with temperate agricultural soils, which can have an indigenous rhizobial population of about one hundred thousand per gram.

Rhizobial effectiveness and inoculum production

It is not always clear why a legume planted in some soils is not adequately nodulated by the indigenous soil microbiota. It seems that these soils often contain few effective rhizobia, often more than half of the population having a moderate or low degree of effectiveness.

Although sound ecological principles indicate that the indigenous microbial population of a soil should be better adapted to the particular soil conditions than most inocula, an inoculum can be introduced in a more viable and effective state and at higher cell densities than the indigenous population of rhizobia. For large legume seeds such as those of soybean, inocula are only really effective with about 1 million viable cells per seed. Sometimes single strain inocula are used, whereas sometimes multiple strains are preferred. The latter tends to be more effective over a broader range of crop and soil conditions. The most common method of inoculum introduction is to incorporate the rhizobial cells with a carrier that can act as a sort of coating for the legume seeds as they are sown. This coating may often be peat, clay, or peat-charcoal based, and enables both prolonged survival of the inoculum (both in storage and in the field) and close contact between legume seed and inoculum. Sometimes, the carrier is stuck to the seed with gum arabic or similar resinous compounds as a true seed coating, sometimes applied in granules, and sometimes sprayed into the seed furrow as a slurry suspension. Crop response to these rhizobial inoculation procedures is greatest when the soil is first planted with a particular legume.

Factors affecting inoculum success

Factors affecting inoculum success include considerations at all stages of inoculum use – strain selection, culturing of the strain, carrier preparation, mixing of the culture and carrier, maturation, storage, transport and application.

Figure 39 demonstrates the main factors that determine the success of a microbial inoculum in soil. A key factor in the success of a rhizobial inoculum will be the level of moisture at which the cells are maintained. This is particularly important in tropical latitudes where desiccation of cells must be avoided until the infection of the legume can occur. Rhizobia are not tolerant to water stress compared to most other soil bacteria and fall into Class 2 in terms of their osmoregulatory strategy (see Chapter 5, pages 160–4). The peat or clay rhizobial carrier must remain moist prior to sowing. After sowing, the water potential regime of the recipient soil will be a fundamental factor in determining inoculum success. Other important factors determining inoculum success include soil temperature, diffusates from legumes and/or other higher plants, microbial antagonism, bacteriophage activity, microbial parasitism and protozoan predation (Nutman, 1971).

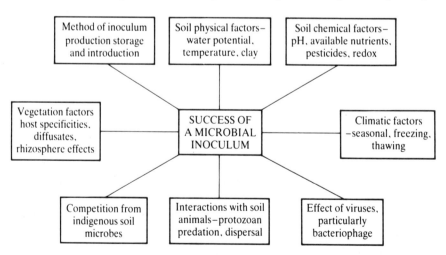

Figure 39. Factors affecting the success of a microbial inoculum in soil.

In many soils, acidity will also play an important part in determining the survival and success of an inoculum. In acid soils, it is generally the high availability of aluminium that provides the biggest problem for the soil biota. Liquid culture growth of cowpea rhizobia and *R. japonicum* is markedly reduced by 50 µM aluminium at pH 4.5. More relevant, however, is to study the effect of aluminium and acidity when the rhizobia are in the presence of the host legume (Andrew, 1978). This approach shows that pH 4.3 can cause death of a rhizosphere population of *R. trifolii* but does not affect root elongation or root hair formation of white clover (*Trifolium repens*) (Wood, Cooper & Holding, 1983). Many legumes, therefore, may not be nodulated by rhizobia in acid soils, largely the result of the high susceptibility of rhizobia to aluminium. The presence of growing roots has a considerable bearing on the survival of rhizobial inocula in soils. Enhanced growth and survival of rhizobia in the rhizosphere is not just restricted to legumes, and even non-leguminous root systems may equally stimulate the rhizobia.

Successful inoculation of a legume may be hampered because of the poor nutrition of the legume itself. Legumes tend to have restricted root systems and are poor nutrient foragers. This is particularly true for phosphorus, which is deficient in most tropical soils. Improved inoculation will often result from either additions of phosphate fertiliser or from VAM infection. Once VAM fungal inocula can be effectively produced, perhaps a combined VAM/rhizobial inoculum will be most effective for tropical legumes.

The soil factors that influence the survival and success of rhizobial inocula are not likely to act independently. For example, there is a strong interaction between soil moisture status and soil temperature (Danso & Alexander, 1975) and the strength of this interaction is modified by the clay content of the soil environment.

Improvement of rhizobial inocula

Considerable research effort is being made into improving the success of rhizobial inocula (Hodgson & Stacey, 1987). Improving rhizobial tolerance to aluminium would certainly seem to be one potentially useful inoculum characteristic. Clues as to how to achieve this may well come from studying the characteristics of strains of rhizobia that have a naturally high tolerance to aluminium.

The ability of the inoculum to lay dormant in the soil or its capacity to produce chemical inhibitors (ammensalism) selective against the indigenous rhizobial population may prove to be the most effective changes to the genetics of the rhizobial inoculum to ensure effective inoculation (Parker, Trinick & Chatel, 1977). Before genetic manipulation of inocula, a greater understanding of soil ecology, rather than of plant/microbial genetics, is required. A great deal more must be known of how soil microbes grow (in the presence of competition) in the rhizosphere of plants, particularly legumes, and of the nature of saprophytic competence, to establish the criteria to ensure persistence of a rhizobial inoculum in the complex and variable soil environment.

Perhaps the most exciting development in N_2-fixation research will come from the possibility of transferring the ability to fix nitrogen from a fixing organism to a non-fixing organism. The genes involved in N_2-fixation by rhizobia include structural *nif* genes for the nitrogenase enzyme, genes for N_2-fixation itself, genes for nodulation, genes for root hair curling, genes for host specificity and genes for nodulation efficiency. The genes involved may be transferred either as a DNA fragment, borne on chromosomal-free plasmids, or perhaps in a whole cell with the cell wall removed (i.e. 'L-forms'). With these aims, clone banks of plasmids that contain clustered *nif* genes have been established (e.g. Singh & Klingmuller, 1986). The plasmids have been isolated from non-symbiotic N_2-fixing bacteria. This genetic engineering is far from the end of the story – it must also be discovered how the new genes can be expressed in the recipient host organism (plant or microbe). Clearly, incorporation of genes for nitrogen fixation into a host must be facilitated by suitable allocation of substrate/energy during periods of active fixation. Apart from these fundamental biochemical considerations, it is also necessary to assess the soil ecological ramifications of the 'new' organism. This is discussed more fully on pages 208–11.

CONTROL OF THE SOIL BIOTA

Pesticidal control

Introduction and definitions

Improved crop yields in world agriculture in the past few decades are probably more the result of pesticidal applications than any other management practice.

A pesticide is any agent that controls one or more pest populations.

Most modern pesticides are chemicals, broadly classified according to their target population (e.g. herbicides, control weeds; fungicides, control fungi; insecticides, control insects etc.).

In addition to removing or controlling target pests in the soil/crop system, pesticides in some way applied to the soil can change the soil ecological balance either by directly affecting non-target soil organisms or by changing the soil's physico-chemical characteristics, which in turn dictates the composition of the soil biota.

Target effects and selectivity

Pesticides can be targeted against many different components of the soil biota (Table 22), although all these agrochemicals will ultimately be broken down and detoxified by the the soil microbial biomass. In some cases, the pesticide is applied directly to the soil, whereas in others the pesticide may be applied to crop foliage. In the latter situation, the pesticide may enter the soil as a result of throughfall or stemflow from the plant, from translocation through the plant to the soil, via the plant roots, or as a result of plant residues entering the soil.

Some pesticides are not intended to be highly selective and have a broad soil organism target range, whereas others are highly selective.

Herbicides

Amongst the herbicides, for example, the widely used 'glyphosate' (Table 22) is a non-selective, post-emergence herbicide. It controls almost all annual and perennial weeds through a variety of possible mechanisms such as reductions in chlorophyll and carotenoid, and increases in ethylene and cellulase activity (Ashton & Crafts, 1981). It is also systemic, meaning it is a pesticide that penetrates deep into plant tissue. The systemic herbicide 2,4-D (2,4-dichlorophenoxyacetic acid) was introduced to be selective against broad-leaved weeds (dicotyledons). It is a 'hormone' herbicide and its mode of action is similar to that of natural plant auxins, promoting cell elongation, so that treated plants show lethally abnormal growth. 'Paraquat' (Table 22) is an example of a non-selective, contact herbicide. Paraquat is active in the presence of light and oxygen; the molecule is reduced to radical ions with associated production of hydrogen peroxide. The peroxide kills the plant through peroxidation of the lipids in the cell membranes. Contact pesticides, like Paraquat, differ from systemic compounds in that they do not markedly penetrate plant tissue.

Table 22. *Some major pesticides and their target soil populations*

Pesticide type	Pesticide (structure)	Target population
INSECTICIDES	Malathion CH_3-O and CH_3-O linked to P (=S) $-S-C-C-OC_2H_5$ with branch $H_2C-C(=O)-OC_2H_5$	Aphids[a], mites, thrips, etc.
	DDT $Cl-$⟨ring⟩$-CH-$⟨ring⟩$-Cl$ with CCl_3	Mosquito larvae
FUNGICIDES	Captan cyclohexene ring fused with imide, $NSCCl_3$, two O	Many moulds (e.g. *Botrytis*) scabs (e.g. *Venturia*) rots (e.g. *Gloeasporium*) rusts (e.g. *Puccinia*) and blights (e.g. *Phytophthora*)
	Carboxin H_3C, ring with O and S, C_6H_5NHCO	Cereal rusts, smuts and bunts (all Basidiomycotina) *Rhizoctonia solani*
HERBICIDES	2,4-D $Cl-$⟨ring, Cl⟩$-OCH_2COOH$	Broad-leaved weeds (dicotyledons)
	Glyphosate $(CHO)_2\overset{O}{\overset{\|}{P}}CH_2NHCH_2CO_2H)$	Broad-leaved weeds and grasses (dicotyledons + monocotyledons)
	Paraquat $\left[CH_3-N⟨ring⟩⟨ring⟩N-CH_3\right]^{2+} 2Cl^-$	Broad-leaved weeds and grasses
NEMATICIDES	Nellite CH_3NH and CH_3NH linked to P (=O) $-O-$⟨ring⟩	Nematodes

Table 22 (*continued*)

Pesticide type	Pesticide (structure)	Target population
MOLLUSCICIDES	Methiocarb	slugs and snails
ACARICIDES	Mitac	Mites and scale insects

a Non-soil organisms.

Fungicides

As with herbicides, fungicides vary greatly in their selectivity and in terms of their systemic properties. Almost all fungicides, however, must be non-phytotoxic. 'Captan' (Table 22) is a non-selective, non-systemic fungicide that reacts with any sulphydryl compound (Figure 40*a*). Reaction with any sulphydryl groups (cellular thiols) produces toxic thiophosgene, which poisons the fungal cell. Many soil fungi may be affected when, as a result of folial spraying of horticultural plants, captan enters the soil. Further soil ecological consequences of Captan entering soil are considered in the section on 'non-target' effects (pages 193–5).

The oxathiin group of heterocyclic fungicides provide an example of a selective, systemic fungicide. 'Carboxin' and 'oxycarboxin' (Table 22) are oxathiins primarily designed to control soil-borne Basidiomycotina diseases (e.g. rusts, bunts and smuts) of cereals. These fungicides interfere with succinate oxidation through inactivation of succinate dehydrogenase, which forms part of the Krebs cycle (Corbett, 1974). Succinate, therefore, accumulates in fungicide-treated Basidiomycotina cells (Figure 40*b*). Carboxin and oxycarboxin are also selective against a pathogen of roots of many seedlings and the causal agent of 'bare-patch' in cereals, the soil fungus

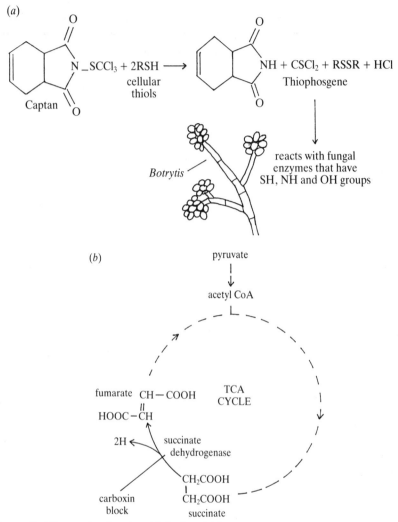

Figure 40. The mode of action of the fungicides captan (*a*) and oxathiins such as carboxin (*b*).

Rhizoctonia solani. It seems that the selective uptake of oxathiins by Basidiomycotina and the imperfect fungus *R. solani* is linked to their lipid content. Electron microscopy of these sensitive fungi shows that the fungicide damages the mitochondria and vacuolar membrane causing respiratory inhibition at the site of succinate dehydrogenase (Marsh, 1977).

The selectivity of some fungicides, such as that of the oxathiins against

Basidiomycotina, suggests they have great potential value in mycorrhizal research as a means of inhibiting the mycobiont while not significantly affecting the free-living soil microbial populations. This is just one example of where pesticides may have an important role to play in soil ecological research, as well as in their use as agrochemicals.

Insecticides

A whole host of soil animals that are known to cause crop diseases, particularly associated with roots, are treated with insecticides. Most of these insecticides are organophosphorus compounds such as 'malathion' (Table 22). Malathion is a non-selective, non-systemic insecticide and its mode of action is shown below.

$$\text{Malathion} \xrightarrow[\substack{\text{(oxidative} \\ \text{desulphuration)}}]{\text{activation}} \text{Malaoxon} \xrightarrow[\substack{\text{(carboxyesterase} \\ \text{activity)}}]{\substack{\text{mammalian} \\ \text{detoxification}}} \substack{\text{excretion} \\ \text{products}}$$

Although Malathion is rapidly activated to Malaoxon through oxidative desulphuration by most soil insects and mammals (Fukuto & Sims, 1971), the soil and other mammals are able to detoxify Malaoxon to water-soluble excretion products through carboxyesterase activity. Malathion is therefore active against soil insects because of their comparatively low carboxyesterase activities. DDT (Table 22) is an insecticide initially developed for control of the malarial mosquito. Although no longer used is many countries, its non-target activity has ensured that the soil ecological ramifications of its use are still being felt. These are discussed as non-target effects of pesticides on pages 193–5.

Pesticidal control of soil processes

Urease activity Costly losses of nitrogen in agricultural systems that receive either urea fertiliser or manures are partly caused by excessively high rates of urea hydrolysis, catalysed by the soil enzyme urease. The nitrogen loss is largely the result of volatilisation of the ammonia formed by the urea hydrolysis. This gaseous loss can often account for more than 50% of the applied fertiliser (Terman, 1979). Losses tend to be highest in tropical situations where urea/manure is often applied to soil under hot, dry conditions. Very high rates of ammonia volatilisation are not only indicative of fertiliser N-loss, but may also cause crop damage. The dramatic increase in the use of urea as a nitrogen fertiliser over recent years, coupled with the known high N-losses associated with urea application, has focused research on developing pesticides to effectively control the rate of urea hydrolysis in soil.

Although many compounds have been patented as urease inhibitors over the last few years, most have proved ineffective (Mulvaney & Bremner, 1981) and only a few have shown real promise. These include the phosphoroamides phenylphosphorodiamidate (PDD) (Martens & Bremner, 1984) as well as N-butylphosphorothioic triamide (NBPT) and N-(diaminophosphinyl)-cyclohexylamine (DPCA).

A second approach to minimising loss of nitrogen from urea fertilisers has been the use of slow-release fertilisers such as ureaform, which is a reaction product of urea and formaldehyde. Ureaform consists of a methylene urea polymer of much lower solubility than urea alone. Sulphur-coated urea is another type of slow-release urea fertiliser. In both cases, the slower dissolution of the urea enables the crop to compete more effectively for the released fertiliser nitrogen.

Nitrification   A range of compounds are now available for the inhibition of nitrification in soil. The aim of their use is to control the nitrification process in order to couple it closely with the rate of nitrate uptake by the plant root. This coupling both ensures the most efficient N-fertilisation/nutrition of the plant and minimises the environmental pollution that can result from excessive nitrification – nitrate not taken up by the plant may be subject to leaching into ground and surface waters, as well as to possible denitrification under anaerobic soil conditions.

The main approach to reducing the potential environmental problems associated with the use of ammonium-based nitrogen fertilisers and to increase the recovery of fertiliser nitrogen by crops has been to use compounds that will effectively inhibit the oxidation of ammonium to nitrite by the microbial nitrifiers in soil. Most compounds tested have not been found to be effective inhibitors (Mulvaney & Bremner, 1981), with only nitrapyrin ('N-serve'), dicyandiamide ('DCD-didin') and etridiazole ('dwell') showing considerable promise.

Acetylene has been found to be an effective inhibitor of ammonium oxidation in soils (Walter, Keeney & Fillery, 1979) and this method of blocking has been used by soil microbiologists worldwide as a means of characterising soil nitrogen dynamics. Non-gaseous, substituted acetylene compounds such as phenylacetylene (C_6H_5C:CH) and ethynylpyridine (C_5H_4N)C:CH, therefore, may prove to be successful soil nitrification inhibitors in the field.

Carbon disulphide has been shown to strongly inhibit nitrification. Compounds such as xanthates and thiocarbamates, which release carbon disulphide, may, therefore, be cheap and effective nitrification inhibitors.

Combined pesticidal control of urease and nitrification Ideally, pesticides are needed that are effective controllers of both urease activity and nitrification in soil although, to date, the most potent inhibitors of nitrification have proved to be ineffective urease inhibitors and vice versa.

Non-target effects of pesticides in soils

Ideally, whether pesticides are selective or broad spectrum, they should have few, if any, non-target effects on the soil biota. Generally, pesticides that tend to have most non-target effects are inevitably those that are most mobile in the soil/plant environment. Systemic fungicides, for example, because they are readily translocated by the plant, may affect non-target soil fungi in the rhizosphere as well as the target fungal disease. The mycobiont of the mycorrhizal symbiosis may be particularly at risk from this type of crop treatment. Some systemic plant growth regulators are also strongly fungicidal and may, also, adversely affect the mycorrhizal symbiosis as well as free-living, rhizosphere soil fungi.

The rhizosphere, because of its chemical dependence on the plant, is a key zone for non-target effects of foliar applied chemicals. These effects may be a direct result of leakage of the molecule from the root system or of some indirect effect such as the chemical causing a change in rhizosphere C-flow. Non-target effects in the rhizosphere may involve free-living and symbiotic organisms and must be monitored to assess the impact of a pesticide on soil ecology (Greaves & Malkomes, 1980).

Sometimes, non-target effects of a particular pesticide have wide soil ecological ramifications. The application of the fungicide Captan, for example, can have detrimental effects on soil rhizobial populations. Nodulation of legumes can be reduced or even totally prevented by this type of organic fungicide and, as a result, the use of Captan is largely restricted to horticulture, where its application can be tightly controlled.

The use of radio-labelled herbicides and insecticides has shown that many of these compounds, which are applied as foliar sprays to plants, are readily translocated to the roots where they are exuded into the soil (Hale, 1978). Many foliar-applied pesticides may, therefore, be having marked non-target effects in the rhizosphere and these may have considerable soil eco-logical ramifications through changes to plant/microbe, plant/animal and plant/plant interactions.

Extreme non-target effects

Possibly the most extreme non-target effects of a pesticide have been through the use of the insecticide DDT, an organochlorine insecticide developed some 50 years ago for the control of malarial mosquitoes.

The soil ecological and other environmental consequences of DDT applications resulted from the fact that, although DDT is relatively insoluble in water, it is much more soluble in fats. This caused DDT to accumulate particularly in animals with fatty tissues. In North America, DDT applications exceeding 30 kg ha^{-1} were used to control the beetle carrying Dutch Elm Disease. Much of this DDT entered the soil and was accumulated, in particular, in the fatty tissues of soil and other animals, leading to a number of serious food-chain effects. These effects were the main reason why DDT, and the closely related insecticide Dieldrin, have now ceased to be used in many countries.

Plant nurseries often practise soil fumigation to prevent pathogenic attack of vulnerable and expensive seedlings. These fumigants such as chloropicrin and carbon disulphide tend temporarily to suppress most of the soil microbial and animal community, although numbers (particularly of soil microbes) tend to recover quickly.

In general, it is the soil fumigants, nematocides and fungicides that are general toxins that cause the most widespread non-target effects, whereas most insecticides and herbicides (under normal application rates) tend to have much fewer non-target effects.

Susceptibility of the soil biota to non-target effects

Some components of the soil biota are more susceptible to non-target effects than others. Nematodes, fungi and nitrifying bacteria are most readily killed by pesticides, whereas spore-forming bacteria and some actinomycetes are more tolerant.

Ideally, pesticides applied to soil, or these entering the soil indirectly, should be highly selective against target pests, with no obvious non-target effects. This is near impossible, although research must continue to refine pesticide selectivity.

Pesticide dynamics in soil

In some cases, non-target effects and movement of pesticides in soil are restricted by strong binding of the pesticide on to soil particles. This is the case for the herbicide Paraquat (1,1′-dimethyl-4,4′-dipyridylium dichloride; see Table 22). Paraquat dissociates to form a cation in soil solution and so is held by cation exchange to negatively charged surfaces such as clays. It is the covalent bonding of the molecule to soil particles that gives Paraquat its great binding strength and ensures that the herbicide is rapidly deactivated in soil. Paraquat is particularly strongly held in soils with a high clay content because the planar nature of the molecule enables it to fit into clay interlayers where it is very strongly held by covalent bonding.

Processes controlling the movement of pesticides in soil

Unfortunately, many pesticides are not deactivated in soil as readily as Paraquat. The proportion of a pesticide application that leaches to ground water is the result of a number of processes that occur in the soil, as follows. (*a*) Transformations including photochemical processes at the soil surface as well as microbial and chemical transformations in the soil. Generally, the fraction of a pesticide leached from the soil decreases with increasing rate of transformation. One therefore expects persistent pesticides to leach more than labile pesticides. (*b*) Plant uptake – systemic pesticides will tend to be readily taken up by the plant root. The extent of this uptake will largely depend on the development of the root system and the bioavailability of the pesticide. (*c*) Distribution and transport: pesticides with a high sorption coefficient (e.g. Paraquat) will tend not to be subject to movement whereas those with a lower sorption coefficient (e.g. substituted urea herbicides) will be more readily mobilised. Movement of pesticides through soils occurs both by diffusion and mass flow. Although diffusion can be the dominant form of herbicide transport in soil, movement via mass flow is generally responsible for the most widespread distribution of pesticides through soils. Transport of non-sorbed pesticides and residues by mass flow will largely depend on the hydraulic properties of the soil and the extent to which rainfall or irrigation exceeds evapotranspiration.

Persistent pesticides with poor sorption properties in soil will tend to be moved through soil into ground and surface waters most readily, particularly in freely draining soils and especially after significant events of rainfall/irrigation. More basic research, however, is required to develop a detailed understanding of the movement of pesticides and residues into ground/surface waters to ensure the acceptable quality of drinking water supplies.

Biological control

Introduction

It is becoming increasingly recognised that many of the pesticides traditionally used for the control of crop pests can cause a range of deleterious effects in the environment. Although chemicals are continually being developed to reduce this environmental risk, an alternative strategy may be required. The use of organisms as biocontrol agents may provide such a strategy and this area of biotechnology offers considerable promise.

A wide range of biological control agents have been identified, although many more remain to be discovered. The key target environment for biological control in the soil is the rhizosphere as it represents the zone where plant infection/attack occurs.

Biological control in the rhizosphere

Control of plant pests in the rhizosphere has been associated with a range of soil bacteria and fungi. These organisms readily appear to utilise rhizodeposited carbon and successfully colonise the rhizosphere. In the case of bacteria, the term 'rhizobacteria' is used to describe aggressive colonisers of the rhizosphere. Most rhizobacteria are Gram-negative.

Improved plant growth due to the introduction of rhizobacteria and rhizosphere-colonising fungi may be caused by a variety of mechanisms, including biological control of pests. In the case of bacteria, the term 'plant-growth-promoting rhizobacteria' or 'PGPR' is used when any beneficial effects on plant growth result from bacterial activity in the rhizosphere. It is clearly difficult, if not impossible, to assess whether plant growth promotion results from biological control of plant pests or some other mechanism such as the production of plant-growth promoting chemicals.

Soil ecology of biological control

Where biological control is identifiable through the rhizosphere activity of bacterial and fungal inocula, the mechanisms of biocontrol may involve a variety of interactions between the control agent and the indigenous soil-borne pest.

Biocontrol by soil bacteria Strains of the bacterium *Arthrobacter* parasitise the plant pathogenic fungi *Fusarium* and *Pythium* by production of enzymes, such as chitinases, which lyse the cell walls of the fungi (Sneh, 1981). In the case of pseudomonad control of seedling infection by the damping-off fungus *Pythium ultimum*, control is thought to be achieved by competition for infection sites (Osburn *et al.*, 1989). The control with fluorescent pseudomonads of 'take-all' of wheat caused by the soil fungus *Gaeumannomyces graminis*, appears linked to an ammensalistic strategy involving antibiotic suppression of the pathogen (Weller, Howie & Cook, 1988).

Biocontrol by soil fungi Control of *Pythium ultimum* by the fungus *Gliocladium virens* has been linked to the production of glyovirin, a diketo-piperazine antibiotic (Howell & Stripanovic, 1983). Ammensalism is also considered to be the mechanism of control by *Trichoderma harzianum* of a broad range of soil-borne plant pathogenic fungi including *Rhizoctonia solani*. The antagonist produces alkyl pyrones, volatiles that appear to act as paramorphagens to assist in penetration of the pathogen (Claydon & Allan, 1987). Competition for infection sites has been proposed as the mechanism by which *Pythium nunn* inhibits the activity of the pathogen *P. ultimum* (Paulitz & Baker, 1988).

Biological control can be achieved through 'induced resistance', where the rhizosphere is inoculated with a weakly virulent, plant pathogenic fungus (Kuc, 1985). After being challenged by the fungus, the plant develops the capacity for future, effective response to more virulent attack. Control of pathogens can also result from use of weakly virulent or hypovirulent strains of the pathogen (Griffin, 1986), through interaction of the fungal hyphae, the hypovirulent characteristics being transferred, with overall reduction in pathogenicity.

Control of nematode pests by mycoparasitism has been documented for many soil fungi (Gray, 1988). *Harposporium*, for example, parasitises nematodes both externally and internally through germination of adsorbed conidia.

Although ammensalism, competition and parasitism (and to a lesser extent, inferred resistance and hypovirulence) will generally be the dominant mechanisms of biological control other, more indirect, factors may also play a part. It may be, for example, that a degree of biocontrol results from the production of iron-chelating substances, or siderophores. These metabolites are produced in order to enable microbes to take up ferric iron (Fe^{3+}) as an organic complex that is available through recognition by specific membrane receptors. Siderophore production will reduce the availability of iron to other rhizosphere microbes, including plant pathogens.

When a potential biological control agent is identified, its soil ecology must be thoroughly characterised. Many aspects to be tested are similar to those for potential chemical pesticides. Pathogen and plant response, effects on non-target organisms, as well as persistence and dispersal in soil, must all be characterised both for environmental considerations and to assess the efficacy of biological control.

Ultimately, the full potential of biological control may only be realised through identification of the molecular basis of the control mechanisms so that genetic modifications can be carried out both to enhance the efficacy of control and to introduce the trait into different organisms (see pages 205–6).

BIOFERTILISATION BY MYCORRHIZAL FUNGAL INOCULATION

Potential benefits of mycorrhizal fungal inoculation

The potential benefits of mycorrhizal fungal inoculation for biofertilising arable and forest crops are very considerable. Some of the plant host responses to mycorrhizal fungal infection, and hence some of the possible benefits of an effective inoculation programme, are outlined in Table 23. These benefits to the plant host range from enhanced nutrient uptake, through increased tolerance of the host to environmental stresses such as soil water stress and heavy-metal toxicity, to enhanced resistance to many of the soil-borne pathogenic microbes.

With a trend towards less intensive agriculture in the UK and much of Europe, the associated application of lower levels of fertilisers and pesticides should increase the importance of mycorrhizal associations of crops, both in terms of enhancing crop nutrient uptake from soil, and also of combatting

Table 23. *Known plant host responses to mycorrhizal fungal infection*

Host response	Mycorrhizal association	Reference
↑ N-uptake	ectomycorrhizas	Rygiewicz *et al.*, 1984
↑ P-uptake	ectomycorrhizas	Bowen, 1973
	endomycorrhizas	Hayman & Mosse, 1972
↑ K-uptake	ectomycorrhizas and endomycorrhizas	Lamb & Richards, 1971
↑ S-uptake	endomycorrhizas	Rhodes & Gerdemann, 1978
↑ root phosphatase	ectomycorrhizas	Bartlett & Lewis, 1973
↑ trace and minor element uptake	ectomycorrhizas endomycorrhizas	Bowen, 1973 Killham, 1985
↑ drought tolerance	ectomycorrhizas endomycorrhizas	Bowen, 1973 Safir *et al.*, 1971
↑ resistance to extreme temperatures	endomycorrhizas	Marx & Krupa, 1978
↑ heavy-metal tolerance	endomycorrhizas	Bradley *et al.*, 1981
↑ resistance to soil toxins	endomycorrhizas	Marx & Krupa, 1978
↑ resistance to soil-borne pathogens	ectomycorrhizas and endomycorrhizas	Marx, 1973 Graham & Menge, 1982
↑ root longevity	ectomycorrhizas and endomycorrhizas	Harley & Smith, 1983
inter-plant nutrient transfer	endomycorrhizas and ectomycorrhizas	Read *et al.*, 1985
↑ N₂-fixation (legumes and other hosts only)	ectomycorrhizas and endomycorrhizas	Bowen, 1984

soil-borne crop disease. Mycorrhizally infected plants can also be linked via their mycorrhizal fungal hyphae and these links can provide the means of inter-plant transfer of photosynthate and other nutrients (Whittingham & Read, 1982). Inter-plant transfer for both ectomycorrhizal and VAM systems has been demonstrated and the suggestion made that these mycorrhizal pathways facilitate nutrient conservation at the ecosystem level (Read *et al.*, 1985). In arable situations, however, mycorrhizal fungal transfer of nitrogen from legumes to non-legumes is unlikely to offer a realistic alternative to conventional fertilising (Figure 41). This is because the transfer is unlikely

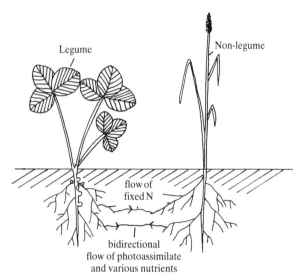

Figure 41. VAM-mediated flow of nitrogen between legumes and non-legumes via hyphal connection of roots.

to make a major contribution to the overall N-nutrition of the non-legume, because the high concentrations of available phosphorus (and other nutrients) often associated with arable soils will suppress mycorrhizal infection, and because many non-leguminous crops are not strongly mycotrophic. More research is required, however, to identify the full significance of nutrient transfer strategies between plants with a common mycorrhizal network.

Successful production and application of mycorrhizal fungal inocula presents a great challenge both to the microbiologist and to the soil ecologist, because of the need not only to mass produce pure cultures of the fungi but also to understand the complexity of soil ecological factors that determine the success of the inoculum in the field or nursery soil.

Ectomycorrhizas

Most mycorrhizal inoculation has been restricted to the ectomycorrhizal-forming fungi (largely Basidiomycotina) and most of this work has been carried out in nurseries where tree seedlings are either being produced 'bare-rooted' or 'container-grown'.

Although soil and spore inocula have been prepared, most researchers (e.g. Marx, 1980) recommend a vegetative or mycelial inoculum as the most effective means of producing mycorrhizal infection. Liquid culturing of these fungi, however, is often difficult, with growth-media conditions very different from one fungus to another (Stevens, 1974).

Figure 39 illustrates some of the many factors and criteria involved in selecting a suitable fungal inoculum for release into the field. Much of the technology required for the culturing of these inocula comes from the work of Moser (1963), one of the first mycologists successfully to produce large quantities of ectomycorrhizal fungal mycelium, with the final inoculum being transferred from laboratory to nursery using a peat-moss carrier in which the nutrient medium containing the fungus had been soaked (other workers have used vermiculite in place of, or as well as, peat).

The scale of an operation to inoculate tree seedlings in a nursery, and especially trees in the field, is considerable. Even a small operation, designed to supply a small group of nurseries in the southern United States requires an annual inoculum production for about 1 billion trees (Marx *et al.*, 1982).

In the early 1980s, the United States Department of Agriculture, Forest Service produced a commercial inoculum, trade named 'MycoRhiz®', of *Pisolithus tinctorius* in conjunction with Abbot Laboratories (Marx *et al.*, 1982). The system used for growth and inoculation involved the large-scale production of an inoculum in a vermiculite/peat/moss/nutrient carrier, and with the application technology for either inoculation of container grown seedlings or of the soil of nursery beds.

'MycoRhiz®' and other large-scale attempts to inoculate tree seedlings have not fulfilled their potential in terms of enhanced seedling growth, partly owing to problems in culturing and preparing an effective inoculum (e.g. inoculum desiccation, contamination etc.), but more likely because of a lack of understanding of soil ecology. This principally relates to the way in which an introduced organism, in this case a member of the Basidiomycotina, competes with the indigenous soil microbial population and interacts with other components of the soil biota, roots, microbes and animals, across a broad range of soil physicochemical conditions.

Endomycorrhizas

Endomycorrhizal fungal inoculation has been limited only to research because of inability to culture these fungi (Zygomycotina of the family *Endogonaceae*) commercially. Research has made use of both soil and spore inocula. Soil inocula consist of spores, soil and mycorrhizal fungal hyphae as well as mycorrhizal root fragments, and are usually obtained from a pot system in which a mycorrhizally infected plant has previously been grown. Spore inocula are obtained from fungal sporocarps and usually isolated through density-gradient centrifugation. A soil inoculum is thought to infect the target host crop most rapidly, possibly because of the greater range of infective propagules (Hall, 1976).

The VAM-forming fungi are generally much more promiscuous, in terms of their host specificity/range, than ectomycorrhizal-forming fungi and far fewer fungi (there are only six known VAM-forming genera compared with over thirty ectomycorrhizal-forming fungal families) need be cultured to provide inocula for a wide range of VAM associations compared with ectomycorrhizal associations.

Effective VAM fungal inoculation can be achieved in pot trials, in laboratory systems, and in the field as long as a viable inoculum is positioned in the root zone of growing plants. The degree of infection by the introduced VAM-forming fungus on the target host plant will largely depend, as with ectomycorrhizal-forming fungi, on how well the introduced organism competes with the indigenous microbial population (including VAM-forming fungi) in different soils.

Factors affecting the competitiveness of mycorrhizal fungal inocula

Some of the factors contributing to the competitiveness of an inoculum are properties of the inoculum itself and include inoculum potential, and the density and form of the inoculum (Marijunath & Bagyaraj, 1981). Interactions with the indigenous soil microbial population are highly complex. One of the most direct of these interactions is parasitism of the VAM-forming fungal inocula, largely by chitridiaceous soil fungi (Ross, 1980), but also by bacteria and actinomycetes (Sneh, Humble & Lockwood, 1977). Mycorrhizal fungal inocula will also interact with the animal component of the soil biota. Mycorrhizal fungi are both physically disrupted and killed by mycophagous nematodes, which feed only on the fungi, and soil animals such as collembola (springtails), which graze on the hyphae of endomycorrhizal fungi (Findlay, 1985). One of the key soil physico-chemical parameters controlling inoculum success will be the soil nutrient status. High levels of available soil phosphorus are generally highly inhibitory to development of VAM, as are high levels of available soil nitrogen (Hayman, 1982). High available concentrations of these nutrients can often also be inhibitory to ectomycorrhizal development although the relationship is not simple, the balance between the nutrients (and also other nutrients that may be limiting) being an important consideration (Reid & Haiskaylo, 1982).

Conclusions

A great deal more research is required before routine production of mycorrhizal fungal inocula for crop systems under a wide range of field conditions can be carried out and the soil ecological factors that control how effectively inocula compete with the indigenous soil biota evaluated. In the short term, most success will probably come from systems where competition from the indigenous soil biota is low. Such systems include industrial wastelands such as coal and other mine-spoil, reclaimed desert lands and sites where the soils have been sterilised by fumigation. There are some indications that these systems have much to offer in terms of enhanced growth of target host plants (Maronek, Hendrix & Kierman, 1981).

Genetic engineering of mycorrhizal-forming fungi may provide future improvements, both in terms of plant host response and infectivity of the mycorrhizal inoculum (i.e. inoculum potential). The genetics of mycorrhizal fungi are poorly understood, however, and so advances of this kind are not short-term prospects. Even with such advances, the benefits of genetically modified mycorrhizal inocula can only be realised with a more complete understanding of basic soil ecology.

GENETICALLY MODIFIED PLANTS AND MICROBES FOR USE IN THE ENVIRONMENT

Introduction

Genetic modification of plants to improve crop yields and increase efficiency of agriculture represents one of the most rapidly developing areas of biotechnology. Great advances have been made with regard to modification of crop plants to enhance resistance to pests such as fungi, viruses and insects (Primrose, 1991) as well as to the chemicals (pesticides) currently used to control these pests (Gasser & Fraley, 1992). Ultimately, it may be possible to carry out genetic modifications to the photosynthetic mechanisms of plants to enable more efficient fixation of atmospheric carbon dioxide and hence increase the potential of agriculture for primary production (Lindsey & Jones, 1989).

As more potential is identified for the use (agricultural and otherwise) of microbial inocula in soils, so too will increase the possibility of refining these systems (and developing new systems) through the use of genetic engineering. Even genetically modified viruses may be used in pest control in crop and tree production.

In many cases, genetic manipulation of plants may be preferred to that of microbial inocula because any microbial inoculum must be able to compete successfully with the indigenous population of the soil, and because any risks associated with genetically modified organisms in the environment are generally more predictable and more easily controlled for plants compared with microbes. There will be situations, however, where genetic manipulation of the plant is not possible or where a microbial inoculum will be more effective. In these situations, microbial inocula may be prepared from natural isolates, through selective enrichment and other procedures. In many cases, however, greater efficiency of selection and improved efficacy may result from genetic modification.

Soil inocula involving genetically modified microbes (GMMs) may be used in the soil environment in a variety of potential ways.

Microbial symbionts such as N_2-fixing rhizobia and mycorrhizal fungi

Rhizobia and mycorrhizal fungi seem obvious targets for recombinant DNA technology. Field tests with an engineered strain of *Rhizobium meliloti*, for example, have yielded considerable improvement in both N_2-fixation and growth of alfalfa (Ezzel, 1987). The more complex and less studied eucaryotic genetics of the mycorrhizal fungi suggest that it will be some considerable time before genetically manipulated strains can be of any practical value. Inability to culture VAM-forming Zygomycotina fungi effectively must be overcome before worthwhile gains can be made with respect to these fungi. The ectomycorrhizal-forming fungi (largely Basidiomycotina) currently seem the most likely target for genetic engineering, although their genetics are poorly understood.

In the case of microbial symbionts such as rhizobia and mycorrhizal fungi (and, indeed, all soil inocula) the ultimate aim of the genetic engineer is to improve plant growth, either by improving the performance of the microbial symbiont in its association with the plant root or through improving the performance (competitiveness) of the inoculum in the soil. The latter may be achieved by manipulation of the *Rhizobium* itself or by some indirect strategy such as through co-inoculation of the *Rhizobium* with antibiotic-producing bacteria to increase colonisation and nodulation of the legume by rhizobia (De-Ming & Alexander, 1988).

Genetic enhancement of the effectiveness of microbial inocula for antagonistic control of soil-borne plant pathogens

An inoculum of the fungus *Peniophora gigantea* has been used over the past three decades to antagonistically control root rot in pine caused by *Fomes annosum* (Rishbeth, 1979). *Trichoderma harzianum* is an imperfect soil fungus with a broad range antagonism against many soil-borne fungal pathogens of crops. The antagonism is caused by production of an organic volatile (see page 197) and gene technology may be used to enhance this production as well as introduce inoculum resistance to fungicides in order that *T. harzianum* can be used as an effective biological control under normal farming conditions where pesticides are applied (Claydon *et al.*, 1987). The fungus *Gliocladium* also has potential for bio-control of soil-borne pathogens (Papavizas, 1985) and, again, this may only be fully realised through genetic manipulation, to enhance the antagonistic strategy of the inoculum and to ensure competitive ability in the presence of other soil microbes.

There is considerable potential for the control of soil-borne root pathogens using rhizosphere-inhabiting bacteria, particularly fluorescent pseudomonads, strains of which are antagonistic against a wide range of pathogens including *Erwinia carotovora* (black leg in potatoes), species of *Pythium* (damping-off fungi), *Rhizoctonia solani* (cereal bare patch) and *Thielaviopsis basicola* (tobacco black root rot). Figure 42 shows antagonistic colonisation of the take-all fungus *Gaeumannomyces* by rod-shaped bacteria in rhizosphere soil of wheat. Analysis of the molecular genetics of these antagonistic responses may enable genetic manipulation to provide improved biocontrol (Schippers, 1988).

Figure 42. Scanning electron micrograph of bacterial (B) antagonism of the take-all fungus (*Gaeumannomyces graminus*) (× 20 000).

Cloning of genes involved in the bacterial production of insecticidal toxins

The cloning of these genes (from the soil bacterium *Bacillus thuringiensis*) into a strain of *Pseudomonas fluorescens* that lives in the maize rhizosphere can provide protection against soil insect pests of roots (Watrud *et al.*, 1985). Similar technology applies to phylloplane protection of crops. A proportion of GMMs (bacteria and viruses) on the phylloplane will inevitably be transported into the soil through a variety of mechanisms.

Genetic modification of microbial inocula for the production of plant growth regulators

Plant growth regulators are produced by a number of rhizosphere bacteria (Holl *et al.*, 1988). For *Azotobacter chroococcum* (and probably other bacteria), production is activated by root exudation (Martinez-Toledo *et al.*, 1988) and may well be enhanced through genetic manipulation of bacterial inocula or through a genetic change of the plant that alters the quantity/ quality of root exudates.

Genetic modification of microbial inocula for the detoxification of contaminated soil – bioremediation

Genetic modification can enable development of bacteria that have an enhanced capacity for xenobiotic degradation (Jain & Sayler, 1987), and GMMs have been constructed, for example, that can degrade chloro- and methylaromatic compounds, which form the basis of pesticides and other industrial pollutants (Rojo *et al.*, 1987). It is uncertain whether such inocula will be used in soils other than the those heavily polluted because a reasonable substrate concentration of the pollutant will be required. Soils with low-level pesticide contamination may be unrealistic for microbial inoculation.

As well as intentional introduction, GMMs may enter soil even though they are not intended as a soil inoculum, such as through their use as a foliar treatment to crops. A well-documented example of this is the use of the now well-known ice-minus mutants of the phylloplane bacterium *Pseudomonas syringae*. This organism, prepared by deleting the gene responsible for use-forming protein, can be sprayed on to frost-sensitive crops to prevent ice crystals forming (Lindow, 1983). Normally, the phylloplane population of *Ps. syringae* and other bacteria produces a protein that causes the formation of ice crystals under frosty conditions. By deleting the gene responsible for production of the ice-forming protein, frost protection is mediated when the leaves of frost-sensitive plants are sprayed with the ice-minus mutants. Field monitoring after application to field crops has shown that, although these organisms freely enter the soil, competitive exclusion ensures poor survival and dispersal (Lindow & Panopoulos, 1988).

As well as from foliar spraying, GMMs will also inevitably enter the soil if they are used as a means of accelerating metal leaching from ores in the mining industry. Species from the chemoautotrophic bacterial genus *Thiobacillus* may be engineered for increased ore-leaching efficiency (Brierley, 1985). In addition to 'field-released' GMMs entering the soil, those used in industrial processes may contaminate the soil as a result of accidental release.

SOIL ECOLOGICAL EFFECTS OF THE USE OF GENETICALLY MODIFIED PLANTS AND MICROBES

The biotechnological development and use of genetically modified plants and microbes, although offering a wide range of potential benefits to agricultural and other systems, may have adverse environmental effects. This must be assessed (usually in contained trials) before any environmental introduction can be made.

Assessment of the ecological effects of modified plants and microbes should include monitoring of: competition (persistence and invasion of indigenous communities), pathogenicity and toxicity (to non-target organisms), gene transfer (to indigenous organisms) and dispersal (beyond the intended target environment). The techniques required to do this for plants are much better established than for microbes and additionally, assessment of the soil ecological effects of GMM's necessitates sensitive detection in the soil environment.

Detection and monitoring of GMM's in soil involves a range of both extractive and *in situ* techniques such as those outlined in Figure 43, as well as development of new techniques with improved power and sensitivity. Ideally, techniques are needed that can detect single cells *in situ*, assay their activity, and facilitate genomic tracking. One such technique invvolves the cloning of *lux* genes for bioluminescence from marine vibrios into the selected soil inoculum (Grant *et al.*, 1991). Because there is little or no background bioluminescence, cells can be imaged with the degree of bioluminescence (catalysed by the enzyme luciferase) proportional to their metabolic activity. The bioluminescence marker system has the additional advantage that it does not give rise to the environmental concerns associated with antibiotic resistance markers.

The survival and dispersal of GMMs will depend on interaction with indigenous soil biota (plants, microbes and animals) as well as the soil physico-chemical environment (Figure 39). Inocula added to soil generally

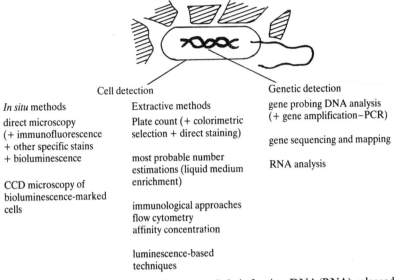

Cell detection | Genetic detection

In situ methods
direct microscopy
(+ immunofluorescence
+ other specific stains
+ bioluminescence

CCD microscopy of
bioluminescence-marked
cells

Extractive methods
Plate count (+ colorimetric
selection + direct staining)

most probable number
estimations (liquid medium
enrichment)

immunological approaches
flow cytometry
affinity concentration

luminescence-based
techniques

Genetic detection
gene probing DNA analysis
(+ gene amplification–PCR)

gene sequencing and mapping

RNA analysis

Figure 43. Methods of detecting GMMs (and their foreign DNA/RNA) released into soil.

have poor survival characteristics because of the frequently unfavourable nature of this interaction. For example, if a GMM inoculum is introduced under wet conditions, the cells will be predominantly located in the larger soil pores where protozoal grazing may rapidly deplete the added population. In terms of microbial dispersal, soil water potential is the dominant control (most movement of cells will be restricted to periods close to rainfall or irrigation events when much of the soils pore space is water filled), although ingestion and egestion by soil animals such as earthworms and protozoa will also transport GMMs through the soil profile.

It seems unlikely that the use of GMMs will, in most cases, markedly change the functional integrity of the soil – differences between constructed and wild strains will generally be very small (maybe only one gene will be added or deleted in 2000), unless some major ecological property (e.g. pathogenicity) of the strain is modified. As with assessing the soil ecological effects of a pesticide or other chemical, however, it is necessary to ensure that a GMM introduction has no marked effect on a range of 'non-target' organisms and processes that particularly contribute to soil functional integrity. These may include soil aggregation, nitrification, xenobiotic degradation as well as mycorrhizal and rhizobial infection.

The possible problems from GMM introduction into the soil environment can be minimised by ensuring limited persistence, such as through insertion of suicide genes (where cell death is triggered by some environmental control) into inocula (Fox, 1989).

The fate of recombined DNA in soil

The soil ecological consequences of release of genetically engineered organisms also extend to the fate of the recombined DNA. Figure 43 indicates some possible strategies for study of dispersal and transfer of genetic material in soil. Dispersal may be over a great range of scale, from over a few micrometres in soil microsites to dispersal through agents such as soil and other animals, birds and wind erosion.

Transfer of genetic material from one organism to another can occur in three ways: by conjugation, transduction or transformation.

Transfer of recombined DNA from a GMM to another soil organism is most likely via conjugative transfer of plasmids (pieces of chromosomal-free DNA), and so much of this potential problem can be avoided by ensuring that foreign DNA is restricted to chromosomal insertions.

Expression of DNA transferred from a GMM to an indigenous soil organism is unlikely and so the frequency of gene transfer must be assessed by gene-probing organisms isolated from the soil. Use of highly sensitive systems such as the Polymerase Chain Reaction (PCR) can theoretically enable single copies of genes to be amplified and detected from environmental samples. Great difficulties can be encountered in trying to obtain soil-free DNA (for gene probing/PCR) from microbes extracted from soil, although these problems are continually being overcome (e.g. Holben *et al.*, 1988). Screening for possible gene transfer should logically begin with isolation of soil organisms for gene probing that are most genetically compatible with the released GMM. In releasing an engineered *Rhizobium*, for example, gene probing of the soil wild-types of that species should identify the highest frequency of gene transfer.

Because of strong adsorption on to soil particles, it is possible that cell-free DNA may remain viable for long periods of time. Protection of DNA, which would normally be rapidly attacked in soil by nuclease enzymes, may be mediated by complexation with resistant organic matter and clays so that foreign genes may persist long after the parent cell has died. It is unlikely, however, that such genes are recoverable from this pool in a viable state.

Conclusions

There is considerable potential for use of genetically modified plants and microbes for agricultural and other purposes. The greater hurdle to overcome for safe and effective use of this technology is developing an understanding of how introduced organisms, genetically modified or otherwise, interact and compete with indigenous soil organisms and how this interaction varies across the full ecological range of soil conditions.

References

Chapter 1

Anderson, J. M. 1987. In *Ecology of Microbial Communities* (eds. M. Fletcher, T. R. G. Gray & J. G. Jones). SGM Symp. 42. Cambridge University Press, pp. 125–46.

Curl, E. A. & Truelove, B. 1986. *The Rhizosphere.* Springer-Verlag, Berlin.

Greenwood, D. J. 1975. *In* Soil physical conditions and crop production. *MAFF Bulletin,* **29**, 261–72.

Hook, D. D. & Crawford, R. M. M. (eds) 1978. *Plant Life in Anaerobic Environments.* Ann Arbor Science.

Kühnelt, W. 1961. *Soil Biology with Special Reference to the Animal Kingdom.* Faber, London.

Lambers, H. 1987. In *Root Development and Function* (eds P. J. Gregory, J. V. Lake & D. A. Rose). Cambridge University Press, pp. 125–46.

Read, D. J., Francis, R. & Finlay, R. D. 1985. In *Ecological Interactions in Soil – Plants, Microbes and Animals* (ed. A. H. Fitter). BES Special Publication 4, Blackwell, Oxford, 193–217.

Rowell, D. L. 1981. In *The Chemistry of Soil Processes* (eds. D. J. Greenland & M. H. B. Hayes). Wiley, New York.

Russell, E. W. 1973. *Soil Conditions and Plant Growth* (10th edition). Longman, London.

Scott Russell, R. 1977. *Plant Root Systems – Their Function and Interactions with the Soil.* McGraw-Hill.

Swift, M. J., Heal, O. W. & Anderson, J. M. 1979. *Decomposition in Terrestrial Ecosystems.* Studies in Ecology, Vol. 5. Blackwell, Oxford.

Tisdale, S. L., Nelson, W. L. & Beaton, J. D. 1985. *Soil Fertility and Fertilizers* (4th Edition). Macmillan, New York.

Wallwork, J. A. 1970. *Ecology of Soil Animals.* McGraw-Hill, London.

Williams, S. T. 1985. *In* Bacteria in their natural environments (eds M. Fletcher & G. D. Floodgate). *Special Publication SGM,* **16**, 81–110.

Chapter 2

Cooke, R. C. & Rayner, A. D. M. 1984. *Ecology of Saprophytic Fungi.* Longman.

Hattori, T. 1973. *Microbial Life in The Soil – An Introduction.* Marcel Dekker, New York.

Hiltner, L. 1904. *Arbeiten der Deutschen Landwirtschaftsgesellschaft Berlin,* **98**, 59–78.

Lee, K. E. 1985. *Earthworms – Their Ecology and Relationships with Soils and Land Use.* Academic Press, Sydney.

Sparling, G. P. 1985. In *Soil Organic Matter and Biological Activity* (eds. D. Vaughan & R. E. Malcolm). *Developments in Plant and Soil Sciences* **16**, 223–62.

Swift, M. J., Heal, O. W. & Anderson, J. M. 1979. *Decomposition in Terrestrial Ecosystems.* Studies in Ecology, Vol. 5. Blackwell, Oxford.

Verhoeff, H. A. & De Goeda, R. G. M. 1985. In *Ecological Interactions in the Soil – Plants, Microbes and Animals* (ed. A. H. Fitter). BES Special Publication 4. Blackwell, Oxford, pp. 367–76.

Weaver, J. E. 1926. *Root Development of Field Crops.* McGraw-Hill, New York.

Chapter 3

Alexander, I. J. & Fairley, R. I. 1983. *Plant and Soil*, **71**, 49–53.

Atkinson, D. 1985. In *Ecological Interactions in Soil – Plants, Microbes and Animals* (ed. A. II. Fitter). BES Special Publication 4. Blackwell, Oxford, pp. 43–65.

Barber, D. A. & Lynch, J. M. 1977. *Soil Biology and Biochemistry*, **9**, 305–8.

Barber, D. A. & Martin, J. K. 1976. *New Phytology*, **76**, 69–80.

Booth, R. G. 1983. *Pedobiologia*, **25**, 187–95.

Bowen, G. D. & Rovira, A. D. 1973. In *Methods in the Study of Microbial Ecology* (ed. T. Rosswall). Swedish Nat. Sci. Res. Council, Stockholm, pp. 443–50.

Campbell, R. 1985. *Plant Microbiology.* Arnold, London.

Cooke, R. C. & Rayner, A. D. M. 1984. *Ecology of Saprophytic Fungi.* Longman, London.

Day, P. R., Doner, H. E. & McLaren, A. D. 1978. In *Nitrogen in the Environment* (eds. D. R. Nielsen & J. G. Macdonald). Academic Press, New York, pp. 305–92.

Elliot, E. T. & Coleman, D. C. 1988. *Ecology Bulletin*, **39**, 23–32.

Finlay, R. D. 1985. In *Ecological Interactions in Soil – Plants, Microbes and Animals* (ed. A. H. Fitter). BES Special Publication 4. Blackwell, Oxford, pp. 319–31.

Fogel, R. 1983. *Plant and Soil*, **71**, 75–85.

Fogel, R. 1985. In *Ecological Interactions in Soil – Plants, Microbes and Animals* (ed. A. H. Fitter). BES Special Publication 4. Blackwell, Oxford, pp. 23–36.

Killham, K., Amato, N. & Ladd, J. N. 1993. *Soil Biology and Biochemistry*, **25**, 57–62.

Newman, E. I. & Watson, A. 1977. *Plant and Soil*, **48**, 17–56.

Nye, P. H. & Tinker, P. B. 1977. *Solute Movement in the Soil–Plant System.* Blackwell, Oxford.

Parry, G. D. 1981. *Oecologia*, **48**, 260–4.

Pate, J. S. 1977. In *A Treatise on Dinitrogen Fixation* (eds. R. W. F. Hardy & W. S. Silver), Section 3. Wiley, New York, pp. 473–517.

Paul, E. A. & Kucey, R. M. N. 1981. *Science*, **213**, 473–4.

Postgate, J. R. 1975. *Microbes and Man.* Penguin.

Read, D. J., Francis, R. & Finlay, R. D. 1985. In *Ecological Interactions in Soil – Plants, Microbes and Animals* (ed. A. H. Fitter). BES Special Publication 4. Blackwell, Oxford, pp. 193–217.

Rovira, A. D., Newman, E. I., Bowen, H. J. & Campbell, R. 1974. *Soil Biology and Biochemistry*, **6**, 211–16.

Stribley, D. P. & Read, D. J. 1980. *New Phytology*, **86**, 365–71.

Vogt, K. A., Grier, C. C., Meier, C. E. & Edmonds, R. L. 1982. *Ecology*, **63**, 370–80.
Winogradsky, S. 1924. *Compte Rendu*, **178**, 1236.

Chapter 4

The carbon cycle

Anderson, J. M. 1973. *Oecologia*, **12**, 251–88.
Edwards, C. S. & Heath, G. 1963. In *Soil Organisms* (ed. J. Doekson & J. van der Drift). North Holland, Amsterdam, pp. 76–84.
Jenkinson, D. S. & Rayner, J. H. 1977. *Soil Science*, **123**, 298–305.
Kirk, T. K. & Fenn, P. 1982. In *Decomposer Basidiomycetes: Their Biology and Ecology* (eds. J. C. Farnkland, J. N. Hedger & M. J. Swift). Cambridge University Press, pp. 67–89.
Paul, E. A. & Voroney, R. P. 1980. In *Contemporary Microbial Ecology* (eds. D. C. Ellwood, J. N. Hedger, M. J. Latham, J. M. Lynch & J. H. Slater). Academic Press, London, pp. 215–37.
Richards, B. N. 1987. *The Microbiology of Terrestrial Ecosystems*. Longman, New York.
Schlesinger, W. H. 1984. In *The Role of Terrestrial Vegetation in the Global Carbon Cycle: Measurement and Remote Sensing* (ed. G. M. Woodwell). Wiley, Chichester, pp. 111–27.
Swift, M. J., Heal, O. W. & Anderson, J. M. 1979. *Decomposition in Terrestrial Ecosystems*. Studies in Ecology, Vol. 5, Blackwell, Oxford.
Whittaker, R. H. 1975. *Communities and Ecosystems* (2nd edition). Macmillan, New York.

The nitrogen cycle

Anderson, J. M., Huish, S. A., Ineson, P., Leonard, M. A. & Splatt, P. R. 1985. In *Ecological Interactions in Soil – Plants, Microbes and Animals* (ed. A. H. Fitter). BES Special Publication 4. Blackwell, Oxford, pp. 377–92.
Batey, T. 1982. *Philosophical Transactions of the Royal Society, London*, **B296**, 551–6.
Berg, B. & Staaf, H. 1981. *Ecology Bulletin*, **33**, 163–78.
Bowen, G. D. 1973. In *Ectomycorrhizae* (eds. G. C. Marks & T. T. Kozlowski). Academic Press, London, pp. 151–208.
Brookes, P. C., Kragt, J. F., Powlson, D. S. & Jenkinson, D. S. 1985. *Soil Biology and Biochemistry*, **17**, 831–5.
Clarholm, M. 1985. *Soil Biology and Biochemistry*, **17**(2), 181–7.
Foster, S. S. D., Cripps, A. C. & Smith-Carrington, A. 1982. *Philosophical Transactions of the Royal Society, London*, **B296**, 477–89.
Harmer, R. & Alexander, I. J. 1985. In *Ecological Interactions in Soil – Plants, Microbes and Animals* (ed. A. H. Fitter). BES Special Publication 4. Blackwell, Oxford, pp. 377–92.
Hart, S. C. & Binkley, D. 1985. *Plant and Soil*, **85**, 11–21.

Hulm, S. C. & Killham, K. 1988. *Journal of Soil Science*, **39**, 417–24.
Killham, K. 1987. In *Soc. Gen. Microbiol. Spec. Pub. Nitrification* (ed. J. Prosser). Cambridge University Press, pp. 117–26.
Killham, K. 1990. *Plant and Soil*, **128**, 31–44.
Malhi, S. S. & McGill, W. B. 1982. *Soil Biology and Biochemistry*, **14**, 393–9.
Martikainen, P. J. 1984. *Soil Biology and Biochemistry*, **16**, 577–82.
Olson, R. A. 1979. In *Isotope and Radiation in Research on Soil–Plant Relationships*. IAEA (Vienna), pp. 3–32.
Paul, E. A. 1976. In *Carbon, Nitrogen, Phosphorus, Sulfur and Selenium Cycles. Proc. 2nd Int. Symp. Environ. Biogeochem.* (ed. J. O. Nrigu).
Rachhpal-Singh & Nye, P. H. 1986. *Journal of Soil Science*, **37**, 9–20.
Rice, E. L. 1974. *Allelopathy*. Academic Press, New York.
Robertson, L. A., van Kleef, B. H. A. & Kuenen, J. G. 1986. *Journal of Microbial Methods*, **5**, 237–42.
Royal Society. 1983. *The Nitrogen Cycle of the United Kingdom – A Study Group Report*. The Royal Society, London.
Ryden, J. C. 1981. *Nature*, **292**, 235–7.
Ryden, J. C., Lund, L. J., Letey, J. & Focht, D. D. 1979. *Journal of the American Society of Soil Science*, **43**, 110–18.
Smith, M. S. & Tiedje, J. M. 1979. *Journal of the American Society of Soil Science*, **43**, 951–5.
Stribley, D. P. & Read, D. J. 1980. *New Phytology*, **86**, 368–71.
Syers, J. K. & Springett, J. A. 1984. In *Biological Processes and Soil Fertility*. Developments in Plant & Soil Sciences, Vol. 11 (eds. J. Tinsley & J. F. Darbyshire). Nijhoff-Junk, The Hague, pp. 93–104.
Tiedje, J. M., Sextone, A. J., Myrold, D. D. & Robinson, J. A. 1982. *Antonie van Leeuwenhoek*, **48**, 569–83.
Tisdale, S. L., Nelson, W. L. & Beaton, J. D. 1985. *Soil Fertility and Fertilisers* (4th edition). Macmillan, New York.
Vitousek, P. M. 1984. *Ecology*, **65**, 285–98.
Wood, M., Cooper, J. E. & Holding, A. J. 1983. *Soil Biology and Biochemistry*, **15**, 123–4.
Wood, P. M. 1988. In *SGM Symp. 42* (eds. J. A. Cole & S. J. Ferguson). Cambridge University Press, pp. 219–44.

The sulphur cycle

Biederbeck, V. O. 1978. In *Soil Organic Matter* (eds. M. Schnitzer & S. U. Khan). Elsevier, New York, pp. 273–310.
Friedrich, C. & Mitrenga, G. 1981. *Fems Microbiology Letters*, **10**, 209–12.
Goldhaber, M. B. & Kaplan, I. R. 1974. In *The Sea, Vol. 5, Marine Chemistry* (ed. E. D. Goldberg). Wiley, New York, pp. 569–655.
Hoque, S. & Killham. K. 1987. *Plant and Soil*, **101**, 3–8.
Killham, K., Lindley, N. D. & Wainwright, M. 1981. *Applied Environmental Microbiology*, **42**, 629–31.
Kimura, M., Wada, H. & Takai, Y. 1979. *Soil Science and Plant Nutrition*, **25**, 145–53.
Stevenson, F. J. 1986. *Cycles of Soil Carbon, Nitrogen, Phosphorus, Sulfur, Micronutrients*. Wiley, New York.

Stewart, B. A., Porter, L. K. & Viets, F. G., Jr. 1966. *Proceedings of the American Society of Soil Science,* **30**, 355–8.
Tisdale, S. L., Nelson, W. L. & Beaton, J. D. 1985. *Soil Fertility and Fertilisers* (4th edition). Macmillan, New York.
Tuovinen, O. H. & Kelly, D. P. 1973. *Archiv für Mikrobiologie,* **88**, 285.
UNEP, 1991. *United Nations Environment Programme Environmental Report.* Blackwell, Oxford.
Yagi, S., Kitai, S. & Kimura, T. 1971. *Applied Microbiology,* **22**, 157–9.

Chapter 5

Allen, M. F., Smith, W. K., Moore, Jr., T. S. & Christensen, M. 1981. *New Phytology,* **88**, 683–93.
Barber, D. A. & Martin, J. K. 1976. *New Phytology,* **76**, 69–80.
Bowen, G. D. 1973. In *Ectomycorrhizae – Their Ecology and Physiology* (eds. G. C. Marks & T. T. Kozlowski). Academic Press, New York, pp. 151–205.
Brown, A. D. 1978. *Advances in Microbial Physiology,* **17**, 181–242.
Darbyshire, J. F. 1976. *Journal of Soil Science,* **27**, 369–76.
Foster, R. C. & Bowen, G. D. 1982. In *Phytopathogenic Prokaryotes* (eds. M. S. Mount & G. H. Lacy). Academic Press, New York, pp. 159–85.
Hardie, K. & Leyton, L. 1981. *New Phytology,* **89**, 599–608.
Harris, R. F. 1980. In *Water Potential Relations in Soil Microbiology.* Soil Sci. Soc. Amer. Madison, Wisconsin, pp. 23–95.
Hsaio, T. C. 1973. *Annual Review of Plant Physiology,* **24**, 519–70.
Killham, K. & Firestone, M. K. 1984*a*. *Applied Environmental Microbiology,* **47**, 301–6.
Killham, K. & Firestone, M. K. 1984*b*. *Applied Environmental Microbiology,* **48**, 239–41.
Lee, K. E. (ed.) 1985. *Earthworms, Their Ecology and Relationships with Soils and Land Use.* Academic Press, Sydney.
Levitt, J. 1972. *Responses of Plants to Environmental Stresses.* Academic Press, New York.
Levy, J. & Krikun, J. 1980. *New Phytology,* **85**, 25–31.
Martin, J. K. 1977. *Soil Biology and Biochemistry,* **9**, 303–4.
Mexal, J. & Reid, C. P. P. 1973. *Canadian Journal of Botany,* **51**, 1579–88.
Mosse, B. & Hayman, O. S. 1971. *New Phytology,* **70**, 29–34.
Nelson, C. E. & Safir, G. R. 1982. *Planta,* **154**, 407–13.
Patrick-Read, C. P. 1974. *Plant Physiology,* **54**, 44–9.
Powell, C. L. & Bagyaraj, D. J. 1986. *VA mycorrhiza.* CRC Press Inc., Florida.
Read, D. J. & Boyd, R. 1986. In *Water, Fungi and Plants* (eds. J. C. Ayres & L. Boddy). Cambridge University Press.
Safir, G. R., Boyer, J. S. & Gerdemann, J. W. 1971. *Science,* **172**, 581–3.
Sanders, F. E., Mosse, B. & Tinker, P. B. 1975. *Endomycorrhizas.* Academic Press, London.
Scott Russell, R. 1977. *Plant Root Systems – Their Function and Interaction with the Soil.* McGraw-Hill, London.
Tesche, Von M. & Gomell, C. 1973. *Flora,* **162**, 371–80.
Tisdall, S. L. & Oades, J. M. 1979. *Australian Journal of Soil Research,* **17**, 429–41.

Chapter 6

Ecology of soils polluted from acid deposition

Assink, J. W. & van den Brink, W. J. (eds.) 1986. *Contaminated Soil, 1st Int. TNO Conf. on Contaminated Soil*, November, 1985, Utrecht, The Netherlands. Martinus Nijhoff, Dordrecht.

Baath, E., Berg, E., Lohm, U., Lundgren, E., Lundkvist, H., Soderstrom, B. & Wiren, A. 1980. *Pedobiologia*, **20**, 85–90.

Babich, H. & Stotzky, G. 1978. *Environmental Research*, **15**, 405–17.

Bradley, R., Burt, A. J. & Read, D. J. 1981. *Nature*, **292**, 335–7.

Firestone, M. K., Killham, K. & McColl, J. G. 1983. *Applied Environmental Microbiology*, **46**, 758–63.

Firestone, M. K., McColl, J. G., Killham, K. & Brooks, P. D. 1984. In *American Chemical Society Special Publication on Acid Rain*, pp. 51–63.

Francis, A. J., Olson, D. & Bernatsky, R. 1980. In *Ecological Impact of Acid Precipitation* (eds. D. Drables & A. Tollan). Proc. Int. Conf. Sandefjord, Norway, pp. 166–7.

Gadd, G. M. & Griffiths, A. J. 1978. *Microbial Ecology*, **4**, 303–17.

Hovland, J. 1981. *Soil Biology and Biochemistry*, **13**, 23–6.

Killham, K. 1985. *Environmental Pollution Series B*, **38**, 283–94.

Killham, K. & Firestone, M. K. 1983. *Plant and Soil*, **72**, 39–48.

Killham, K., Firestone, M. K. & McColl, J. G. 1983. *Journal of Environmental Quality*, **12**, 133–7.

Likens, G. E., Bormann, F. H. & Johnson, N. M. 1972. *Environment*, **14**, 33–44.

Lohm, U. 1980. In *Ecological Impact of Acid Precipitation* (eds. D. Drablos & A. Tollan). Proc. Inst. Conf. Sandefjord, Norway, pp. 166–7.

Pancholy, S. K., Rice, E. L. & Turner, J. A. 1975. *Journal of Applied Ecology*, **12**, 337–42.

Shriner, D. S. 1978. *Phytopathology*, **68**, 213–18.

Shriner, D. S. & Johnston, J. W. 1981. *Environmental and Experimental Botany*, **1**, 199–209.

Strayer, R. F. & Alexander, M. 1981. *Journal of Environmental Quality*, **10**, 460–5.

Strayer, R. F., Lin, C. J. & Alexander, M. 1981. *Journal of Environmental Quality*, **10**, 547–51.

Tamm, C. O. 1976. *Ambio*, **5**, 235–8.

Tuovinen, O. H., Niemela, S. I. & Gyttenberg, H. G. 1971. *Antonie van Leeuwenhoek*, **37**, 489–96.

Ulrich, B. & Pankrath, J. (eds.) 1983. *Effects of Accumulation of Air Pollutants in Forest Ecosystems*. Reidel, Dordrecht.

Ecology of soils polluted with radionuclides

Bell, J. N. B., Minski, M. J. & Grogan, H. A. 1988. *Soil Use & Management*, **4**, 76–84.

Bowen, G. D. 1984. In *The Nutrition of Plantation Forests*. Academic Press, London, pp. 147–79.

Bunzl, K. & Kracke, W. 1986. *Health Physics*, **50**, 540–2.

Carbol, P., Ittner, T. & Skalberg, M. 1987. In *Proc. Inst. Conf. Chemistry and*

Migration of Actinides and Fission Products in the Geosphere, Munich, Preprint 870911.

Clark, M. J. 1986. *Journal of the Society of Radiological Protection*, **6**, 157–66.

Cremers, A., Elsen, A., De Preter, P. & Maes, A. 1988. *Nature*, **335**, 247–9.

Crossley, O. A. Jr. & Witkamp, M. 1966. *Pedobiologia*, **6**, 293–303.

Haselwandter, K. 1978. *Health Physics*, **34**, 713–15.

Haury, G. & Schikarski, W. 1977. In *Global Chemical Cycles and their Alterations by Man* (ed. W. Stumm). Dahlem Konferenzen, Berlin, p. 165.

Killham, K. 1985. In *Ecological Interactions in the Soil*. BES Special Publication 4. (ed. A. H. Hitter). Blackwell, London.

Kirk, G. J. O. & Staunton, S. 1989. *Journal of Soil Science*, **40**, 71–84.

Livens, F. R. & Loveland, P. J. 1988. *Soil Use & Management*, **4**, 69–75.

Malone, C. R. & Reickle, D. E. 1973. *Soil Biology and Biochemistry*, **5**, 629–39.

Martin, C. J., Heaton, B. & Robb, J. D. 1988. *Journal of Environmental Radioactivity*, **6**, 247–59.

Tinker, P. B. 1978. *Physiologie Vegetale*, **16**, 743–51.

Chapter 7

Biofertilisation by rhizobial inoculation

Andrew, C. S. 1978. In *Limitations and Potentials for Biological Nitrogen Fixation in the Tropics* (eds. J. Dobereiner, R. H. Burns & A. Hollaender). Plenum Press, New York, pp. 135–60.

Cooper, D. R., Hill-Cottingham, D. E. & Lloyd-Jones, C. P. 1976. *Physiology of the Plant*, **38**, 313–18.

Danso, S. K. A. & Alexander, M. 1975. *Proceedings of the American Society of Soil Science*, **38**, 86–9.

Hodgson, A. L. & Stacey, G. 1987. *CRC Critical Reviews of Biotechnology*, **4**, 1–73.

Nutman, P. S. 1971. In *Soil Microbiology* (ed. N. Walker). Butterworth, London.

Nutman, P. S. 1976. In *Symbiotic Nitrogen Fixation in Plants* (I.B.P. Vol. 7, ed. P. S. Nutman). Cambridge University Press, pp. 211–37.

Parker, C. A., Trinick, M. J. & Chatel, D. L. 1977. In *A Treatise on Dinitrogen Fixation, Section IV: Agronomy & Ecology* (eds. R. W. F. Hardy & A. H. Gibson). Wiley, New York.

Singh, M. & Klingmuller, U. 1986. *Plant and Soil*, **90**, 235–42.

Wood, M., Cooper, J. E. & Holding, A. J. 1983. *Soil Biology and Biochemistry*, **15**, 123–4.

Control of the soil biota

Ashton, F. M. & Crafts, A. S. 1981. *Mode of Action of Herbicides*. Wiley, New York.

Claydon, N. & Allan, M. 1987. *Transactions of the British Mycological Society*, **88**, 503–13.

Corbett, J. R. 1974. *The Biochemical Mode of Action of Pesticides*. Academic Press, London.

Fukoto, T. R. & Sims, J. J. 1971. In *Pesticides in the Environment* (ed. R. White-Stevens). Dekker, New York.

Gray, N. F. 1988. In *Diseases of Nematodes, Vol. 2* (eds. G. O. Poinar & H. B. Jansson). CRC Press, Boca Raton, pp. 3–14.

Greaves, M. P. & Malkomes, H. P. 1980. In *Interactions Between Herbicides and the Soil* (ed. R. J. Hance). Academic Press, London, pp. 223–53.

Griffin, G. J. 1986. *Horticulture Review*, **8**, 291–336.

Hale, M. G. 1978. *Interactions Between Non-Pathogenic Organisms and Plants.* Elsevier.

Howell, C. R. & Stripanovic, R. D. 1983. *Canadian Journal of Microbiology*, **29**, 321–4.

Kuc, J. 1985. In *Cellular and Molecular Biology of Plant Stress* (eds. J. L. Key & T. Kosuge). Alan R. Liss, New York, pp. 303–18.

Marsh, R. W. (ed.) 1977. *Systemic Fungicides* (2nd edition). Longman, London.

Martens, D. A. & Bremner, J. M. 1984. *Journal of the American Society of Soil Science*, **48**, 302–5.

Mulvaney, R. L. & Bremner, J. M. 1981. In *Soil Biochemistry, Vol. 5* (eds. J. N. Ladd & E. A. Paul). Marcel Dekker, New York, pp. 153–96.

Osburn, R. M., Schroth, M. N., Hancock, J. G. & Hendson, M. 1989. *Phytopathology*, **79**, 709–16.

Paulitz, T. C. & Baker, R. 1988. *Canadian Journal of Microbiology*, **34**, 947–51.

Sneh, B. 1981. *Phytopathologische Zeitschrift*, **100**, 251–6.

Terman, G. L. 1979. *Advances in Agronomy*, **31**, 189–223.

Walter, H. M., Keeney, D. R. & Fillery, I. R. 1979. *Journal of the American Society of Soil Science*, **43**, 195–6.

Weller, D. M., Howie, W. J. & Cook, R. J. 1988. *Phytopathology*, **78**, 1094–100.

Biofertilisation by mycorrhizal fungal inoculation

Bartlett, E. M. & Lewis, D. H. 1973. *Soil Biology and Biochemistry*, **5**, 249–57.

Bowen, G. D. 1973. In *Ectomycorrhizae – Their Ecology and Physiology* (eds. G. C. Marks & T. T. Kozlowski). Academic Press, London, pp. 151–205.

Bowen, G. D. 1984. In *Nutrition of Plantation Forests* (eds. G. D. Bowen & E. K. S. Nambiar). Academic Press, London, pp. 147–79.

Bradley, R., Burt, A. J. & Read, D. J. 1981. *Nature*, **292**, 335–7.

Findlay, R. D. 1985. In *Ecological Interactions in the Soil – Plants, Microbes and Animals* (ed. A. H. Fitter). BES Special Publication 4. Blackwell, Oxford, pp. 319–31.

Graham, J. H. & Menge, J. A. 1982. *Phytopathology*, **72**, 95–8.

Hall, I. R. 1976. *Transactions of the British Mycology Society*, **67**, 409–11.

Harley, J. L. & Smith, S. E. 1983. *Mycorrhizal Symbiosis*. Academic Press, London.

Hayman, D. S. 1982. *Phytopathology*, **72**, 1119–25.

Hayman, D. S. & Mosse, B. 1972. *New Phytology*, **71**, 41–7.

Killham, K. 1985. In *Ecological Interactions in the Soil – Plants, Microbes and Animals* (ed. A. H. Fitter). BES Special Publication 4. Blackwell, Oxford, pp. 225–33.

Lamb, R. J. & Richards, B. N. 1971. *Australian Forestry*, **35**, 1–7.

Marijunath, A. & Bagyaraj, D. J. 1981. *New Phytology*, **87**, 355–63.

Maronek, D. M., Hendrix, J. E. & Kierman, J. 1981. *Horticulture Reviews*, **3**, 172–213.

Marx, D. H. 1973. In *Ectomycorrhizae – Their Ecology and Physiology* (eds. G. C. Marks & T. T. Kozlowski). Academic Press, London, pp. 351–82.

Marx, D. H. 1980. In *Tropical Mycorrhizal Research* (ed. P. Mickola). Oxford University Press, London, pp. 13–71.

Marx, D. H. & Krupa, S. V. 1978. In *Interactions Between Non-pathogenic Soil Microorganisms and Plants* (eds. R. Dommergues & S. V. Krupa). Elsevier, Amsterdam, pp. 373–400.

Marx, D. H., Ruehle, J. L., Kenney, D. S., Cordell, C. E., Riffle, J. W., Molina, R. J., Pawuck, W. H., Nauratil, S., Tinus, R. W. & Goodwin, O. C. 1982. *Forest Science*, **28**, 373–400.

Moser, M. 1963. In *Mykorrhiza* (eds. W. Rawald & H. Lyr), Fischer, Jena, pp. 497–524.

Read, D. J., Francis, R. & Finlay, R. D. 1985. In *Ecological Interactions in Soil – Plants, Microbes and Animals* (ed. A. H. Fitter). BES Special Publication 4. Blackwell, Oxford, pp. 193–217.

Reid, C. P. P. & Haiskaylo, E. 1982. In *Methods and Principles of Mycorrhizal Research* (ed. N. C. Schenck). Amer. Phytopath. Soc., St. Paul, Minnesota, pp. 175–87.

Rhodes, L. L. & Gerdemann, J. W. 1978. *Soil Biology and Biochemistry*, **10**, 361–4.

Ross, J. P. 1980. *Phytopathology*, **70**, 1200–5.

Rygiewicz, P. T., Bledsoe, C. S & Zasoski, R. J. 1984. *Canadian Journal of Forest Research*, **14**, 893–9.

Safir, G. R., Boyer, J. S. & Gerdemann, J. E. 1971. *Science*, **172**, 581–3.

Sneh, B., Humble, S. J. & Lockwood, J. L. 1977. *Phytopathology*, **67**, 622–8.

Stevens, R. B. (ed.) 1974. *Mycology Guidebook*. University of Washington Press, Seattle.

Whittingham, J. & Read, D. J. 1982. *New Phytology*, **90**, 277–84.

Genetically modified plants and microbes for use in the environment

Brierley, J. A. 1985. In *Engineered Organisms in the Environment: Scientific Issues* (eds. H. O. Halvorson, D. Pramer & M. Rogul). American Society of Microbiology, Washington D.C., pp. 141–6.

Claydon, N., Allan, M., Hanson, J. R. & Avent, A. G. 1987. *Transactions of the British Mycology Society*, **88**, 503–13.

De-Ming, L. I. & Alexander, M. 1988. *Plant and Soil*, **108**, 211–19.

Ezzel, C. 1987. *Nature*, **327**, 90.

Fox, J. L. 1989. *Biotechnology*, **55**, 259–61.

Gasser, C. S. & Fraley, R. T. 1992. *Scientific American*, **266**, 34–9.

Grant, F. A., Glover, L. A., Killham, K. & Prosser, J. I. 1991. *Soil Biology and Biochemistry*, **23**, 1021–4.

Holben, W. E., Jansson, J. K., Chelm, B. K. & Tiedge, J. M. 1988. *Applied Environmental Microbiology*, **54**, 703–11.

Holl, F. B., Chanway, C. P., Turkington, R. & Radley, R. 1988. *Soil Biology and Biochemistry*, **20**, 19–24.

Jain, R. K. & Sayler, G. S. 1987. *Microbiological Science*, **4**, 59–63.

Lindow, S. E. 1983. *Plant Disease*, **67**, 327–33.

Lindow, S. E. & Panopoulos, N. J. 1988. In *The Release of Genetically-Engineered Micro-organisms* (eds. M. Sussman, C. H. Collins, F. A. Skinner & D. E. Stewart-Tull). Academic Press, London.

Lindsey, K. & Jones, M. G. K. 1989. *Plant Biotechnology in Agriculture*. Open University Press, Milton Keynes.

Martinez-Toledo, M. V., de La Rubia, T., Moreno, J. & Gonzalez-Lopez, J. 1988. *Plant and Soil*, **110**, 149–52.

Papavizas, G. C. 1985. *Annual Review of Phytopathology*, **23**, 23–54.

Primrose, S. G. 1991. *Molecular Biotechnology*. Blackwell, Oxford.

Rishbeth, J. 1979. *European Journal of Forest Pathology*, **9**, 331–40.

Rojo, F., Pieper, D. H., Engesser, K. H., Knackmuss, H. J. & Timmis, K. N. 1987. *Science*, **238**, 1395–7.

Schippers, B. 1988. *Philosophical Transactions of the Royal Society, London* **B318**, 285–93.

Watrud, S., Perlak, F. J., Tran, M. T., Kusano, K., Mayer, E. J., Miller-Widman, M. A., Obukowicz, M. E., Nelson, D. R., Kreitinger, J. P. & Kaufman, R. J. 1985. In *Engineered Organisms in the Environment: Scientific Issues* (eds. H. O. Halvorson, D. Pramer & M. Rogul). Washington, D.C., pp. 40–6.

Further reading

Chapter 1

Anderson, J. M. 1981. *Ecology for Environmental Science. Biosphere, Ecosystems and Man.* Arnold.

Foster, R. C. 1988. Microenvironments of soil microorganisms. *Biology and Fertility of Soil*, **6**, 189–203.

Jeffrey, D. W. 1987. *Soil–Plant Relationships – An Ecological Approach.* Croom Helm, London.

Richards, B. N. 1974. *Introduction to the Soil Ecosystem.* Longman, New York.

Wild, A. (ed.) 1988. *Russell's Soil Conditions and Plant Growth* (11th edition). Longman, London.

Wild, A. 1993. *Soils and the Environment – An Introduction.* Cambridge University Press.

Chapter 2

Plant roots and their ecology

Fitter, A. H. (ed.) 1985. *Ecological Interactions in the Soil – Plants, Microbes and Animals.* BES Special Publication 4. Blackwell, Oxford.

Jeffrey, D. W. 1987. *Soil–Plant Relationships – An Ecological Approach.* Croom Helm.

Russell, E. W. 1973. *Soil Conditions and Plant Growth* (10th edition). Longman, London.

Scott Russell, R. 1977. *Plant Root Systems. Their Function and Interaction with the Soil.* McGraw-Hill, London.

Vancura, V. & Kunc, F. (eds.) 1989. *Interrelationships between Micro-organisms and Plants in Soil.* Developments in Soil Science 18. Elsevier, Amsterdam.

Soil microbes and their ecology

Alexander, M. 1977. *Introduction to Soil Microbiology.* Wiley and Son, New York.

Blaine Metting, F., Jr. 1993. *Soil Microbial Ecology.* Marcel Dekker, New York.

Bold, H. C. & Wynne, M. J. 1979. *Introduction to the Algae.* Prentice-Hall, New Jersey.

Domsch, K. H., Gams, W. & Anderson, T. H. 1981. *Compendium of Soil Fungi.* Academic Press, New York.

Garrett, S. D. 1981. *Soil Fungi and Soil Fertility.* Pergamon.

Gray, T. R. G. & Williams, S. T. 1971. *Soil Microorganisms*. Oliver & Boyd, Edinburgh.
Griffin, D. M. 1972. *Ecology of Soil Fungi*. Chapman and Hall.
Lynch, J. M. & Poole, N. J. 1979. *Microbial Ecology – A Conceptual Approach*. Blackwell, Oxford.
Paul, E. A. & Clark, F. E. 1989. *Soil Microbiology & Biochemistry*. Academic Press, San Diego.
Richards, B. N. 1987. *The Microbiology of Terrestrial Ecosystems*. Longman, Harlow.
Round, F. E. 1973. *The Biology of the Algae*. Arnold, London.
Webster, J. 1980. *Introduction to Fungi*. Cambridge University Press.
Williams, S. T. 1978. In *Nocardia and Streptomyces* (eds. M. Mordarski, W. Kurylowicz & J. Jeljaszewicz). Fischer Verlag, New York, pp. 137–44.
Wood, M. 1989. *Soil Biology*. Blackie, Glasgow.

Soil protozoa and their ecology

Darbyshire, J. F. 1975. Soil protozoa – animalcules of the subterranean microenvironment. In *Soil Microbiology* (ed. N. Walker). Butterworth, London.
Peterson, H. 1982. Quantitative ecology of microfungi and animals in soil and litter. *Oikos*, **39**, 288–482.
Stut, J. D., Bamforth, S. S. & Lousier, J. D. 1982. *Protozoan Agronomy Monographs* 9.

Soil mesofauna and their ecology

Eisenbeis, G. & Wichard, W. 1985. *Atlas on the Biology of Soil Arthropods*. Springer Verlag, Berlin.
Finlay, B. J. 1990. In *Advances in Microbial Ecology*, Vol. 11 (ed. K. C. Marshall). Plenum, New York.
Freckman, D. W. (ed.) 1982. *Nematodes in Soil Ecosystems*. University of Texas Press, Austin.
Kevan, D. K. McE. 1965. In *Ecology of Soil-Borne Pathogens* (eds. K. F. Baker & W. C. Snyder). University of California Press, Berkeley, pp. 33–51.
Kuhnelt, W. 1961. *Soil Biology with Special Reference to the Animal Kingdom*. Faber, London.
Satchell, J. E. 1983. *Earthworm Ecology – From Darwin to Vermiculture*. Chapman and Hall, London.
Sims, R. W. & Gerard, B. M. 1985. *Earthworms*. Linnean Society, London.
Syers, J. K. & Springett, J. A. 1984. In *Biological Processes and Soil Fertility* (eds. J. Tinsley & J. F. Darbyshire). Developments in Plant and Soil Science, Vol. 11, pp. 93–104.
Wallwork, J. A. 1976. *The Distribution and Diversity of Soil Fauna*. Academic Press, London.

Chapter 3

The legume/*Rhizobium* association

Child, J. 1981. In *Soil Biochemistry* (eds. E. A. Paul & J. N. Ladd). Marcel Dekker, New York, Vol. 5, pp. 247–322.

Gresshoff, P. M., Roth, L. E., Stacey, G. & Newton, G. (eds.) 1990. *Nitrogen Fixation: Achievements and Objectives*. Chapman & Hall, New York.

Postgate, J. R. (ed.) 1982. *Fundamentals of Nitrogen Fixation*. Cambridge University Press.

Stacey, G., Burns, R. & Evans, H. J. (eds.) 1992. *Biological Nitrogen Fixation*. Chapman & Hall, New York.

The mycorrhizal association

Harley, J. L. & Smith, S. E. 1983. *Mycorrhizal Symbiosis*. Academic Press, London.

Reid, C. P. P. 1990. In *The Rhizosphere* (ed. J. M. Lynch). Wiley, New York, pp. 218–315.

Sanders, F. E., Mosse, B. & Tinker, P. B. (eds.) 1975. *Endomycorrhizae*. Academic Press, London.

Schenck, N. C. (ed.) 1982. *Methods and Principles and Mycorrhizal Research*. Am. Phytopath. Soc. St. Paul, Minnesota.

The rhizosphere

Balandreau, J. & Knowles, R. 1978. In *Interactions Between Non-Pathogenic Micro-organisms and Plants* (eds. Y. R. Dommergues & S. V. Krupa). Elsevier, New York, pp. 243–8.

Bowen, C. D. 1980. In *Contemporary Microbial Ecology* (eds. D. C. Ellwood, J. N. Hedger, M. J. Latham, J. M. Lynch & J. S. Slater). Academic Press, London, pp. 283–304.

Curl, E. A. & Truelove, B. 1986. *The Rhizosphere*. Springer-Verlag, New York.

Lynch, J. M. (ed.) 1990. *The Rhizosphere*. Wiley, Chichester.

Werner, D. 1992. *Symbiosis of Plants and Microbes*. Chapman & Hall, London.

Other interactions of the soil biota

Ahmadjian, V. & Paracer, S. 1986. *Symbioses: An Introduction to Biological Systems*. University of New England Press, Hannover.

Dommergues, Y. R. & Krupa, S. V. (eds.) 1978. *Interactions Between Non-Pathogenic Organisms and Plants*. Elsevier, Amsterdam.

Edwards, C. A., Stinner, B. R., Stinner, D. & Rabatin, S. 1988. *Biological Interactions in Soil*. Elsevier, Amsterdam.

Fitter, A. H. (ed.) 1985. *Ecological Interactions in Soil – Plants, Microbes and Animals*. BES Special Publication 4. Blackwell, Oxford.

Fletcher, M., Gray, T. R. G. & Jones, J. G. (eds.) 1987. *Ecology of Microbial Communities, SGM Symp. 41*, Cambridge University Press.

Lynch, J. M. & Poole, N. J. (eds.) 1979. *Microbial Ecology – A Conceptual Approach*. Blackwell, Oxford.

Mitchell, M. J. & Nakas, J. P. (eds.) 1986. *Microbial Interactions in Natural and Managed Ecosystems*. Nijhoff/Junk, Dordrecht.

Soil microbial and animal population dynamics

Andrews, J. H. 1984. In *Current Perspectives in Microbial Ecology* (eds. M. J. Klug & C. A. Reddy). ASM publication, Washington, D.C., pp. 1–7.

Slater, J. H. & Bull, A. T. 1978. In *Companion to Microbiology* (eds. A. T. Bull & P. M. Meadow). Longmans, London, 181–206.
Usher, M. B. 1985. In *Ecological Interactions in Soil – Plants, Microbes and Animals* (ed. A. H. Fitter). BES Special Publication 4. Blackwell, Oxford, pp. 243–66.

Chapter 4

The global carbon cycle

Bolin, B., Degens, E. T., Kempe, S. & Ketner, P. (eds.) 1979. *The Global Carbon Cycle*. Wiley, New York.
Pearman, G. I. (ed.) 1988. *Greenhouse Planning for Climate Change*. CSIRO, Melbourne.
Woodwell, G. M. & Pecan, E. V. 1973. *Carbon and the Biosphere*. U.S. Atomic Energy Commission, Springfield.
Zehnder, A. J. B. 1983. In *The Natural Environment and Biogeochemical Cycles* (ed. O. Hutzinger). Springer-Verlag, Berlin.

The soil carbon cycle and the nature/decomposition of soil organic carbon

Allison, F. E. 1973. *Soil Organic Matter and its Role in Crop Production*. Elsevier, New York.
Chen, Y. & Avnimelech, Y. 1986. *The Role of Organic Matter in Modern Agriculture*. Martinus Nijhoff, The Hague.
Schnitzer, M. & Khan, S. U. (eds.) 1978. *Soil Organic Matter*. Elsevier, New York.
Stevenson, F. J. 1982. *Humus Chemistry: Genesis, Composition, Reactions*. Wiley, New York.
Tate, R. L. 1987. *Soil Organic Matter. Biological and Ecological Effectors*. Wiley, New York.
Vaughan, D. & Malcolm R. E. 1985. *Soil Organic Matter and Biological Activity*. Developments in Plant and Soil Sciences, Vol. 16. Nijhoff & Junk, Dordrecht.
Williams, S. T. & Gray, T. R. G. 1974. In *Biology of Plant Litter Decomposition* (eds. C. H. Dickinson & G. J. F. Pugh), Vol. 2. Academic Press, London.

Soil N-cycling

Clark, F. E. & Rosswall, T. (eds.) 1981. *Terrestrial Nitrogen Cycles. Ecology Bulletin Stockholm*, Vol. **23**.
Nielsen, D. R. & MacDonald, J. G. (eds.) 1978. *Nitrogen in the Environment*, Vols 1 & 2. Academic Press, New York.
Sprent, J. R. 1987. *The Ecology of the Nitrogen Cycle*. Cambridge Studies in Ecology, Cambridge University Press.
Stevenson, F. J. (ed.) 1982. *Nitrogen in Agricultural Soils*. Agronomy, Vol. 22. Am. Soc. Agron., Madison, Wisconsin.

N₂-fixation

Burns, R. F. & Hardy, R. W. F. 1975. *Nitrogen Fixation in Bacteria and Higher Plants*. Springer-Verlag, Berlin.

Child, J. 1981. In *Soil Biochemistry*, Vol. 5 (eds. E. A. Paul & J. N. Ladd). Marcel Dekker, New York.
Gresshoff, P. M., Roth, L. E., Stacey, G. & Newton, W. E. (eds.) 1990. *Nitrogen Fixation: Achievements and Objectives.* Chapman & Hall, New York.
Stewart, W. D. P. 1965. *Nitrogen Fixation by Free-Living Micro-organisms.* Cambridge University Press.

Plant N-uptake, N-immobilisation/mineralisation

Bremner, J. M. 1967. In *Soil Biochemistry*, Vol. 1 (eds. A. D. McLaren & G. H. Petersen). Marcel Dekker, New York, pp. 19–66.
Nye, P. H. & Tinker, P. B. 1977. *Solute Movement in the Soil-Root System.* Blackwell, Oxford.
Paul, E. A. & Juma, N. 1981. In *Terrestrial Nitrogen Cycles* (eds. F. E. Clark & T. Rosswall). *Ecology Bulletin Stockholm*, **33**, 179–95.

Nitrification

Focht, D. D. & Verstraete, W. 1977. In *Advances in Microbial Ecology*, Vol. 1, Plenum Press, New York, pp. 135–99.
Prosser, J. I. 1986. (ed.) *Nitrification.* IRL Press, Oxford.
Verstraete, W. 1981. In *Terrestrial Nitrogen Cycles. Processes, Ecosystem Strategies, and Management Impacts* (eds. F. E. Clark & T. Rosswall). *Ecology Bulletin Stockholm*, **33**, 303–14.

Gaseous N-loss via denitrification and ammonia volatilisation

Freney, J. R. & Simpson, J. R. 1983. *Gaseous Loss of Nitrogen from Plant–Soil Systems.* Developments in Plant and Soil Sciences, Vol. 9. Nijhoff-Junk, The Hague.
Knowles, R. 1980. In *Soil Biochemistry*, Vol. 5 (eds. E. A. Paul & J. N. Ladd). Marcel Dekker Inc., New York, pp. 323–70.
Payne, J. W. 1981. *Denitrification.* Wiley, New York.

Assimilatory and dissimilatory reduction of nitrate to ammonium

Cole, J. A. 1988. In *SGM Symp. 42* (eds. J. A. Cole & S. J. Ferguson). Cambridge University Press, pp. 281–330.

Measurement of N-fluxes and the use of ^{15}N

Harrison, A. F. & Ineson, P. 1990. *Nutrient Cycling in Terrestrial Ecosystems – Field Methods, Application and Interpretation.* Elsevier, London.
IAEA, 1971. *Nitrogen-15 in Soil-Plant Studies.* International Atomic Energy Agency, Vienna.
Jansson, S. L. 1971. In *Soil Biochemistry*, Vol. 2. (eds. A. D. McLaren & J. Skujins). Marcel Dekker, New York.

Soil S-cycling

Bettany, J. R. & Stewart, J. W. B. 1982. *Proceedings of the International Sulfur Institute*, **2**, 767–85.

Brown, K. A. 1982. *Environmental Pollution Series* B **3**, 47–80.
Freney, J. R. 1967. In *Soil Biochemistry* (eds. A. D. McLaren & G. H. Peterson). Marcel Dekker, New York, pp. 229–59.
Zehnder, A. J. B. & Zinder, S. H. 1980. In *Handbook of Environmental Chemistry* (ed. D. Hutchinson). Springer-Verlag, Berlin.

S-mineralisation/immobilisation

McGill, W. B. & Cole, C. V. *Geoderma*, **26**, 267–86.
Swift, R. S. 1985. *Sulphur in Agriculture*, **9**, 20–4.

S-oxidation

Roy, A. B. & Trudinger, P. A. 1970. *The Biochemistry of Inorganic Compounds of Sulphur*. Cambridge University Press.
Wainwright, M. 1984. *Advances in Agronomy*, **37**, 349–96.
Wier, R. G. 1975. In *Sulphur in Australasian Agriculture* (ed. K. D. McLachlan). Proc. Symp. Sulphur in Australian Agric., Canberra. Sydney University Press, pp. 40–9.

S-reduction

Krouse, H. R. & McCready, R. G. L. 1979. In *Biogeochemical Cycling of Mineral Forming Elements* (eds. P. A. Trudinger & D. J. Swaine). Elsevier, Amsterdam, pp. 315–68.

Chapter 5

Adaptation to extreme environments

Crawford, R. M. M. 1989. *Studies in Plant Survival: Ecological Histories of Plant Adaptation to Adversity*. Blackwell, Oxford.
Heinrich, M. R. (ed.) 1976. *Extreme Environments. Mechanisms of Microbial Adaptation*. Academic Press, New York.
Kushner, D. J. (ed.) 1978. *Microbial Life in Extreme Environments*. Academic Press, London.

Soil water stress and the plant

Fitter, A. H. & Hay, R. K. M. 1983. *Environmental Physiology of Plants*. Academic Press, London.
Kozlowski, T. T. (ed.) 1983. *Water Deficits and Plant Growth*. Academic Press, New York.
Kramer, J. 1983. *Water Relations of Plants*. Academic Press, New York.
Lange, O. L., Kappen, L. & Schulze, D. (eds.) 1976. *Water and Plant Life – Problems and Modern Approaches*. Ecological Studies, 19, Springer-Verlag, Berlin.
Paleg, L. G. & Aspinall, D. (eds.) 1982. *The Physiology and Biochemistry of Drought Resistance in Plants*. Academic Press, Sydney.
Turner, N. C. & Kramer, P. J. (eds.) 1980. *Adaptations of Plants to Water and Higher Temperature Stress*. Wiley, New York.

Soil water stress and microbes/animals

Fairbridge, R. & Finkl, Jr. C. W. (eds.) 1979. *Encyclopaedia of Soil Science*. Dowden, Hutchinson & Ross, Stroudsburg, Pennsylvania.

Griffin, D. M. 1981. In *Advances in Microbial Ecology* (ed. M. Alexander). Plenum, New York.

Parr, J. F., Gardner, W. R. & Elliot, L. F. (eds.) 1981. *Water Relations in Soil Microbiology*. Soil Science Society of America, Madison, Wisconsin.

Chapter 6

The soil ecological effects of acid deposition

Hutchinson, T. C. & Havas, M. (eds.) 1980. *Effect of Acid Precipitation on Terrestrial Ecosystems*. Plenum, New York.

Legge, A. H. & Krupa, S. V. (eds.) 1986. *Air Pollutants and their Effects on the Terrestrial Ecosystem*. Wiley, New York.

Mathy, P. (ed.) 1988. *Air Pollution and Ecosystems*. Reidel, Dordrecht.

Mellanby, K. (ed.) 1988. *Acid Pollution, Acid Rain and the Environment*. Watt Committee Rep. No. 18. Elsevier, London.

Tabatabai, M. A. 1985. In *CRC Critical Review of Environmental Control* (ed. R. A. Olson). No. 15, pp. 65–110.

Wellburn, A. 1988. *Air Pollution and Acid Rain – The Biological Impact*. Longman, New York.

Radionuclide pollution

Eisenbud, M. 1987. *Environmental Radioactivity*. Academic Press, Orlando.

Hewitt, C. N. 1990. In *Pollution – Causes, Effects and Control* (ed. R. M. Harrison). Royal Society of Chemistry, Cambridge.

Kathren, R. 1984. *Radioactivity in the Environment: Sources, Distribution, and Surveillance*. Harwood, Amsterdam.

OECD, 1987. *The Radiological Impact of the Chernobyl Accident in OECD Countries*. OECD Nuclear Energy Agency, Paris.

Chapter 7

Rhizobial inoculation

Beringer, J. R. 1982. In *Advances in Agricultural Microbiology* (ed. N. S. Subba Rao). Butterworth, London, pp. 26–52.

Burton, J. C. 1979. In *Recent Advances in Biological Nitrogen Fixation* (ed. N. S. Subba Rao). Oxford and IBH Publishers, New Delhi, pp. 380–405.

FAO, 1984. *Legume Inoculants and Their Use*. Food and Agriculture Organisation of the United Nations, Rome.

Thompson, J. A. 1980. In *Methods of Evaluating Biological Nitrogen Fixation* (ed. F. J. Bergersen). Wiley, Chichester, pp. 489–533.

Pesticides and soil ecology

Brown, A. W. A. 1978. *Ecology of Pesticides.* Wiley, New York.
Perring, F. H. & Mellanby K. (eds.) 1977. *Ecological Effects of Pesticides.* Academic Press, London.
Saltzman, S. & Yaron, B. 1986. *Pesticides in Soils.* Van Nostrand Reinhold, New York.
Somerville, L. & Greaves, M. P. 1987. *Pesticides Effects on Soil Microflora.* Taylor & Francis, London.

Biological control

Chet, I. (ed.) 1987. *Innovative Approaches to Plant Disease Control.* Wiley, New York.
Delucci, V. (ed.) 1987. *Integrated Pest Management.* Parasitis, Geneva.
Hornby, D. (ed.) 1990. *Biological Control of Soil-Borne Plant Pathogens.* CAB International.
Keister, D. L. & Cregan, P. B. (eds.) 1991. *The Rhizosphere and Plant Growth.* Kluwer, Dordrecht.

Mycorrhizal inoculation

Hall, I. R. 1988. In *Biotechnology in Agriculture.* Alan. R. Liss Inc., pp. 141–74.
Schenck, N. C. (ed.) 1982. *Methods and Principles of Mycorrhizal Research.* American Pathology Society, St. Paul, Minnesota.
Sieverding, E. 1991. *Vesicular–Arbuscular Mycorrhiza Management in Tropical Agrosystems.* Deutsche Gesellschaft für Technische Zusammerarbeit, Eschborn.
Trappe, J. M. 1977. *Annual Review of Phytopathology,* **15**, 203–22.

The use of genetically modified plants and microbes in the environment

Ginsburg, L. R. (ed.) 1991. *Assessing Ecological Risks of Biotechnology.* Butterworth-Heinemann, Boston.
Grierson, D. (ed.) 1991. *Plant Genetic Engineering.* Blackie, Glasgow.
Halvorson, H. O., Pramer, D. & Rogul, M. (eds.) 1985. *Engineered Organisms in the Environment: Scientific Issues.* American Society of Microbiology, Washington, D.C.
Kung, S.-d. & Arntzen, C. J. (eds.) 1989. *Plant Biotechnology.* Butterworth, Boston.
Lycett, G. & Grierson, D. (eds.) 1990. *Genetic Engineering of Crop Plants.* Butterworth, London.
Nakas, J. P. & Hagerdorn, C. (eds.) 1990. *Biotechnology of Plant–Microbe Interactions.* McGraw-Hill, New York.
Royal Commission, 1989. *13th Report of the Royal Commission on Environmental Pollution: The Release of Genetically Engineered Organisms to the Environment.* HMSO, London.
Sussman, M., Collins, C. H., Skinner, F. A. & Stewart-Tull, D. E. (eds.) 1988. *The Release of Genetically-Engineered Micro-Organisms.* Academic Press, London.

Index